TEACHING WORD RECOGNITION SKILLS

SEVENTH EDITION

Cindy Hendricks
Bowling Green State University

Lee Ann Rinsky
late of De Anza College

Upper Saddle River, New Jersey
Columbus, Ohio

Library of Congress Cataloging-in-Publication Data
Hendricks, Cindy.
Teaching word recognition skills / Cindy Hendricks, Lee Ann Rinsky.—7th ed.
p. cm.
Rev. ed. of: Teaching word recognition skills / Lee Ann Rinsky.
Includes bibliographical references and index.
ISBN 0-13-119597-2
1. Word recognition. 2. Reading (Elementary) I. Rinsky, Lee Ann. Teaching word recognition skills. II. Title.
LB1573.6.H46 2007
372.46'2—dc22 2006021754

Vice President and Executive Publisher: Jeffery W. Johnston
Senior Editor: Linda Ashe Bishop
Senior Production Editor: Mary M. Irvin
Senior Editorial Assistant: Laura Weaver
Design Coordinator: Diane C. Lorenzo
Cover Designer: Candace Rowley
Cover Image: SuperStock
Production Manager: Pamela D. Bennett
Director of Marketing: David Gesell
Senior Marketing Manager: Darcy Betts Prybella
Marketing Coordinator: Brian Mounts

This book was set in Jansen Text by Carlisle Communications, Ltd. It was printed and bound by Banta Books, Inc. The cover was printed by Phoenix Color Corp.

Pearson Education Ltd.
Pearson Education Singapore Pte. Ltd.
Pearson Education Canada, Ltd.
Pearson Education—Japan
Pearson Education Australia Pty. Limited
Pearson Education North Asia Ltd.
Pearson Educación de Mexico, S.A. de C.V.
Pearson Education Malaysia Pte. Ltd.

10 9 8 7 6 5 4 3 2 1
ISBN: 0-13-119597-2

To Jimmy . . . I love you and thank you for your support and patience.
To Papa and Mame . . . thanks for keeping the hotel lobby open all night.
To Sherrie, Terrie, Ralph, Dave, Lynn, Andy, Cody, Cassie, and Little Runt . . . thanks for always being there for me.

Preface

This new edition of *Teaching Word Recognition Skills* includes substantial revisions and updates in all areas. It has benefited from the suggestions offered by preservice and inservice teachers and by faculty who use the text, and has been strengthened by findings from current reading research.

Balance in the Reading Program

This text was written in response to the preservice and inservice teachers' need for a self-instructional manual in word recognition skills. The organization, presentation of information, and suggested learning methods facilitate acquisition of the needed background. In addition, the linguistic and historical insights provided clarify some of the more complicated sound-symbol relationships.

As in previous editions, this new edition teaches the benefits of systematic instruction in word recognition strategies, of which phonics is a key element. It stresses reading instruction in an environment that has comprehension as its goal, with quality reading materials constituting the core of the reading program. Phonics is put in its proper perspective in this edition, with increased emphasis on sight words, context clues, structural analysis, and the dictionary.

Good phonics instruction enables students to move from a decoding strategy in which individual letters and sounds are used initially to one in which words can be identified as subunits of language through patterns. As children move into content areas such as social studies and science, they do not always become successful decoders of the more demanding vocabulary that is essential to comprehension. Lacking the tools to unlock these words can make reading in these areas distasteful. Knowing the building blocks of the English language, students can read and learn independently without frustration.

New to This Edition

This edition contains new information and features including:

- an in-depth exploration of the history of word recognition instruction
- a more balanced approach to word recognition, emphasizing multiple word recognition strategies
- updated references with more citations included within the text for a more research-based presentation
- additional suggestions for beginning readers
- activities in blending, context clues, structural analysis, and sight-word instruction, among others
- improved self-checks within chapters and review questions at the end of each chapter

All resources, materials, and references have been checked for accuracy and timeliness.

Organization of the Text

The first section of the text provides a historical examination of word recognition from the Hornbook through No Child Left Behind. The two following sections about our English language provide the needed background to enable teachers-in-training and teachers-in-service to learn or review the variant consonants, blends, consonant digraphs, single vowel sounds, vowel digraphs, and diphthongs; the variety of ways the *y* and *w* are used; the controlling effect of the letter *r*; and the special combinations *ci*, *ti*, and *si*. This section is also designed to review how consonants and vowels are produced.

The next section of the text begins with an explanation of the prerequisites necessary for phonics instruction. Following this discussion, procedures for introducing beginning sound-symbol relationships are detailed. The differences among analytic, synthetic, embedded, and analogy phonics are explained, and sample lessons are provided. The importance of sight words is detailed, and basic sight word lists are included, with suggestions for teaching these critical words. Structural analysis focuses on compound words, affixed words, and syllabication. Difficulties that students encounter with these words are explained with suggested procedures for teaching. The text discusses the importance of context as an aid in decoding and enumerates types of clues. The final chapter puts the word recognition skills into perspective as a way of achieving fluency and discusses the impact of word recognition on comprehension.

The research conducted during the revision of the textbook reemphasizes that success in reading is based not only on the method and materials used, but also on teacher competency and the amount of time students actually spend reading. As teachers engage students in word recognition instruction, they must supplement that instruction with authentic reading experiences. It is critical that teachers remember that the goal of reading instruction is to develop readers who enjoy reading.

Acknowledgments

We are indebted to teachers and students who have offered ideas for continued improvement of the text. For this edition, we would like to thank the individuals who reviewed the manuscript at various stages and offered constructive suggestions; the book is greatly improved as a result of their help: Paz I. Bartolome, UNC–Wilmington; Scott Beesley, Grand Canyon University; Annette L. Bubeck, The Richard Stockton College of NJ; Nell Carvell, Southern Methodist University; Judith A. Crowe, California Lutheran University; Laurie A. Elish-Piper, Northern Illinois University; Joan K. Juralewicz, Worcester State College; William Kist, Kent State University; Linda Kleemann, Harris-Stowe State University; Linda Jones McCoy, Pittsburg State University; Martha McGovern, Georgia Southern University; Beth Musser, West Liberty State College; Elizabeth Wadlington, Southeastern Louisiana University; and Ann A. Wolf, Gonzaga University.

We also wish to thank the members of the editorial and production departments of Merrill/Prentice Hall and at Carlisle for their help during the publication process: Linda Bishop, Editor; Mary Irvin, Production Editor; Laura Weaver, Editorial Assistant; Diane Lorenzo, Design Coordinator; Candace Rowley, Cover Designer; and Mary Tindle, Project Coordinator.

Brief Contents

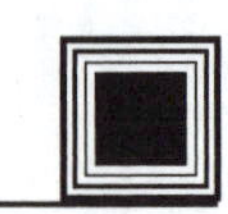

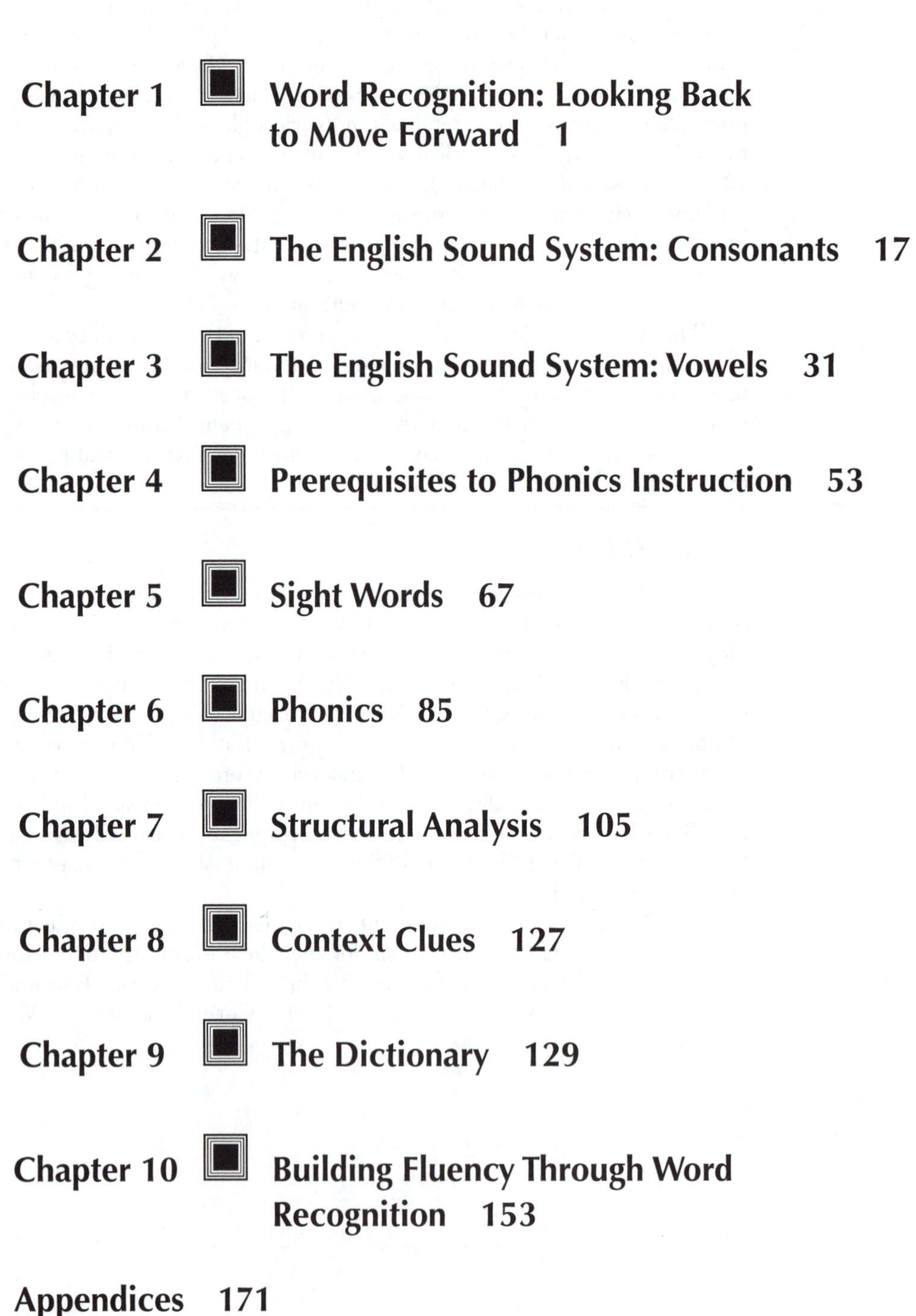

Contents

Chapter

Sight Words 67

Chapter

Phonics 85

Chapter

Word Recognition: Looking Back to Move Forward

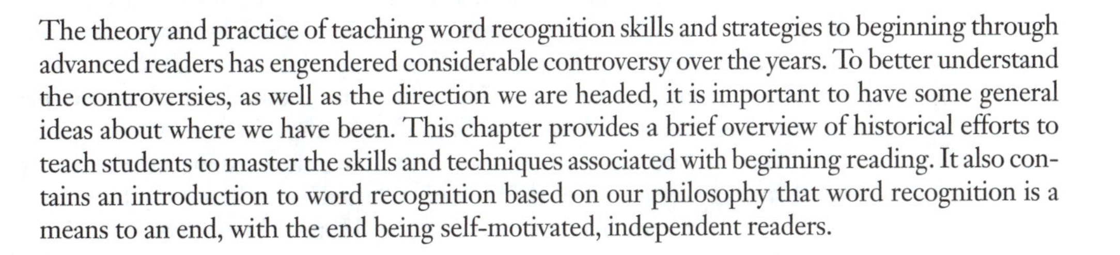

The theory and practice of teaching word recognition skills and strategies to beginning through advanced readers has engendered considerable controversy over the years. To better understand the controversies, as well as the direction we are headed, it is important to have some general ideas about where we have been. This chapter provides a brief overview of historical efforts to teach students to master the skills and techniques associated with beginning reading. It also contains an introduction to word recognition based on our philosophy that word recognition is a means to an end, with the end being self-motivated, independent readers.

Understanding the Past

Colonial Times

In the mid-15th century in Europe, and later in the New England colonies, reading instruction took place using a hornbook, which was a wooden paddle with lessons attached and covered by a thin piece of transparent ox or cow horn (Blackwell Museum, 1999). Generally, a hole was cut into the handle so a leather string could be tied to it to enable the child to carry it on a belt or around the neck (Austin, n.d.). Hornbooks were sometimes made of metal (including silver), stone, ivory, leather, or cardboard and were decorated with jewels by the wealthy. According to Andrew Tuer (1897), some hornbooks were even made of gingerbread. As children learned each letter of the alphabet, they were rewarded with letters to eat. Tuer includes lines from Matthew Prior's Canto II of *Alma*:

> *To Master John the English Maid*
> *A Horn Book gives of Ginger-bread:*

And that the Child may learn the better,
As he can name, he eats the Letter;
Proceeding thus with Vast Delight,
He spells, and gnaws from Left to Right. (p. 264)

The lessons consisted of the alphabet in upper and lower case, vowels, vowel and consonant combinations, the Lord's Prayer, a cross (in the upper left corner of the hornbook and where the term crisscross originates), and religious verses (Chisholm, 1911). These were handwritten on a piece of parchment and affixed to the wooden paddle. The hornbook was used to teach children to read. First, the children learned the alphabet, and then they learned how letters sounded when they were put together. After they had mastered the letters and sounds, they moved to real words (Blackwell Museum, 1999). The Lord's Prayer was printed on the hornbooks because children already knew the prayer, and it was believed to be better to learn how to read with familiar text.

Reading instruction in the American colonies continued to be delivered using the alphabetic method, defined as a teaching method that emphasizes knowing the letter names and attaching sounds to the letter names (Savage, 2004). Using *The New England Primers* as a focal point of instruction, children learned the letters of the alphabet, sounds made by the letters, and words that corresponded to the letters. After learning the letters, rhyming couplets (religious and moralistic in nature) were used to reinforce learning. In fact, the children's prayer beginning, "Now I lay me down to sleep," was included in *The New England Primer* as a series of couplets. The purpose of *The New England Primers* can best be described using an 1805 cover page, which explained the book was "For the more easy attaining the True Reading of English" while the 1807 cover includes the "The New-England Primer Improved, Being an Easy Method to Teach Young Children the English Language" (Shannon, 2001. http:// public.gettysburg.edu/~tshannon/his341/colonialamer.htm). Also emphasized during the early years of the colonies was spelling. Noah Webster introduced *The New American Spelling Book*, which focused on teaching children to read and spell by learning the sounds of letters and syllables. The alphabetic method remained the primary method of teaching beginning reading through the beginning of the 1800s.

Overseas, however, a different method, a whole word method (learning whole words before learning the sounds of the individual letters), was being used and was gaining popularity. Upon his return from visiting Europe, Horace Mann, considered the father of public education, advocated the use of this new method of teaching beginning reading. He believed the whole word method was superior to the alphabetic method (Savage, 2004). During the 1800s, teachers struggled with the alphabetic and whole word schools of thought regarding the teaching of beginning reading.

Then came the *McGuffey Eclectic Readers*. This textbook series, published between 1836 and 1844, was the most popular of the day. The series presented the letters of the alphabet (sequentially) to be memorized. Then, children were taught to form and pronounce words. The lessons began with learning the words used in the reading selection. Each of the new words was written with diacritical markings to show correct pronunciation and syllabication (McGuffey's Readers, n.d.).

The readers (organized according to reading levels) emphasized phonetic elements in the early grades; however, within the pages of text, it was explained that the materials enabled ". . . the teacher to pursue the Phonic Method, the Word methods, the Alphabetic Method, or any combination of these methods" (*McGuffey Eclectic Primer*, 1909, p. iii).

The Modern Era

For the next 60 years or so, the *McGuffey Electic Readers* dominated reading instruction (Savage, 2004). It was not until the arrival of Dick, Jane, and Sally that a major change in reading instruction took place. The popular Scott Foresman series revitalized the whole word method that had been so strongly advocated by Horace Mann years earlier. Children learned words by sight, instead of sounding them out letter by letter. Due to the popularity of the series, other publishing companies supported the look-say, or whole word, method, by creating their own characters and their character's families, such as Alice and Jerry. The look-say, or whole word, method, dominated reading instruction through the 1960s (Savage, 2004).

In 1936, Dolch published his basic sight vocabulary word list. This list consisted of 220 of the most common words to appear in print, excluding nouns. Teachers were urged to use this word list with all students, but especially with struggling readers. It was believed that memorizing these sight words would reduce the amount of time that students would have to spend decoding frequently occurring words in the texts. Many of these words continue to appear often within text.

Although the look-say method was still dominating reading instruction in the 1950s, rumblings of a movement back to phonics instruction were beginning to be heard. A strong pro-decoding, code-emphasis, or phonics movement was regaining momentum, due in part to Rudolph Flesch's book *Why Johnny Can't Read* (1955) in which he berated school administrators for abandoning phonics for a "look-see" model. According to Flesch, Johnny cannot read because he was taught using the look-say method without phonics instruction.

The Distant Past

During the 1960s, perhaps in response to Flesch, code-emphasis programs began to appear in an attempt to help students make connections between phonemes and graphemes, also known as "breaking the code." The Initial Teaching Alphabet (i.t.a.), developed by Sir James Pitman, was first used in British schools in 1961. I.T.A. is a phonemic alphabet based on the sound system of the English language. The i.t.a. consists of 44 letters. Each letter represents a single phoneme (see Figure 1.1). Pitman's alphabet was designed to provide a logical and reliable reading and writing system for the beginning reader and writer. Pitman envisioned that children would first learn to read using the i.t.a. and then be introduced to standard English orthography at age seven. The efficacy of the i.t.a. has never really been established as it failed to garnish any type of wide-reaching support. Two main problems plagued the i.t.a.; first, there was a lack of materials written in i.t.a., which made it difficult to use, and second, the transition to traditional orthography was difficult for children.

FIGURE 1.1 Pitman's Initial Teaching Alphabet

b	c	d	f	g	h	j	k	l	m	n
bed	**c**at	**d**og	**f**ish	**g**oat	**h**at	**j**ug	**k**ey	**l**ion	**m**an	**n**est
p	r	s	t	v	w	y	z	a	e	i
pet	**r**ock	**s**un	**t**able	**v**oice	**w**in	**y**et	**z**ip	**a**pple	**e**ngine	**i**nsect
o	u	æ	ee	ie	œ	ue	wh	ch	ʃh	th
hot	**u**mbrella	**a**ngel	**ee**l	**i**ce	**oa**t	**u**niform	**wh**eel	**ch**air	**sh**oe	**th**umb
th	au	oi	ou	ŋ	ƨ	ʒ	ɹ	ɑ	ω	ω
that	**au**to	**oi**l	**ow**l	ri**ng**	dog**s**	gara**g**e	bi**r**d	f**a**ther	b**oo**k	m**oo**n

Ager. Simon. Omniglot Writing Systems & Languages of the World. Pitman Initial Teaching Alphabet (i.t.a.). Retrieved September 27, 2006, from http://www. omniglot.com/writing/ita.htm. Reprinted with permission.

Words in Color, another code-emphasis approach to teaching sound-symbol relationships was developed by Caleb Gattegno, a mathematician. The Words in Color system consists of color-coded spelling wall charts (called the Fidel), color-coded word wall charts, and a pointer. (Une Educat Poor Demain, Associatim, 2002, http://assoc.orange.fr/ une.education.pour.demain/lectureenc/wcprese.htm). The color-coded spelling wall charts included all the possible graphemes (letters) of each phoneme (sound) in columns so that the whole system could be viewed at one time. The word charts were also organized based on spelling patterns. Through the use of color, children could work on developing phonemic awareness equating one phoneme with one color. This provided a visual cuing system for students who could use color to help in pronouncing an unknown word.

Another method for breaking the code that also appeared in the 1960s was identified as the Linguistic Method, or more specifically, structural linguistics, which emphasized regularity and consistency between the sounds and the symbols of the written language. Popularized by the publication of *Let's Read: A Linguistic Approach* (Bloomfield & Barnhart, 1961), this method focused on teaching decoding through the use of phonograms, or word families. Students began with simple, regularly spelled patterns whose symbols always represented the same speech sounds, to more complex, sophisticated, and irregularly spelled patterns. For example, students would learn *cap*, and then learn *gap*, *lap*, *map*, *nap*, *rap*, *sap*, and *tap* before they moved to the more complex *chap*, *clap*, *snap*, *trap*, and *wrap*.

While the code-emphasis programs were being developed and piloted, Theodore Clymer, a reading researcher, conducted his landmark study that concluded that the phonics generalizations were not very dependable (1963). In his study, Clymer examined more than 2600 words from four popular reading programs to determine which words could be decoded using the 45 phonics generalizations that he was required to teach. For his investigation, he wanted to know how useful the generalizations were so he set the criteria at 75%. If a rule worked 75% of the time, then he believed it was worth teaching. Of the 45 generalizations that he examined, only 18 worked at the 75% level. The common "when two vowels go walking, the first one does the talking" worked 45% of the time, but "when *c* is followed by *o* or *a*, the sound of /k/ is likely to be heard" worked 100% of the time in Clymer's investigation. Clymer's research, as well as the research of others who replicated his work, led educators to question the efficacy of teaching children to memorize phonics rules.

In response to the controversy involving phonics/decoding skills versus the look-say approach, Bond and Dykstra (1967) conducted research sponsored by the U.S. Office of Education. The First Grade Studies examined numerous approaches to beginning reading instruction. Identical achievement tests and measures were used in 27 different centers across the country to determine the best method of teaching beginning readers. Their findings led to a number of conclusions. First, the individual classroom teacher had more impact on beginning reading success than the materials used for beginning reading instruction. This finding supports the notion that there simply is no substitute for effective teaching and that the emphasis in beginning reading instruction should be on quality teachers, rather than on instructional materials or methodologies. A good teacher can be successful with beginning readers regardless of materials, and a poor teacher will have little success even with the best of materials. A second conclusion reached was that a combination of phonics and whole word methods was superior to one or the other by itself. According to Bond and Dykstra, reading programs and materials are not equally effective with all students in all situations. In an article published in 1968, Dykstra concluded, "Data from the Cooperative Research Program in First Grade Reading Instruction tend to support Chall's conclusion that code-emphasis programs produce better overall primary grade reading and spelling achievement than meaning-emphasis programs" (p. 21).

Simultaneous with but independent of the research conducted by Bond and Dykstra (1967), Jeanne Chall, a Harvard professor of education, convinced the Carnegie Corporation to sponsor her synthesis of past research related to the best way to teach beginners to read. This investigation led to the 1967 publication of her now classic book, *Learning to Read: The Great*

Debate. Chall's debate was whether children learned better from teachers who taught using a code-emphasis approach (synthetic phonics) or whether they learned better from teachers who used a meaning-emphasis approach (analytical phonics). After reviewing relevant research, Chall concluded that in beginning to read, learning to decode by direct teacher instruction using phonics showed superior results. Chall revised her book (1983, 1996) and confirmed her earlier findings as did continuing research by others: Johnson and Bauman (1984); Williams (1985); Jacobs, Baldwin, and Chall (1990); Samuels and Farstrup (1992); and Adams and Bruck (1995). Chall (1999) pointed out that although she and Bond and Dykstra (1967) completed their investigations independent of one another, they both came to the same conclusions: (1) stronger phonics or decoding programs produced higher reading achievement, and (2) learning the alphabetic code (phonics, word analysis, decoding, sound-symbol relations) was essential in beginning reading, but was not sufficient. Chall's critics were concerned that such emphasis on breaking the code and on workbook pages might impede the important goals of reading instruction: obtaining meaning from the text and enjoying reading.

Stahl (1998) notes that in the 1970s, Scott Foresman was overtaken by the Ginn 720 series to become the dominant basal series. He provided several reasons for this change including more diverse settings, loosening controlled vocabulary, and an earlier introduction to phonics through word patterns and analytic phonics. This represented a shift from the sight vocabulary (look-say) approach to an emphasis on decoding due, in part, to the work by Flesch (1955), Chall (1967), and Bond and Dykstra (1967).

Also in the 1970s, however, a movement de-emphasizing decoding and the basal text, called whole language, was endorsed by the National Council of Teachers of English. The movement stressed a pedagogy that moved from a focus on sub-skills in teaching reading to an emphasis on holistic concerns for language development (Beck & Juel, 1995; Clark, 1995). Reading was not viewed as a separate subject with a set of discrete and isolated skills; rather, it was viewed as part of an integrated whole called the language arts, which incorporated reading, writing, listening, and speaking. Whole language instruction also emphasized the use of authentic children's literature as opposed to the controlled vocabulary in basal readers. Although phonics was never supposed to be omitted from the whole language classroom, it was limited to teaching only what students needed to construct meaning (Savage, 2004). Whole language instruction became popular among educators in the 1980s.

In 1985, another significant publication appeared—*Becoming a Nation of Readers* (Anderson, Hiebert, Scott, & Wilkinson, 1985). In this report, the authors spoke of implicit (intrinsic, analytical, meaning-emphasis) and explicit (intensive, synthetic, code-emphasis) phonics. The Commission on Reading concluded that phonics instruction improves children's ability to identify words: "... on the average, children who are taught phonics get off to a better start in learning to read than children who are not taught phonics" (p. 37). The commission identified useful phonics strategies as those designed to teach children the sounds of letters both in isolation and in words, and to teach children to blend the sounds together to pronounce words. The commission recommended that children be encouraged to identify words by thinking of other words with similar spellings. They supported the notion that phonics instruction should include the identification of words in meaningful sentences and stories. Finally, the commission recommended that phonics instruction should occur early and should be kept simple.

The Not-So-Distant Past

During the 1980s and 1990s, fueled by popular magazines such as *Newsweek* and *Time*, the reading wars began and raged on for years. Educators and politicians alike debated the phonics versus whole language issue. Finally, even the federal government became involved in the continuing controversy, commissioning reading researcher Marilyn Adams to re-examine, re-evaluate, and issue a new report on *The Great Debate*. Her published report, *Beginning to*

Read: Thinking and Learning about Print (1990) supported Chall, as did her subsequent critique published a year later. According to Adams, researchers reported superior results in teaching children to read when phonics was emphasized. As a result of this investigation and the subsequent publication of the report, various state legislatures, including California and Ohio, enacted legislation mandating phonics instruction for all children.

In 1998, a significant step was made toward ending the reading wars—the publication of *Preventing Reading Difficulties in Young Children* (Snow, Burns, Griffin, 1998). Endorsed by the National Research Council, this work is the result of a collaborative effort by more than a dozen leaders in reading research. The preface to the book referred to the end of the reading wars, "The unpleasantness of the conflicts among reading researchers was moderated, if not eliminated, by the realization that all the participants are primarily interested in ensuring the well-being of young children and in promoting optimal literacy instruction" (p. v). All the members of this group agreed on two basic issues:

> Reading should be defined as a process of getting meaning from print, using knowledge about the written alphabet and about the sound structure of oral language for purposes of achieving understanding.
>
> Early reading instruction should include direct teaching of information about sound-symbol relationships to children who do not know about them and that it must also maintain a focus on the communicative purposes and personal value of reading. (p. vi)

The researchers suggested adequate initial reading instruction requires that children:

- ❒ Use reading to obtain meaning from print,
- ❒ Have frequent and intensive opportunities to read,
- ❒ Are exposed to frequent, regular spelling-sound relationships,
- ❒ Learn about the nature of the alphabetic writing system, and
- ❒ Understand the structure of spoken words. (p. 4)

Further, the reading researchers asserted that adequate progress in learning to read English beyond the initial level depends on:

- ❒ Understanding how sounds are represented alphabetically,
- ❒ Sufficient practice in reading to achieve fluency with different kinds of texts,
- ❒ Sufficient background knowledge and vocabulary to render written texts meaningful and interesting,
- ❒ Control over procedures for monitoring comprehension and repairing misunderstandings, and
- ❒ Continued interest and motivation to read for a variety of purposes. (p. 4)

The researchers recommended that every primary grade teacher should attend to the following: the alphabetic principle, sight words, reading words by mapping speech sounds to parts of words, achieving fluency, and comprehension. They added that failure to master word recognition may limit comprehension.

Before the National Research Council's findings were published, another panel had already been convened. In collaboration with the Secretary of Education and the National Institute of Child Health and Human Development (NICHHD), the U.S. Congress once again commissioned work in the name of effective reading instruction. The National Reading Panel (NRP), formed in 1997, began its investigation by taking into account the work completed by the National Research Council. The topics to be explored by the NRP included alphabetics (phonemic awareness instruction, phonics instruction), fluency, comprehension (vocabulary instruction, text comprehension instruction, teacher preparation, and comprehension strategies instruction), teacher education and reading instruction, and computer technology and reading instruction. After setting research methodology standards, the panel divided into subgroups and began reviewing research. Of interest here are the results of the alphabetics research investigations.

Alphabetics included both phonemic awareness instruction and phonics instruction. Phonemic awareness instruction was selected because previous researchers had suggested that phonemic awareness instruction and letter knowledge were the two best predictors of reading performance during the first two years of reading instruction (NICHHD, 2000). The NRP reviewed 52 phonemic awareness articles that met the established criteria. The panel reported that the meta-analyses show the following:

- ❒ Focusing instruction on one or two skills was significantly more effective for teaching Phonemic Awareness (PA) than focusing on multiple skills;
- ❒ Teaching children to manipulate phonemes with letters was more effective than teaching children without letters;
- ❒ Teaching PA in small groups was the most effective grouping pattern;
- ❒ Training in PA does not need to be lengthy;
- ❒ Teaching PA to students is effective;
- ❒ Training in PA improved children's ability to read and spell both short term and long term;
- ❒ Teaching PA is a means rather than an end; it is not acquired for its own sake but rather for its value in helping children understand and use the alphabetic system to read and write;
- ❒ Acquiring PA will happen in the course of learning to read and spell even though there is no explicit PA instruction;
- ❒ Instructing children in PA will differ; some children will need more instruction than others; and
- ❒ Making the connection between the PA skills taught and their application to reading and writing tasks is essential (NICHHD, 2000).

According to the NRP (NICHHD, 2000), phonics instruction, which stresses the acquisition of letter-sound correspondences, has been accomplished through several instructional approaches including synthetic phonics (converting letters to sounds and blending sounds to form words), analytic phonics (identifying words and then analyzing letter-sound relations), embedded phonics (learning phonics in context), analogy phonics (using parts of known words to identify new words), onset-rime phonics (connecting words through linguistic/word families), and phonics through spelling (transforming sounds into letters to write words). The NRP defines systematic phonics as the identification of a full array of letter-sound correspondences (p. 2-99) including consonant letters and sounds, short and long vowel letters and sounds, and vowel and consonant digraphs. The NRP conducted a meta-analysis of 38 studies to seek answers to questions regarding the effectiveness of systematic phonics instruction compared with other forms of instruction. Results of the meta-analyses led to the following conclusions:

- ❒ Systematic phonics instruction produced gains in reading and spelling not only in the early grades but also in the later grades and among children having difficulty learning to read.
- ❒ Systematic phonics instruction made a more significant contribution to children's growth in reading than do alternative programs providing unsystematic or no phonics instruction (p. 2-132).
- ❒ Various types of systematic phonics approaches were more effective than non-phonics approaches.
- ❒ Systematic phonics instruction was effective when delivered through tutoring, through small groups, and through teaching classes of students.
- ❒ Systematic phonics instruction had the biggest impact on reading when it was begun in kindergarten or first grade before children learn to read independently.

- Systematic phonics instruction was significantly more effective than non-phonics instruction in helping to prevent reading difficulties among at-risk students and in helping to remediate reading difficulties in disabled readers and in those living in low socioeconomic conditions.

The NRP did provide several warnings: (a) the goal of phonics instruction is "to provide children with some key knowledge and skills and to ensure that they know how to apply this knowledge in their reading and writing" (p. 2-135), (b) "programs that focus too much on the teaching of letter-sounds relations and not enough on putting them to use are unlikely to be very effective" (p. 2-135), and (c) "educators must keep the *end* in mind and ensure that children understand the purpose of learning letter-sounds and are able to apply their skills in their daily reading and writing activities" (p. 2-135).

The NRP explains that phonics is not a reading program: ". . . phonics instruction should be integrated with other reading instruction to create a balanced reading program" (p. 2-136). The final point made is one worth repeating, "Phonics should not become the dominant component in a reading program neither in the amount of time devoted to it nor in the significance attached" (p. 2-136).

These two major reports, *Preventing Reading Difficulties in Young Children* and the *National Reading Panel*, have received much public attention, but not all of the attention has been positive (Garan, 2001; Yartvin, 2002). Debates continue regarding "scientifically-based reading research," the selection of studies used for the meta-analyses, the exclusion of studies for the meta-analyses, and the conclusions reached by the panel. One thing that seems to be evident, however, is that no single method of teaching works adequately for all readers.

Eldredge (2005) explains that a new movement began in the early 1990s because educators liked the ideals of whole language, but recognized the need for phonics instruction as well as direct instruction. This new movement was called Balanced Literacy, or a balanced approach to the teaching of reading. It is not clear, however, what educators mean when they speak of balanced instruction. For example, Honig (1996) defines a balanced approach as one that combines language and literature-rich activities with explicit teaching of the skills needed to decode words. He stresses that a balanced reading program provides both separate, explicit skill instruction and language-rich literature instruction.

According to Pressley (2002), "Balanced-literacy teachers combine the strengths of whole language and skills instruction, and in doing so create instruction that is more than the sum of its parts" (p. 1). Perhaps the most complete definition of balanced literacy instruction was written by Spiegel (1998):

> A balanced approach to literacy development is a decision-making approach through which the teacher makes thoughtful choices each day about the best way to help each child become a better reader and writer. A balanced approach is not constrained by or reactive to a particular philosophy. It is responsive to new issues while maintaining what research has already shown to be effective. It is an approach that requires and frees a teacher to be a reflective decision maker and to fine tune and modify what he or she is doing each day in order to meet the needs of the child. (p. 115)

Current Day

The most significant impact on reading instruction in the past few years has been the bipartisan reauthorization of the Elementary and Secondary Education Act (ESEA) in 2001 (U.S. Department of Education [DOE], 2005). Referred to as the No Child Left Behind Act (NCLB), this is clearly a change in role for the U.S. government, which for all practical purposes has added reforming K–12 education to its previous role of funding agency. The goal of the NCLB act is to ensure that all students (regardless of background) have the opportunity to obtain a quality education and to become proficient in core academic subjects. The

NCLB act specifically requires that all students through the eighth grade progress in six areas of reading: phonemic awareness, phonics, spelling and writing, fluency, text comprehension, and vocabulary. Schools who wish to continue to receive federal funds need to document student growth in these six areas.

NCLB is focused on principles of stronger accountability, more choices for parents and students, greater flexibility for states and school districts, and the use of "research-based instructional methods" (U.S. DOE, 2005). Starting with the 2005–2006 school year, all students in grades three through eight were assessed in reading and math. All students are expected to be proficient in reading and mathematics by 2013–2014. Under the accountability provisions, states must describe how they will close the achievement gap and make sure all students achieve academic proficiency, and they must produce annual state and school district report cards.

NCLB (U.S. DOE, 2005) supports "scientifically based reading instruction programs" through two programs: Early Reading First (preschool) and Reading First (early grades). Early Reading First funds support preschool programs that not only provide for children's social, emotional, and physical development, but also support a high-quality (grounded in "scientifically based research") education to young children, especially those from low-income families. Early Reading First supports programs that stress the importance of early reading skills, including phonemic awareness, phonics, fluency, vocabulary, and comprehension. Funds may be used for professional development as well as for instructional activities and instructional materials. Programs must be grounded in "scientifically based research," and their success must continually be evaluated.

Reading First monies are dedicated to helping states and local school districts establish high-quality (based on scientific research), comprehensive reading instruction for all children in kindergarten through third grade. Reading First funds must be spent to implement reading instruction based on "scientifically based reading research."

"Scientifically based reading research" is defined as research that uses rigorous, systematic, and objective procedures to obtain knowledge relevant to reading development, reading instruction, and reading difficulties (U.S. DOE, 2005). It also includes research that employs systematic, empirical, observational or experimental methods; involves rigorous data analyses; relies on measurements or observational methods that provide valid data across evaluators and observers and across multiple measures and observations; and has been accepted by a peer-reviewed journal or an approved panel.

Available funds may be used for diagnostic assessments, for professional development for teachers, for purchasing reading materials, and for ongoing support to improve reading instruction. Reading First students are systematically and explicitly taught phonemic awareness, phonics, fluency, vocabulary, and comprehension.

Quick Self-Check 1

1. Why do you think the McGuffey readers were formally titled *The McGuffey Eclectic Readers*?
2. What events in reading added to the emphasis on "breaking the code" in the 1960s?
3. What two recent publications have significantly impacted reading instruction during the initial years of the new millennium?
4. Examine Figure 1.2, a timeline of significant events with word recognition. There are two 15-year time spans that account for major activities (1955–1970 and 1985–2000). Can you speculate why this is so? Is there a connection between the two?

FIGURE 1.2 Timeline of Significant Events Connected with Word Recognition

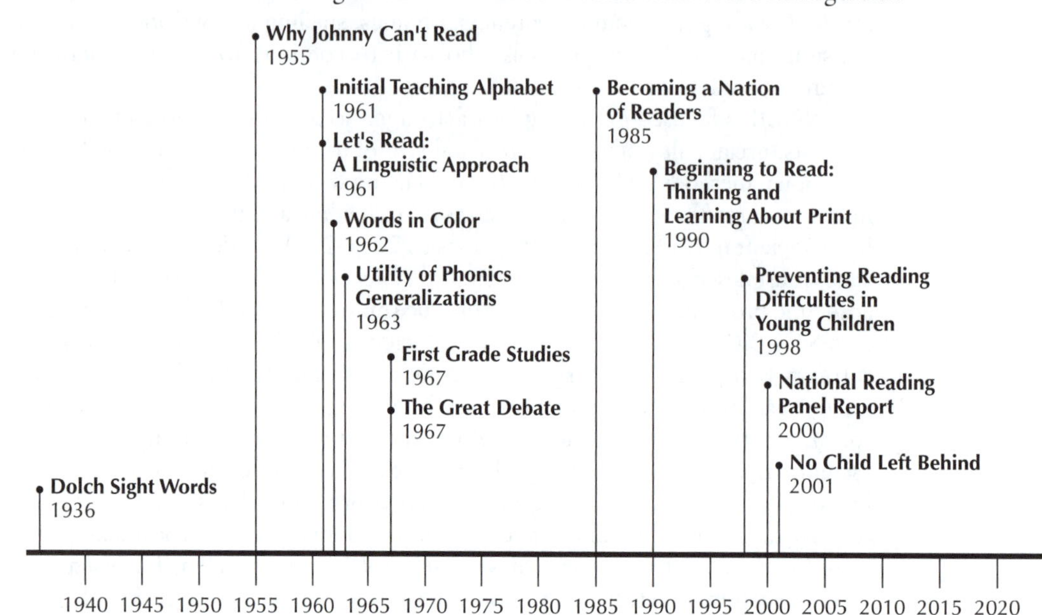

Understanding Issues with Word Recognition

Stages of Word Recognition

Numerous researchers have attempted to identify various stages through which developing readers pass on their way to becoming proficient at reading words. Five explanations of word recognition stages will be presented to compare and contrast the researchers' perceptions of word recognition stages.

Ehri and McCormick

After extensive research, Ehri and McCormick (1998) identified five stages through which they believe children pass as they develop their word recognition skills.

1. *Pre-alphabetic stage:* Children rely on visual, contextual, or graphic features to read words (a stop sign, the oo in look that appears to be like eyes). They attempt to read words by looking only at the shape or length of the word and selectively use cues. Most students remember a word only after many exposures to it.
2. *Partial-alphabetic stage:* Children begin to apply the alphabetic principle, associating some letters with sounds and connecting printed letters to sounds and pronunciations. Reading is limited to sight words, because the alphabetic principle is just beginning to develop.
3. *Full-alphabetic stage:* Children read words using grapheme-phoneme relationships. Reading speed increases because strategies become more automatic and the size of the sight vocabulary increases. One characteristic of this phase is that students begin to use analogies to identify unknown words (dare/scare).
4. *Consolidated-alphabetic stage:* Children continue using alphabetic principles but focus on patterns and groupings larger than the phoneme-grapheme unit. Larger units

assist in analyzing multisyllabic words, and speed up the process of reading words. Children at this stage clearly understand the alphabetic principle and rhyme-based patterns.

5. *Automatic-alphabetic stage:* Students automatically recognize most words in text by sight. They are able to apply multiple strategies to attack unfamiliar words. This stage characterizes the mature reader.

Stahl

Stahl (1998) identified three stages he believes readers go through as they develop word recognition skills. He calls his first stage the awareness stage. In this stage, readers develop knowledge about how print *functions* (to tell stories, to inform, to provide direction) as well as the *conventions* of print (top to bottom, left to right, punctuation). It also involves learning about the *form* of print (letters of the alphabet) and learning that spoken words can be broken into individual sounds, which we call *phonemes*. Stahl believes this stage usually occurs in kindergarten and can best be accomplished with holistic methods.

Stahl's (1998) second stage includes accurate decoding. In this stage, readers are focused on accurately decoding the words they encounter. During this stage, the focus is on learning about words and sound-symbol correspondences, and on applying that knowledge to read text. Stahl explains that the transition from the accuracy stage to the automaticity stage generally lasts from first through third grade. Because of the emphasis on phonemic awareness in this stage, some direct instruction is recommended. Strategy development, as well as practice with phonemic awareness, is necessary.

The final stage as identified by Stahl (1998), is the automaticity stage. Here, children begin to develop automatic word recognition skills that will enable them to concentrate more on the meaning of the text rather than on the mechanics of reading. This stage requires that students have lots of opportunities for reading so that they can apply what they have learned to authentic reading situations.

Juel

The three stages of word reading identified by Juel (1991a) are similar to those recognized by Stahl. The first stage is the Selective Cue Stage. During this stage, readers rely on random cues (any visual cue that helps students remember the word), environmental cues (where the word is on the page), and distinctive letter cues (such as the two *ll*s in yellow). During the Spelling-Sound Stage, readers rely on graphophonic clues to learn phoneme-grapheme relationships. They learn to blend words and rely heavily on phonics. The final stage is the Automatic Stage in which readers use context and graphophonic cues as they develop fluency (accuracy and speed).

Frith

Frith's (1985) stages of word recognition consist of three categories:

1. *Logographic:* Children tend to recognize words as whole displays; they are not yet reading but are searching for identifiable features to remember words. Readers at this stage do not have strategies for sounding out words.
2. *Alphabetic:* Children focus on more of the letters in words as they try to pronounce them. As readers, the children are developing a cache of sight words. During this stage, children are sounding out words, which is also known as phonological recoding.
3. *Orthographic:* Children look at words in terms of spelling patterns. In the orthographic stage, children are able to use analogies to help them identify unknown words.

Bear, Invernizzi, Templeton, Johnston

The final category of stages is the word study approach as explained by Bear, Invernizzi, Templeton, and Johnston (2004). These authors believe that word study is developmental and the level of instruction must match the level on which the learner is operating. Their premise is that one of the easiest ways to know what students need is to look at their spelling.

Stage I is the emergent spelling stage as well as the emergent reader stage. This stage is defined as describing anyone who is not reading conventionally. There is a lack of correspondence between the letters they make and the sounds they are intended to represent. This stage is best characterized by the terms prephonetic and prereading.

Stage II is the letter name-alphabetic spelling stage and beginning reader stage, typically characteristic of students during kindergarten through the middle of second grade. This stage reflects students' use of the names of the letters in combination with the alphabetic principle when they spell. Students begin to match sounds and symbols and move from partial to full phonemic segmentation. Reading at this stage is generally disfluent and word-by-word.

Stage III is the within word pattern spelling and transitional reader stage, occurring toward the end of first grade and throughout second and third grade. Students are developing a sight vocabulary, and their knowledge of letter sounds and vowel patterns is becoming automatic. Onsets, rimes, and word families are familiar to learners. Reading moves from word-by-word to phrase-by-phrase.

Stage IV is the syllables and affixes spelling stage as well as the intermediate reading stage. This stage is generally achieved in the intermediate grades. At this stage, students begin to examine multisyllabic words and patterns. Syllables and affixes are the focal point of this stage, and word recognition becomes more automatic.

The final stage is the derivational relations spelling stage and the advanced reader stage. The authors indicate that most students in this stage are found in the middle school, high school, and college. This stage is characterized by accuracy in spelling and the continued development of a large sight vocabulary. The focus is also on word meaning. This stage continues to develop and be refined as students move through the grades and encounter various reading opportunities.

Table 1.1 helps to put the various stages in perspective.

Why is it important to consider developmental stages? Hempenstall (2004) explains that not all students require the same level or kind of instruction. She adds that understanding and considering developmental stages can help ensure that each student receives assistance appropriate to his or her needs, while containing the costs of providing optimum support. Attention

TABLE 1.1 Comparison of Word Recognition Stages

Authors	Stages				
Ehri and McCormick	Pre-alphabetic	Partial alphabetic	Full alphabetic	Consolidated alphabetic	Automatic
Stahl	Awareness	Awareness	Accuracy	Accuracy	Automaticity
Juel	Selective cue	Spelling-sound	Spelling-sound	Spelling-sound	Automatic
Frith	Logographic	Alphabetic	Alphabetic	Orthographic	
Bear, Invernizzi, Templeton, Johnston	Emergent spelling; Emergent reader	Letter-name alphabetic spelling; Beginning reader	Within word pattern spelling; Transitional reader	Syllables and affixes spelling; Intermediate reader	Derivational relations spelling; Advanced reader

to developmental stages also reduces the likelihood that students who are having difficulty will be overlooked or that students will waste time with tasks they have already mastered.

Some disagree with the notion of developmental stages, mainly because stage theories tend to assume that all children develop in a similar manner and receive similar instruction. Factors such as age, culture, educational background, and home environment are likely to affect performance, or movement from one developmental stage to the next. Alternative theoretical orientations include dual-route theories, which suggest that students develop two different routes as they become skilled readers: lexical (whole word) and sublexical (phonological). The point is that even those who agree with developmental stage theory do not agree on what those stages are or how many there should be. And some don't agree that developmental stage theory accurately explains how children learn word recognition strategies.

Evidence-Based Reading Instruction

According to the U.S. Department of Education (2005), scientifically based reading research uses rigorous, systematic, and objective procedures to obtain knowledge relevant to reading development, reading instruction, and reading difficulties. The U.S. DOE includes research that employs systematic, empirical observational or experimental methods. Additional characteristics of scientifically based reading research involves rigorous data analyses—a reliance on measurements or observational methods that provide valid data across evaluators and observers and across multiple measures and observations. Finally, to be scientifically based reading research, the research must be accepted by a peer-reviewed journal or an approved panel.

In 2002, the International Reading Association (IRA) issued a position statement that identified what they believe is "evidence-based reading instruction." IRA suggests that research-based instruction and scientifically based research are terms used to reflect the same construct. According to IRA, evidence-based reading instruction means that a program, strategy, or technique has a record of success. This means that there is reliable, trustworthy, and valid evidence to suggest that when the program, strategy, or technique is used with an appropriate group, successful outcomes can be expected. The confusion lies in identifying what evidence can be used to claim success. IRA believes the evidence must be objective (identified and interpreted similarly by any evaluator), valid (representative of tasks important for successful reading), reliable (results don't change based on day or assessor), systematic (data collection follows a rigorous design of experimentation or observation), and refereed (approved for publication by independent reviewers).

Concerns about what constitutes scientifically based reading research affect research practices and instructional practices in word recognition. Results from the National Reading Panel may have yielded contrasting results if different criteria were used to define the research-based reading instruction.

Word Recognition Strategies

The act of reading involves multiple processes enacted simultaneously to obtain meaning from text. Competence in multiple skills, including the ability to identify and recognize words, is necessary to obtain meaning from text as well as to develop independence with text. Groff (1991) claims that through extensive research, no higher positive correlations have been found than that between word recognition and reading comprehension. He adds that decoding ability becomes most effective in the word recognition process when it reaches the automatic stage.

Decoding competency of the written language may be defined as the ability to recognize letters and their related sounds as *meaningful words*. Word recognition is an interaction of (1) word knowledge, (2) knowledge of letter sounds, (3) knowledge of word parts, (4) receptive vocabulary, (5) sight vocabulary, and (6) the use of context clues (DeVries, 2004). Children who do this automatically and with little apparent effort get the meaning from the pages they are reading because they are able to concentrate on the text rather than on identifying individual words. Children cannot achieve independence in reading until they can identify unknown words they encounter while reading. An inability to reorganize words not only limits a child's understanding of what is being read, but may lead to frustration and a distaste for reading.

In this text, word recognition is defined as the strategies that students use when they are attempting to read words. These include sight words, context clues, phonics, structural analysis, and context. These five strategies are not absolute; controversy exists as to how many word recognition skills there are, and even what constitutes word recognition. Decoding is what one does when attempting to decipher an unknown word using the clues identified as phonics, syllabic analysis or morphemic analysis. The five areas that we consider when evaluating the word recognition competency of students include the following:

knowledge of basic sight words
ability to use phonetic clues
ability to use structural clues
ability to use context clues
ability to use a dictionary

The separation of these areas is arbitrary and are not endorsed by all educators. By focusing on one strategy at a time, it is easier for teachers to develop a thorough understanding of each one. Children will find some strategies to be more suited to their abilities than others. As students learn to read, however, teachers should encourage them to be flexible and to use a variety of word recognition skills. Students should know that sometimes a single clue works best to decode an unknown word, but at other times, a combination of clues is necessary. Often the effectiveness of a word recognition skill is enhanced when it is used in combination with others. Research supports the notion that no method or strategy exists that is best for teaching all children; therefore, students should be taught to use a number of word recognition strategies and to select those that work best for them. See Appendix D for a Teacher's Test of Decoding Skills to evaluate your own knowledge in these areas.

To help understand word recognition and decoding, we will introduce the foundations of word recognition and then introduce briefly word recognition skills that will be discussed in more depth in Section 2 of this text. It is important to remember that the goal of word recognition instruction is automaticity. This means that students can read a text using various strategies automatically so that they are able to concentrate on the meaning of the text rather than on the mechanics of reading the text.

Quick Self-Check 2

1. Why is understanding developmental stage theory important for teachers?
2. How is scientifically based research defined? How is evidence-based research defined?

SUMMARY

The strong evidence in favor of a code-emphasis approach in beginning reading cannot be discounted. Writer and researcher Stanovich (1993-1994) is quoted as follows:

> That direct instruction in alphabetic coding facilitates early reading acquisition is one of the most well-established conclusions in all of behavioral science. . . . The

> idea that learning to read is just like learning to speak is accepted by no responsible linguist, psychologist, or cognitive scientist in the research community. (p. 285–286)

Furthermore, the evidence shows that a strong phonics program seems to work especially well for children whose background experiences have not prepared them for beginning to read. Although it is true that some students learn to read without being directly taught, it can be attributed to their predisposition to learn to read and their experiences before attending school.

Although researchers do not all agree on the number of stages of word recognition or characteristics describing each stage, one thing is clear: children begin using whatever clues they have available to them to begin to make sense of the print world around them. Through home and school experiences, they refine their limited rough tactics and learn to use more sophisticated strategies for unlocking the meaning of unknown words.

In the final analysis, a successful classroom *depends on the teacher*. It has always been so and will continue to be so. To paraphrase an old cliché: For forms of teaching, let fools contest, that which is best taught, is best. Knowledgeable and competent teachers are the key. Such teachers understand the English sound-symbol system so they know *how* to teach phonics, *when* to teach it, and *how much* of it to teach (Moats, 1995). Accordingly, we will examine the five areas of word recognition needed to develop the necessary background for supporting student learning, no matter which program or program combination is used.

Review Questions

1. There is an old adage, "What goes around comes around." Based on the brief history of word recognition provided in this chapter, what are your predictions for the future regarding phonemic awareness, phonics, and word recognition instruction?

2. After reading about the various stage theories and thinking of your own experiences, do you ascribe to the notion of stage theories to explain the development of word recognition skills?

3. Examine the definitions of scientifically based reading research and evidence-based reading instruction. Can you find differences? Where? Do you have a preference? Which one? Why?

The English Sound System: Consonants

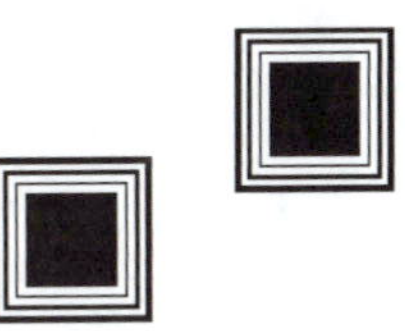

There are 26 letters in the alphabet. Of these 26, 5 are called vowels and 21 are called consonants. The word *consonant* originated as a Latin word meaning *to sound together*. Consonants must be sounded together with vowels to create words. Because they are influenced by the letters that come after them (carriage, city, soak, see), it may be difficult to sound most consonants in isolation.

Understanding Consonants

Consonants are speech sounds produced by a partial or complete obstruction of the air stream by the lips, teeth, tongue, gums, palate (roof of the mouth), and vocal cords. The air is completely blocked and released to form /b/, forced through a small opening to form /s/, redirected through the nasal cavity for /m/, and allowed to flow around the obstruction for /l/. As shown, the sound a letter makes is written with slash marks before and after (see Figure 2.1).

Consonants can be voiced or unvoiced. If the vocal cords are vibrated to utter consonant sounds, the sounds are said to be voiced. Consonant sounds are voiceless when the vocal cords do not vibrate. When two consonants are produced in the same way, with one voiced and one voiceless, they are called equivalent phonemes. The nine pairs include: /b/ and /p/; /f/ and /v/; /z/ and /s/; /d/ and /t/; /k/ and /g/; /th/ and /~~th~~/; /w/ and /hw/; /sh/ and /zh/; /ch/ and /j/. Consonants are generally divided into five groups: glides, liquids, nasals, fricatives, and stops. To ensure that pre-service and in-service teachers understand how sounds are produced the consonant groupings will be reviewed.

Fricatives and Affricates

Fricatives are consonants that are formed by friction in the mouth. Affricates are a combination of a fricative and a stop. Wilde's (1997) graphic representation of these sounds helps illustrate their relationships.

FIGURE 2.1 Where Sounds Are Formed

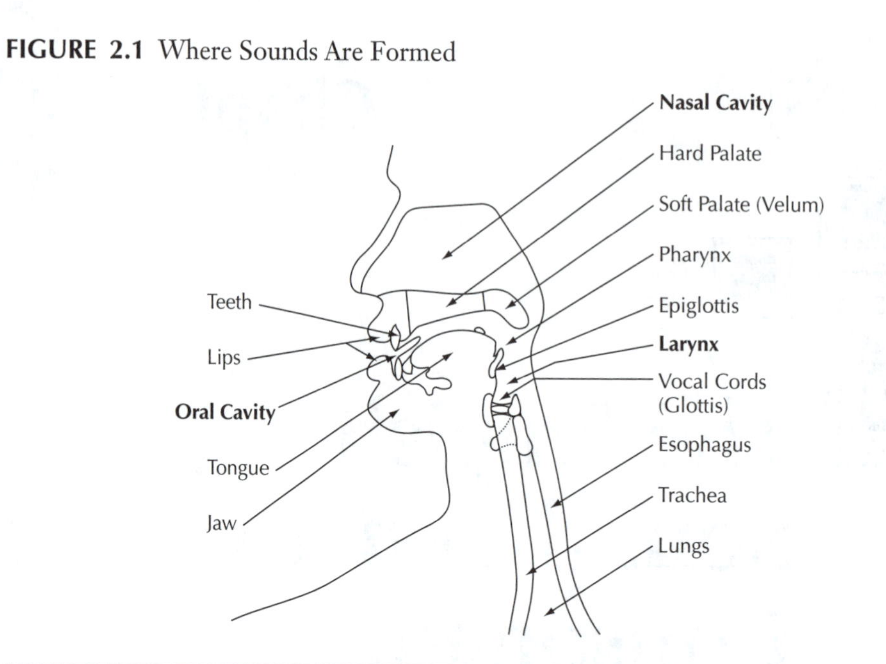

Location	Voiced	Unvoiced
Lips and teeth (labiodental) verse liver	/v/ fire cough	/f/
Teeth (dental) /d/ this bother	/q/ thin faith	
Front of mouth (alveolar) zoo as	/z/ sin fuss	/s/
Roof of mouth (palatal) pleasure fusion	/z/ crush machine	/s/
Affricates—Roof of mouth (palatal) chin matched	/c/ gym fudge	/j/

Stops

A stop is formed by completely closing off the stream of breath; therefore, stops cannot be sounded in isolation, only in combination with a vowel. Wilde's (1997) graphic aid provides a clearer understanding of the stops.

Location	Voiced	Unvoiced
Lips (bilabial)	/b/ bus begin	/p/ petty put
Front of mouth (alveolar)	/d/ dog danger	/t/ tire toad
Back of mouth (velar)	/g/ goat gas	/k/ king kite

Nasals

Nasal sounds are produced when the mouth is closed off so the air goes through the nose instead. There are three nasal sounds in our language. Wilde (1997) summarizes the characteristics of nasals:

Location	Nasal
Lips (bilabial)	/m/ mother many
Front of mouth (alveolar)	/n/ nature note
Back of mouth (velar)	/ŋ/ sing bank

Glides

Glides, also called semivowels, are /w/, /y/, and /h/. These consonants sometimes behave as vowels, but they generally do not appear in print alone (Wilde, 1997). They either precede or follow a vowel. Some examples include wow, cow, eye, and yes.

Liquids

Liquid consonants have no friction; however, the air stream is still interrupted. The consonants /l/ and /r/ are liquids (Wilde, 1997). Listen while you pronounce the following words: *last*, *fellow*, *rib*, and *sorry*.

Consonants Representing One Sound

The single consonant letters *b*, *d*, *f*, *h*, *j*, *k*, *m*, *n*, *p*, *qu*, *r*, *t*, *v*, *w*, *y*, and *z* are generally decoded as the following sounds:

b	/b/	bat	*l*	/l/	land	*t*	/t/	top
d	/d/	dent	*m*	/m/	mat	*v*	/v/	vane
f	/f/	fall	*n*	/n/	name	*w*	/w/	well
h	/h/	hit	*p*	/p/	pan			
j	/j/	jam	*qu*	/kw/	quite[1]	*y*	/y/	yellow
k	/k/	kite	*r*	/r/	road	*z*	/z/	zebra

[1] Since *q* is always written with *u*, both letters are included with the single consonants.

The consonants *c*, *g*, *s*, and *x* will be discussed thoroughly in the following sections.

Deciding the order for teaching initial consonants varies from publisher to publisher. An examination of several phonics programs shows the following variability among phonics programs in the order of teaching initial consonants:

Program A	Program B	Program C	Program D
f, m, s, t, h, b	s, m, r, t, b, f	m, s, d, g, t, p	n, r, d, m, p, s, t, g
l, d, c, n, g, w	n, p, d, h, c, g, j, l, k,	h, f, b, w, c /k/	c /k/, h, f, w, l, b, k,
p, r, k, j, q, v,	v, w, z	j, r	j, v, qu, x,
y, z	c /s/, g /j/, qu, y	l, n, k v, y, z	y, z

Consonants with More Than One Sound

The letters *c*, *g*, *s* and *x* are sometimes called variant consonants.

The Letter *c*

Examine the words in lists *A* and *B*.

A			*B*		
***c* as /k/**			***c* as /s/**		
*c*at	*c*ot	*c*ut	*c*ell	*c*ity	*c*ycle
*c*ame	*c*old	*c*ub	*c*ent	*c*ircus	*c*yclone
*c*ab	*c*one	*c*url	*c*ement	*c*itrus	*c*ypress

Notice that when the vowel following *c* is an *a*, *o*, or *u*, the letter *c* decodes (reads) as the sound of the letter *k*. The /k/ sound is called the hard sound of the letter *c*. See the examples of *c*at, *c*ot, and *c*ut in list *A*. Repeat these words to yourself and listen to the sound.

When the vowel following the letter *c* is *e*, *i*, or *y*, the letter *c* decodes as the sound of the letter *s* (the sound for *s* is written /s/). This is called the soft *c* sound. See the examples of *c*ell, *c*ity, and *c*ycle in list *B*. Repeat these words to yourself and listen to the sound.

The Letter *g*

A			*B*		
***g* as /g/**			***g* as /j/**		
*g*ang	*g*ot	*g*um	*g*em	*g*iant	*g*ym
*g*as	*g*oat	*g*ull	*g*entle	*g*inger	*g*ypsy
*g*ame	*g*old	*g*uppy	*g*enius	*g*iraffe	*g*yrate

Notice in list *A* that the words begin with the most frequent sound that single *g* encodes. As with the letter *c*, when the vowel following *g* is an *a*, *o*, or *u*, the letter *g* decodes as the hard sound, and this hard sound is written as /g/. Examples from the list are *g*ang, *g*ot, and *g*um. Repeat these words to yourself to hear the sound.

In list *B*, the words begin with a second sound that the letter *g* may encode. When the vowel following the letter *g* is an *e, i,* or *y*, the letter *g* may decode as the sound of the letter *j* and this sound is written as /j/. Examples from the list are gem, giant, and gym. Repeat these words to yourself to hear the sound. This sound is called the soft *g*.

A major difference exists between the two generalizations for *c* and *g*. Some simple but often used words such as *girl, get,* and *give* have the hard *g* sound. There are a few other exceptions to the *g* generalization, but it works a substantial number of times, so it is worth learning. In contrast, the *c* generalization works almost all the time.

Stated simply, then, in regard to the letters *c* and *g*:

1. **When *a, o,* and *u* follow *c* or *g*, these letters (*c* and *g*) encode the hard sound (/k/, /g/).**
2. **When *e, i,* and *y* follow *c* or *g*, these letters (*c* and *g*) encode the soft sound (/s/, /j/). *G* has several exceptions, such as girl, get, and give.**
3. **When *c* or *g* appear at the end of a word, they also represent the hard sound.**

The Letter *s*

The letter *s* encodes three sounds. Pronounce the following words and notice the sound of *s* in each one.

A *s* as /s/	*B* *s* as /z/	*C* *s* as /sh/
*s*ale	hi*s*	a*ss*ure
*s*end	name*s*	*s*ugar
*s*it	rea*s*on	*s*ure
*s*ob	ro*s*e	
u*s*	u*s*e	

Notice the difference between the words in lists *A* and *B*. In list *A* the letter *s* encodes its most common sound written as /s/. As shown, examples are *s*ale, *s*end, and *s*it. Say the words to hear the sound. In list *B*, *s* encodes a second sound called the /z/ sound. Unlike *c* and *g*, the vowels following the *s* consonant do not always affect whether the sound is /s/ as in set or /z/ as in use. Often, when the *s* is followed at the end of the word by an *e* it may encode the sound /z/, as in the word ro*s*e.

Some intensive phonics programs teach a third sound /sh/, such as in the words *s*ugar, *s*ure, and a*ss*ure, shown in list *C*. There are, however, only a few such words.

Stated simply, we may generalize about the single letter *s*.

Single letter *s* can decode as three sounds:

1. **/s/ as in *s*at.**
2. **/z/ as in hi*s*.**
3. **/sh/ as in *s*ugar.**

The Letter *x*

A *x* as /ks/	*B* *x* as /gz/	*C* *x* as /z/
fo*x*	e*x*pand	*X*erox
x-ray	e*x*treme	*x*ylem
fle*x*ible	e*x*it	*x*enon

Say the words in each column aloud to hear the difference in the sound of the letter *x*.

The most common sound of the letter *x* is the /ks/ sound it makes when it appears at the end of words such as ta*x* and o*x* (column *A*). However, it also makes the /gz/ sound when it appears in the medial position, such as in e*x*aggerate, e*x*act, and e*x*cite (column *B*). The letter *x* also makes the /z/ sound at the beginning of some words, such as *x*ylophone (column *C*) and can make the same sound when it appears in the middle of a word, such as an*x*iety. Sometimes the letter *x* is silent as in faux. Because there are so few words that begin with the letter *x*, only one sound, the ending sound heard in bo*x*, is usually taught.

With respect to letter *x*:

1. **The letter *x* makes three sounds (/ks/, /gz/, /z/) or may have no sound.**
2. **When *x* appears at the end of a word, it generally has the /ks/ sound.**
3. **When *x* appears in the middle of a word, it generally makes the /gz/ sound.**
4. **When *x* appears at the beginning of a word, it generally has the /z/ sound.**

Quick Self-Check 1

1. When are the letters *c* and *g* decoded as the soft sound?
2. When are the letters *c* and *g* decoded as the hard sound?
3. When *c* or *g* appears at the end of a word, they generally represent the hard sound. Can you think of words that end with *c* or *g* that represent the hard sound?
4. What are the three sounds of *s*?
5. What are the four possibilities for sounds made by the letter *x*?

Consonant Digraphs

Two consonant letters together encoding only a single sound are called consonant digraphs. In the word *digraph*, the syllable *di* stands for "two" and the syllable *graph* stands for "any written symbol (letter)." Digraph then means "two written symbols or letters that encode a single sound." As you will see, some digraphs encode more than one single sound.

The Unique *h* Digraphs

Look at the following list of words and note the sound/sounds encoded by each digraph.

Words	Digraphs and Sounds			
*ch*air, sc*h*ool, *ch*ef	ch	/ch/	/k/	/sh/
*gh*ost, lau*gh*	gh	/g/	/f/	
*ph*oto	ph	/f/		
*sh*ip	sh	/sh/		
*th*at, *th*in	th	/~~th~~/	/th/	
*wh*at, *wh*o	wh	/w/	/h/	

You will notice that each digraph includes the letter *h*. Each digraph also has distinctive features:

ch This consonant digraph encodes three sounds:

1. /ch/ as in *ch*air.
2. /k/ as in s*ch*ool.
3. sh/ as in *ch*ef.

The most common sound *ch* encodes is the /ch/ as in *ch*air, *ch*amp, and *ch*op. Repeat these words to hear the sound.

A second sound, the /k/ sound, occurs in words such as *ch*aracter and s*ch*eme. These are frequently words of Greek origin. Repeat the words *ch*aracter and s*ch*eme to hear the /k/ sound.

The third sound of /sh/, as in *ch*ef, is usually found in French words, such as *ch*ampagne, *ch*andelier, and *ch*aise. There are only a few such words.

gh This digraph has two sounds:

1. /g/ as in *gh*ost.
2. /f/ as in enou*gh*.

The *gh* digraph causes a lot of problems because it derives from the former gutteral *gh*, a part of Old English. Through the years this gutteral sound has been replaced or modified so that today it appears as the sounds in *gh*ost and enou*gh*. Say these words with *gh* to remember the sounds. Actually, there are few words with the latter sound. Words like thorou*gh* and thou*gh* appear to have the *gh* digraph; however, the *gh* is silent. Since no sound is made, the *gh* in these words is not a digraph. These words are usually learned as sight words.

ph This digraph does not include the sound of /p/ but encodes the sound of /f/ as in *ph*armacy. It often appears at the beginning of words but may also appear in the middle as in *ph*os*ph*orus, or at the end as in gra*ph*. Repeat these words to hear the sound.

sh This digraph encodes only one sound as /sh/ in *sh*ip and da*sh*. Say the words to hear the sound.

th This digraph has two sounds called voiced *th* and unvoiced *th*. Say the words *th*ere and *th*ink, while at the same time placing your hands on your throat. Notice that when you say the word *there* you feel the vibrations of your vocal cords on the /th/ sound. This sound is written /~~th~~/. The /th/ sound that vibrates is called the voiced sound. When you say the word *think*, you do not feel these vibrations. Repeat several times. The /th/ sound that does not vibrate is called the voiceless sound.

Study the following additional examples. Say these words to yourself and again note the difference between the beginning sounds:

A	***B***
Voiced *th* as /~~th~~/	**Voiceless *th* as /th/**
*th*an	*th*ank
*th*at	*th*atch
*th*em	*th*eater
*th*en	*th*ick
*th*ere	*th*ink

wh This digraph has two sounds: the sound of /w/ in *wh*at and the sound of /h/ in *wh*o. In Old English a word such as *wh*at was written as *hw*at and pronounced with the *h* initially. Later the letters *hw* were reversed to become *wh*. In pronunciation, however, we differentiated between *wh*ich and *w*itch by pronouncing the /h/ of *wh*ich first. Today with language still changing, most people pronounce such words as *wh*at, *wh*en, and *wh*ere with only the /w/ sound.

Notice the words below beginning with the digraph *wh* and followed by the letter *o*:

*wh*o
*wh*ole
*wh*olly

When *o* follows the *wh* digraph, this digraph decodes as /h/. These words are generally taught as sight words.

Insofar as the consonant digraphs with *h*, we might generalize as follows:

Digraphs are two consonant letters placed together that encode a single sound or several single sounds. The letter *h* combines to form six digraphs as follows: *ch*, *gh*, *ph*, *sh*, *th*, and *wh*. The digraph

1. ***ch* encodes three sounds as the /ch/ in *ch*air, /k/ in s*ch*eme, and /sh/ in *ch*andelier.**
2. ***gh* encodes two sounds as the/g/ in *gh*ost and the /f/ in rou*gh*.**
3. ***ph* encodes the /f/ sound as in *ph*oto.**
4. ***sh* encodes the /sh/ sound as in *sh*ip.**
5. ***th* encodes two sounds as the /th/ in *th*ere and the /th/ in *th*ick.**
6. ***wh* encodes two sounds as the /w/ in *wh*at and the /h/ in *wh*o.**

See Appendix B for example words to use in teaching consonant digraphs with *h*.

Quick Self-Check 2

1. The letter *h* combines with other consonants to encode unique sounds.
   a. Which combinations encode three sounds? List these with their respective sounds?
   b. Which combinations encode two sounds? List these with their respective sounds.
   c. Which combinations encode one sound? List these with their respective sounds.

Digraphs with a First Silent Letter

There is a second group of consonant digraphs, all of which have a silent letter. These digraphs are *gn*, *kn*, *wr*, and *ck*. Note the following:

A	B	C	D
***gn* as /n/**	***kn* as /n/**	***wr* as /r/**	***ck* as /k/**
*gn*arl	*kn*ack	*wr*ap	ta*ck*
*gn*at	*kn*ee	*wr*eck	che*ck*
rei*gn*	*kn*ife	*wr*inkle	sti*ck*
*gn*ome	*kn*ow	*wr*ist	tru*ck*

gn* and *kn Notice that when the letters *gn* or *kn* are used together, only the sound of /n/ is heard. The *g* is silent in the *gn* digraph as in *gn*arl, and the *k* is silent in the *kn* digraph as in *kn*ack.

wr In the *wr* digraph the *w* is silent. Interestingly enough, most words beginning with *wr*, such as *wr*ap and *wr*inkle, denote a twisting motion in their meanings.

ck The digraph *ck* also has a first silent letter when it appears at the end of a syllable or word (often with one syllable) and *follows a short vowel.* Notice the following two groups of words. In list *A* all the vowels are short and the ending /k/ sound is written as *ck*. In list *B* all the vowels are long and the ending /k/ sound is written as *ke*.

A	*B*
***ck* as /k/**	***ke* as /k/**
sa*ck*	ma*ke*
de*ck*	*eke*[2]
ti*ck*	ti*ke*
do*ck*	po*ke*
lu*ck*	du*ke*

We might generalize about these four digraphs, *gn*, *kn*, *wr*, and *ck* as follows:

1. **In the consonant digraphs, *gn*, *kn*, *wr*, and *ck*, the first letter is always silent.**

Special Combinations

dge* and *tch A third group of three-letter consonant combinations behaves similarly to *ck*. Even though these combinations include three letters and not two, they are still often referred to as digraphs, principally because they encode a single sound. These two combinations are *dge* and *tch*. Note the following:

A	*B*
***dge* as /j/**	***tch* as /ch/**
ba*dge*	la*tch*
le*dge*	stre*tch*
ri*dge*	sti*tch*
do*dge*	blo*tch*
smu*dge*	clu*tch*

In every instance, the vowels preceding these combinations are short, just as with the *ck* digraph. Also, as with the *ck* digraph, these combinations are often found at the end of one-syllable words. The reason for the combination *dge* goes back several hundred years when printers attempted to show whether vowel sounds were long or short. Often, an extra consonant letter was added to indicate that the previous vowel sound was short. The words in column *A* were written as *bagge*, *legge*, etc. The first *g* was eventually turned around and became the letter *d*.

We still see evidence of this printing device—doubling a consonant letter to keep the prior vowel short—in such words as la*dd*er, le*tt*er, li*tt*er, o*tt*er, and ru*dd*er. This is also the reason we usually only pronounce a single consonant letter in English even when it is doubled. (Other reasons for doubling consonant letters will be discussed later.)

We might generalize as follows for the special combinations *dge* and *tch*:

1. **The combination *dge* decodes as the sound of /j/, as in do*dge*.**
2. **The combination *tch* decodes as the sound of /ch/, as in sti*tch*.**
3. **These combinations follow a short vowel, often at the end of a one-syllable word.**

ng The two letters *n* and *g* blur to become one distinctive sound, or digraph. You can hear this unique nasal sound if you pronounce the following words: si*ng*, ra*ng*, lo*ng*.

See Appendix B for example words to use in teaching the consonant digraphs with a first silent letter, and the special combinations *dge* and *tch*.

[2] Very few words end in *eke*.

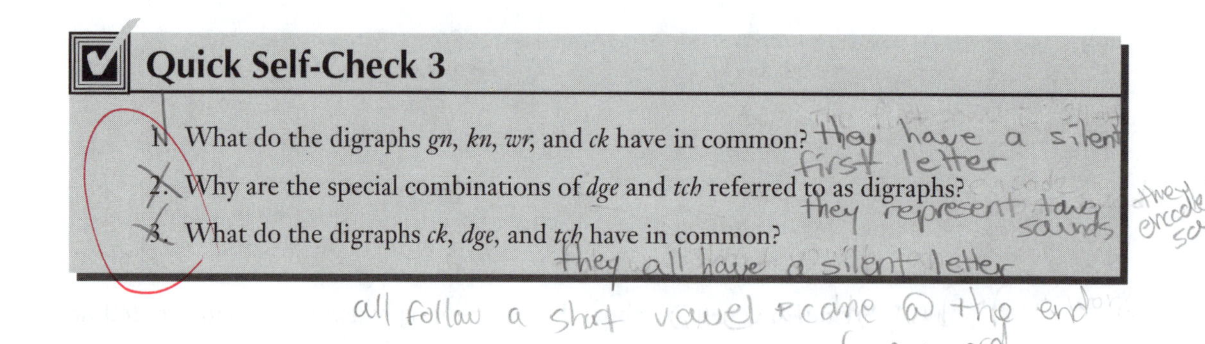

Quick Self-Check 3

1. What do the digraphs *gn*, *kn*, *wr*, and *ck* have in common?
2. Why are the special combinations of *dge* and *tch* referred to as digraphs?
3. What do the digraphs *ck*, *dge*, and *tch* have in common?

Consonant Blends

Two-Consonant Beginning Blends

By definition, a consonant blend occurs when two or three consonant sounds (with their related letters) cluster together and are pronounced rapidly. The English language generally does not permit the blending of two or more consonant sounds at the beginning of a word. However, certain combinations of two-letter and three-letter blends are permitted. The two-letter blend groups that combine at the beginning of words (and sometimes in the middle, or medially) to give us hundreds of words in English are of four major types: the *r* blends, the *l* blends, the *s* blends, and the *tw* blends. Listen as you say the words in columns *A*, *B*, *C*, and *D* aloud.

As you voiced the lists of words, you should have noticed several things. When *r* or *l* is part of a blend, such as *cr* or *cl*, the letters *r* and *l* are second. With the *s* blends, the letter *s* comes first in the consonant cluster, as in *scan*, *slip*, and *small*. As you may have noticed, when *W* is part of a blend, it appears second like the *r* and *l* in words such as *tw*inkle, *tw*irl, and *tw*ist. Only three words represent the *dw* blend: *dw*arf, *dw*ell, and *dw*indle.

The *tw* and *tr* consonant blends are the only *t* blends permitted in English. The *tr* blend is included as an *r* blend. The *tw* is included with the *w* blends.

A *r* blends	*B* *l* blends	*C* *s* blends	*D* *tw* blends
*br*eak	*bl*onde	*sc*an	*tw*eak
*cr*ate	*cl*ean	*sk*ate	*tw*eed
*dr*eam	*fly*	*sl*eet	*tw*in
*fr*ight	*gl*eam	*sm*all	*dw*arf
*gr*im	*kl*utz	*sn*atch	*dw*ell
*kr*emlin	*pl*ease	*sp*urt	*dw*indle
*pr*unes		*st*op	
*tr*ain		*sw*im	

We might generalize about consonant blends as follows:

There are 4 two-letter consonant blend groups found at the beginning (and sometimes in the middle) of words. These are the *r*, *l*, *s*, and *w* blends.

1. **The *r*, *l*, and *w* blends consist of two letters with the *r*, *e*, and *w* coming second.**
2. **The *s* blend consisits of two letters with the *s* coming first.**

See Appendix B for example words to use in teaching the consonant blends *r*, *l*, *s*, and *tw*.

Three-Consonant Beginning Blends

Three consonants may be blended together as well. Many of the *s* blends, as well as *thr* may be combined at the beginning of words such as *scr*ub, *spl*ash, *str*eak, and *thr*oat.

str	*scr*	*spr*	*spl*	*shr*	*squ*	*thr*
*str*ing	*scr*ap	*spr*ing	*spl*ash	*shr*ub	*squ*are	*thr*oat
*str*eet	*scr*ub	*spr*ay	*spl*it	*shr*imp	*squ*eak	*thr*ob

Ending Blends

In addition to the beginning consonant blends, many English words also have ending consonant blends. Learning about final blends is essential for understanding that only certain combinations of letters (graphemes) are used to make a sound.

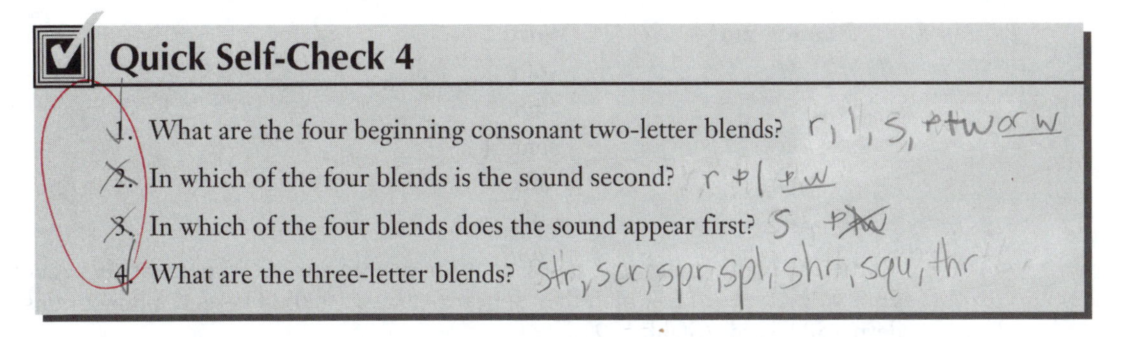

Quick Self-Check 4

1. What are the four beginning consonant two-letter blends?
2. In which of the four blends is the sound second?
3. In which of the four blends does the sound appear first?
4. What are the three-letter blends?

Some phonics programs also include these blends for instructional purposes. Others do not, because certain program writers believe that in decoding strategies, the beginning letter/sounds are more important than the ending letter/sounds. Examples of these combinations are *ld* as in bo*ld*, *nd* as in ba*nd*, *nt* as in se*nt*, *nk* as in tha*nk*,[3] and *lk* as in sta*lk*.

Two-Consonant Final Blends

ct	*ft*	*ld*	*lf*	*lk*	*lm*	*lp*
refle*ct*	le*ft*	co*ld*	e*lf*	mi*lk*	ca*lm*	gu*lp*
a*ct*	si*ft*	ba*ld*	she*lf*	si*lk*	pa*lm*	he*lp*
du*ct*	swi*ft*	yie*ld*	myse*lf*	fo*lk*	rea*lm*	ye*lp*
stri*ct*	the*ft*	to*ld*	se*lf*	su*lk*		

lt	*mp*	*nt*	*nd*	*nk*	*ng*	*pt*
fe*lt*	da*mp*	se*nt*	a*nd*	ba*nk*	sa*ng*	a*pt*
ti*lt*	lu*mp*	mi*nt*	ba*nd*	si*nk*	ri*ng*	cre*pt*
qui*lt*	mu*mp*	ru*nt*	behi*nd*	su*nk*	ru*ng*	sle*pt*
bui*lt*	li*mp*	au*nt*	gra*nd*	mi*nk*	so*ng*	we*pt*

st	*sk*	*sp*	*sm*	*st*
du*st*	ri*sk*	cri*sp*	reali*sm*	ju*st*
lo*st*	du*sk*	gra*sp*	touri*sm*	va*st*
twi*st*	fla*sk*	cla*sp*		mi*st*
tru*st*	de*sk*	a*sp*		fi*st*

[3] Some phonics programs classify this as a consonant digraph.

Three-Consonant Final Blends

Some words end in a consonant blend made of three consonants. Some of the most frequent three-consonant blends are listed below with sample words.

nge	nce	nse	nch	tch
hi*nge*	da*nce*	ri*nse*	pi*nch*	sti*tch*
ra*nge*	fe*nce*	de*nse*	pu*nch*	stre*tch*
fri*nge*	si*nce*	se*nse*	hu*nch*	la*tch*
cri*nge*	sta*nce*		i*nch*	

Phonograms

One way of teaching ending blends is by combining a blend with a vowel. This cluster of vowel and blend is frequently referred to as a phonogram. Some examples of these combinations are:

Phonogram	Word
old	sold
ind	find
ent	sent
ank	rank
alk[4]	walk

Of the 286 phonograms that appear in primary grade texts,[5] 95 percent are pronounced the same in every word in which they appear (Adams, 1990). These 37 phonograms alone can derive 500 words (Stahl, 1992).

-ack	-ain	-ake	-ale	-all	-ame	
-an	-ank	-ap	-ash	-at	-ate	
-aw	-ay	-eat	-ell	-est	-ice	
-ick	-ide	-ight	-ill	-in	-ine	
-ing	-ink	-ip	-ir	-ock	-oke	
-op	-or	-ore	-uck	-ug	-ump	-unk

We might generalize about ending blends as follows:

Certain consonants combine at the ends of words. Some of the more common of these are *ld*, *nd*, *nt*, *nk*, and *lk*. To teach these ending blends, they are sometimes combined with a vowel.

Quick Self-Check 5

1. What are common two-letter blends that occur at the end of words?
2. What are common three-letter blends that occur at the end of words?

[4] Phonograms are sometimes referred to as *rimes* and the letter or syllable before them as an *onset*.

[5] See Appendix C for additional phonograms.

SUMMARY

The scope of the written English language system for reading teachers may be more easily understood by dividing it into categories that include consonants and vowels. Further categorizing consonants may assist in understanding the phoneme-grapheme relationship. The consonant groupings include consonants representing one sound, consonants representing more than one sound, digraphs and blends. Table 2.1 provides a graphic illustration of the consonant divisions.

TABLE 2.1 Overview of English Orthography for the Teacher—Consonants

Consonants Representing One Sound		**Consonants Representing More Than One Sound (Variant Consonants)**		**Digraphs with *h***		**Digraphs With First Silent Letter**		**Digraph Cluster Following a Short Vowel**	
b	bat	c	cat	ch	chair	ck	deck	dge	bridge
d	dent		city		scheme				
f	fall				chandelier	gn	gnome	tch	stitch
h	hit	g	got						
j	jam		giant	gh	ghost	kn	knife		
k	kite								
l	land	s	us	ph	pharmacy	wr	write		
m	mat		his						
n	name		sugar	sh	ship				
p	pan								
qu	quite	x	fox	th	thick				
r	road		exit		these				
t	top		xerox						
v	vane			wh	what				
w	well				who				
y	yellow								
z	zebra								
Two-Consonant Beginning Blends				**Three-Consonant Beginning Blends**		**Two-Consonant Final Blends**		**Three-Consonant Final Blends**	
r	break	s	scan	str	string	ct	duct	nge	hinge
	crate		skate			ft	left		
	dream		sleet	scr	scrap	ld	cold	nce	dance
	fright		small			lf	elf		
	grim		snatch	spr	spring	lk	milk	nse	rinse
	kremlin		spurt			lm	calm		
	prunes		stop	spl	splash	lp	help	nch	pinch
	train		swim			lt	felt		
				shr	shrub	mp	damp	tch	stitch
l	blonde	tw	tweak			nt	sent		
	clean		tweed	squ	square	nd	and		
	fly		twin			nk	sink		
	gleam		twinkle	thr	throat	ng	sang		
	klutz		twirl			pt	wept		
	please		twist			st	lost		
						sk	risk		
						sp	crisp		
						sm	realism		
						st	fist		

How much or how little of this information is directly taught to students depends totally on a teacher's theoretical orientation to the teaching of reading or in some cases, to the teaching materials provided by the school system. For example, a teacher who believes in a more sequential, synthetic approach may teach all the information contained herein in a step-by-step linear fashion. A teacher who uses an embedded or contextual approach may teach some of the contents of this chapter and then wait until a situation presents itself that requires additional knowledge to continue reading instruction. Other teachers allow children to discover this information through meaningful encounters with literature.

Regardless of the theoretical orientation methods or materials used, teachers cannot teach letters and sounds effectively unless they have an in-depth understanding of the information themselves.

Review Questions

1. Is there a connection between the consonant groups (glides, liquids, nasals, fricatives, stops) and the order that consonants appear to be taught as identified by the comparison of phonics programs in this chapter?

2. Can you think of some fun, game-like ways to practice consonants, consonant digraphs, and consonant blends?

Chapter 3

The English Sound System: Vowels

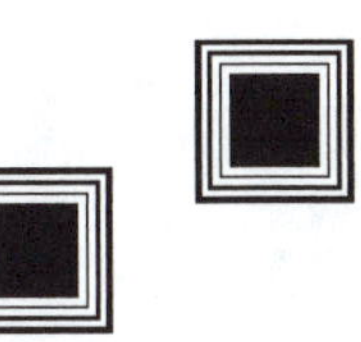

The term *vowel* comes from the Latin word *vocalis*, which means "uttering voice" or "speaking." Unlike consonants, which are characterized by an interruption of airflow at some point in the vocal tract, a vowel is characterized by an opening of the vocal tract and is produced when there is no interference with the column of air within the vocal tract.

Understanding Vowels

The common vowels are *a*, *e*, *i*, *o*, and *u*. Letters that are generally consonants sometimes act like vowels, such as *w* and *y*. To demonstrate how difficult it can be to understand vowels, consider the fact that there are 44 phonemes; 25 of these phonemes are consonant phonemes with 21 letters to represent the sounds. The remaining 19 vowel phonemes have 5 letters to represent their sounds. It should be clear that understanding vowels and the sounds they represent is far more complicated than understanding consonants and more than one-letter graphemes are needed to represent the sounds.

Vowels are generally classified by where they occur in the mouth and by the position of the tongue within the oral cavity. Other factors are also considered, but here we will limit the discussion to these two broad areas. Blevins (1998) explains, "The most important distinguishing characteristic of a vowel is its place of articulation" (p. 47). Vowels are classified according to (a) whether they are produced in the front, central, or back part of the mouth and (b) whether the tongue is raised to a high (closed), mid, or low degree (open). The chart summarizes the vowel sounds and their classifications (Blevins, 1998; Wilde, 1997).

	Front	Central	Back
High (Closed)	long *e*: be, free short *i*: bib, grin long *i*: lime, bite		long *u*: mule, use
Mid	long *a*: bale, face short *e*: well, bed	schwa	long *o*: go, dome
Low (Open)	short *a*: fact, ban	short *u*: bug, thud	short *o*: slob, mop

Louisa Moats also provided a diagram that helps put the location of the vowel in perspective. Figure 3.1 illustrates the location of the vowel sound and the shape of the mouth. Say the following words slowly, noting where they are produced as well as the location of the tongue. Try saying *tree*, and *spoon*. Note where these vowels are located on the chart in Figure 3.1 (*tree* is front and high; *spoon* is back and high). Now, try the word *hot* and then *tree* and *spoon*. Again, where does *hot* appear on the chart? Say each of the following words and locate where it falls on the chart (Figure 3.1): *bee, pin, face, web, bat, tie, dog, sun, saw, toe, book, moon, toy, cow, about.*

The Single Vowels, *a, e, i, o, u,* and the Schwa

Each vowel encodes a short and long sound, and also a schwa sound. While this latter sound has many regional variations, it is usually similar to short *u* as in *up* and is shown in texts as an upside down *e*, or ə. The vowels *a*, *o*, and *u* encode an additional sound, sometimes called a special or third sound, to be discussed later.

FIGURE 3.1 Adaptation of Moats' Vowel Chart (2000)

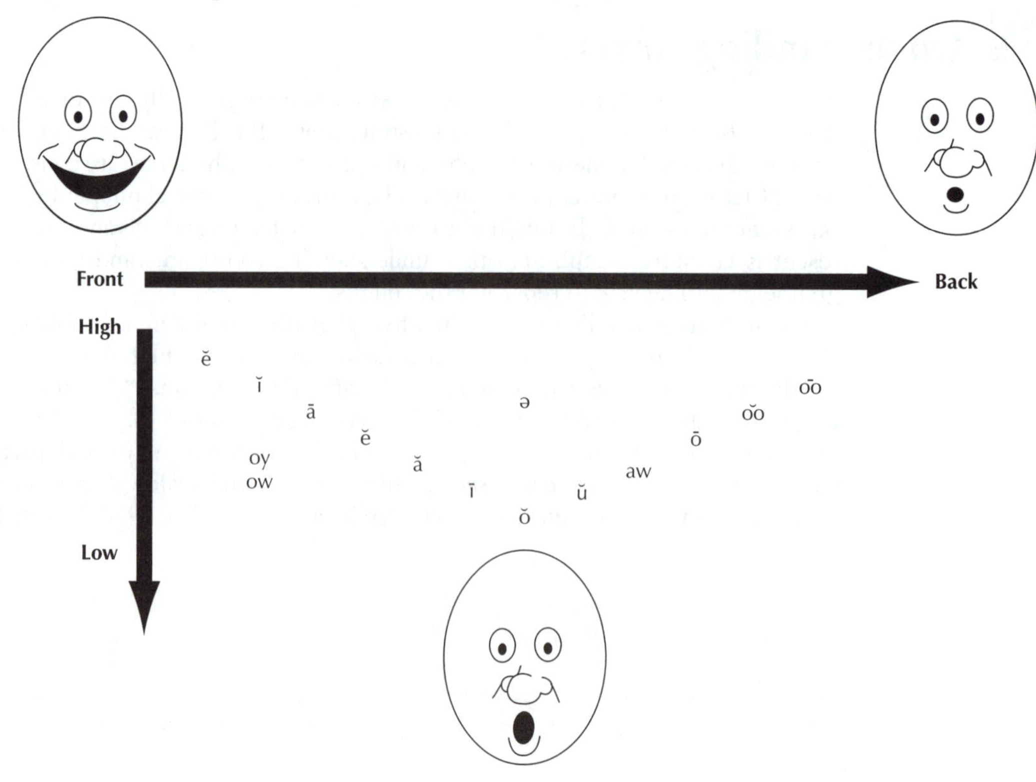

Short Vowel Sound	Long Vowel Sound	Schwa Sound
*a*ct	*a*ble	b*a* na na / ə /
*e*gg	*e*ven	tick *e*t / ə /
*i*t	*i*vy	pen c*i*l / ə /
*o*live	*o*men	*a* pron / ə /
*u*ntil	*u*nit, t*u*lip	

The Short Vowel Sound

The short vowel sound is the most prominent in English. The breve mark (˘) is used in writing to indicate the short vowel. Examples: *ăct*, *ĕgg*.

To aid in recalling vowel sounds, teachers, with the help of their students, often compose fun sentences beginning with these sounds such as:

*A*n *e*gg *i*s *o*ddly *u*neven.

Another way to remember the short vowel sound is by thinking of key words that are similar:

b*ă*t	b*ŏ*p
b*ĕ*t	b*ŭ*t
b*ĭ*t	

The Long Vowel Sound

The macron (¯) is positioned above the vowel to indicate that it is long. Examples are *āble*, *ēven*. The long vowel sound is identical to the name of the vowel as *ā*, *ē*, *ī*, *ō*, *ū*. In addition, sometimes the letter *u* has the long vowel sound /o͞o/ as in the word *tulip*. An examination of the two word lists below will indicate the two long *ū* sounds.

A	***B***
***u* as /yū/**	***u* as /o͞o/**
cūte	brūte
fūture	dūke
hūman	Jūne
mūle	lūte
pūny	nūmeral
ūse	tūbe

Repeat these words to hear the difference between the two sounds. The words in list *A* have the traditional long /yū/ sound, while in list *B*, the long *ū* has the sound of /o͞o/, not /yū/.

In sum, while the vowel letters *ā*, *ē*, *ī*, and *ō* may each decode as one long vowel sound, the letter *ū* may decode as two, /y*ū*/ and /o͞o/.

Special Vowel Sounds

Repeat the following words to hear the special or third vowel sounds of *a*, *o*, and *u*.

***a* as /ä/**	***o* as /o͞o/**	***u* as /o͝o/**
c*a*ll	l*o*se	p*u*sh
w*a*nd	wh*o*m	b*u*llet
f*a*ther	pr*o*ve	b*u*shel

Many reading programs only teach short and long vowel sounds. Words such as those listed previously, representative of special vowel sounds, are sometimes treated as sight words.

A word of caution about these sounds. Except for the long vowels, it is extremely difficult to pronounce the vowel sounds in isolation. When learning or teaching the short vowels, place a consonant sound such as /t/ after each of them to make pronunciation easier. These combinations are often referred to as phonograms.[1] (Refer to Appendix C) The short vowels would then be pronounced in a phonogram or word as follows:

/at/ as in săt
/et/ as in sĕt
/it/ as in sĭt
/ot/ as in tŏt
/ut/ as in hŭt

Key words are very important for remembering sounds, as we do not speak in sounds but in words! Teachers and learners should capitalize on what is familiar.

The Schwa

One of the changes occurring in the English language at the present time is the reduction of the short vowel to the schwa sound. What this means is that in *unaccented* syllables many of the short vowels have an /uh/ kind of sound, similar to short *u* as in *up*?[2]

Consider the following words as spoken in context:

*a*cróss	He walked *a*cross the street.
tíck*e*t	She waited for a tick*e*t.
pénc*i*l	The penc*i*l needed sharpening.
séc*o*nd	Just one sec*o*nd, please.

In each instance the vowel in the unaccented syllable has a schwa sound, written like an upside down e, /ə/. To accurately indicate the sound of the vowel, you will often find words like those in the previous example written in dictionaries, glossaries, and textbooks as follows:

ə cross	tick ət
pen səl	sec ənd

In view of what we have just mentioned in regard to short vowels, long vowels, third sound, and schwa, we might make the following generalizations about single vowels:

1. **Single vowel letters have a short and long sound.**
2. **The short vowel sounds are *ă* (ăct); *ĕ* (ĕgg); *ĭ* (ĭt); *ŏ* (ŏlive); and *ŭ* (ŭntil).**
3. **The long vowel sounds are the same as the names of the vowel letters, /ā/, /ē/, /ī/, /ō/, /ū/. The letter *u* has a second additional long vowel sound of /ōō/ (brute).**
4. **The letters *a* as /ä/ (call); *o* as /ōō/ (prove); and *u* as /ŏŏ/ (push) have a special, or third sound. Sometimes words with these sounds are taught as sight words.**
5. **Unaccented syllables with a single vowel letter may have a schwa sound. The sound is written as /ə/ (tickət).**

See Appendix B for example words to use in teaching vowel sounds.

[1] Sometimes phonograms are referred to as a base.
[2] Regional variations must be considered when discussing the schwa.

Quick Self-Check 1

1. The vowel letters, *a, e, i, o,* and *u* may encode a long or short sound.
   a. In addition, what vowel letter has a second long sound? What is it?
   b. Which vowel letters may encode a third sound? Are words with these sounds taught phonetically or by sight?
   c. What is the schwa sound? In what part of a word is it usually heard?

Final Unpronounced Letter *e*

We sometimes use the single letter vowel and a final *e* to encode the long vowel sound. We do this to differentiate between words such as the following:

A	*B*
măd	māde
mĕt	mēte
rĭd	rīde
nŏt	nōte
cŭt	cūte

Therefore, we might generalize about final *e* changing the preceding vowel sound as follows:

The letter *e* at the end of a word may sometimes indicate that the preceding vowel is long. (Remember, too, that a final *e* may indicate that the preceding *c* or *g* has a soft sound as in stan*c*e and bar*g*e.)[3]

There are other reasons for the unpronounced final *e*. Language is often arbitrary when it comes to spelling. In English we have a rule that English words will not end in the letter *v*. With words such as *have, prove,* and *love,* the *e* does not make the preceding vowel long. It is simply there because English words do not end in *v*. Sometimes, however, the final *e* after *v* does make the preceding vowel long in such words as *shave* and *stove*. In these and other similar words, the *e* plays a dual role.

Another reason an unpronounced final *e* appears after certain words, such as *house* and *awe*, is simply due to historical circumstance and the whims of early printers. When several words began to change during the Middle English period, the final *e*, formerly pronounced as an /ĕ/, became silent, but printers nonetheless retained the written letter. Second, during the earlier printing periods the letter *e* was added to fill up the line when words did not complete the required number of spaces. We still have to struggle with words such as these.

The last reason for unpronounced final *e* can be found in such words as *table, maple,* and *noble*. The *e* follows an *l* and is needed to complete the second syllable; otherwise, the first vowel would be short, and the word would be unpronounceable. For example, try pronouncing *tabl, mapl,* and *nobl*.

We now have five reasons why English words have a final unpronounced letter *e*:

Final Unpronounced *e*

1. **Final *e* may indicate that the vowel before it is long.**
2. **Final *e* may indicate that the preceding *c* or *g* has a soft sound.**

[3] Refer to "Consonants With More Than One Sound," if you do not remember this generalization.

3. **Final *e* is used after *v* because English words do not end in *v*.**
4. **Final *e* may be a historical leftover.**
5. **Final *e* follows *l* in a two-syllable word to complete the syllable.**

A further note on final *e*. While this rule has about 93 percent predictability, most exceptions occur with words that end in *ile* as *facile*, *ine* as *machine*, both derived from French spellings, and words ending in *are* as *mare*.

See Appendix B for example words to use in teaching long vowels with final silent *e*.

Quick Self-Check 2

Next to each word indicate the final *e* generalization.

1. prove
2. stable
3. fence
4. stake
5. else

Vowel Digraphs and Diphthongs

Recall that a consonant *digraph* means two letters encoding only a single sound or several single sounds. In addition to consonant digraphs, there are vowel digraphs. Recall that some digraphs encode more than one single sound. There is also within the vowels a second category called diphthongs.[4]

There is not always agreement as to what a digraph is and what a diphthong is. By definition, a diphthong is a "gliding sound from one vowel to another." If you say the long *o* sound and watch your lips in a mirror, you will see that your mouth formation remains stationary. However, if you pronounce the diphthong /oy/ as in *oil*, your mouth moves or glides as it goes from one sound to the other.

This lack of agreement as to what is a digraph and what is a diphthong comes about because linguists and reading specialists, who define these terms, have different points of reference. Linguists are usually concerned with the nature of the sounds, and those who teach reading are concerned with decoding the letters that encode those sounds.

Learning such terminology as *digraph* and *diphthong* is not that important for children who are learning decoding strategies. What is important is that they see such vowel combinations as *ou* or *au* as units and do not try to read them as individual vowel sounds.

Vowel Digraphs and Diphthongs That Begin with a

Vowel Pair	Word
ai	m*ai*d /ā/
ay	st*ay* /ā/
au	v*au*lt /ä/
aw	dr*aw* /ä/

[4] Diphthongs will be discussed in more detail later.

ai* and *ay As you can see, in addition to the silent *e* pattern, we have ways of writing the long *a* sound using two letters. Examples: m*ai*d and st*ay*. This is one of the difficulties in understanding the English writing-decoding system. We have too many different ways of representing the same sound!

The vowel digraph *ai* may decode as long *a* in the middle of a word while *ay* decodes as long *a* at the end.[5] The reason for this is that English words do not end in *i* except for the foreign words we have borrowed, such as *spaghetti* and *macaroni*.

au* and *aw In some phonics systems the combinations *au* and *aw* are considered digraphs and in others diphthongs. Both *au* and *aw* decode as the sound /ä/. Since English words do not usually end in *u* (as is the case with *v*), *au* is generally used at the beginning and middle of a word, as in *au*thor and f*au*lt, and *aw* usually is used at the end, as in l*aw*.

These four pairs, *ai*, *ay*, *au*, and *aw*, are considered stable in that they almost always decode as these sounds.

We might generalize about these digraphs/diphthongs beginning with the letter *a* as follows:

1. **There are four vowel pairs beginning with *a*: *ai*, *ay*, *au*, and *aw*.**
2. **The digraphs *ai* and *ay* decode as the long /ā/ sound. *Ai* may be used at the beginning or in the middle of a word. *Ay* may be used at the end.**
3. ***Au* and *aw* decode as the /ä/ sound. *Au* is usually used at the beginning or in the middle of a word. *Aw* generally is used at the end.**

See Appendix B for example words to use in teaching vowel digraphs and diphthongs beginning with *a*.

Quick Self-Check 3

1. Why do we have the two digraphs *ai* and *ay*? What sound do they encode?
2. Why do we have the two digraphs *au* and *aw*? What sound do they encode?
3. Why are these combinations considered stable?

Vowel Digraphs with e

Vowel digraphs that contain the letter *e* are as follows:

Digraph	Word		
ee	sl*ee*p /ē/		
ea	h*ea*t /ē/	spr*ea*d /ĕ/	st*ea*k /ā/
ie	bel*ie*f /ē/	t*ie* /ī/	
ei	rec*ei*ve /ē/	v*ei*n /ā/	
	(very irregular digraph)		
ey	donk*ey* /ē/	pr*ey* /ā/	

Since the *e* digraphs are more complicated than the *a* digraphs, we will generalize about each one individually.

[5] When a suffix has been added to the word, *ay* may be in the middle. Example: *playing*.

ee The vowel digraph *ee* is usually the first vowel digraph introduced in reading because of its stability. Since it usually decodes as long /ē/ (sl*ee*p, j*ee*p, st*ee*p), we may generalize as follows:

The vowel digraph *ee* decodes as /ē/.

ea The vowel digraph *ea* is more complicated because it decodes as three sounds. Look at the following lists of words:

A	***B***	***C***
***ea* as /ē/**	***ea* as /ĕ/**	***ea* as /ā/**
cl*ea*n	l*ea*ther	st*ea*k
r*ea*ch	br*ea*th	br*ea*k
s*ea*l	r*ea*dy	gr*ea*t
p*ea*ch	pl*ea*sant	

The first and most common sound is long /ē/ as in cl*ea*n, r*ea*ch, and s*ea*l. About 25 percent of the time this digraph decodes as short /ĕ/, as in l*ea*ther, br*ea*th, and r*ea*dy. A third sound this digraph decodes as is long /ā/, although there are only a few such words. Examples are gr*ea*t and st*ea*k.

We might generalize about the *ea* digraph as follows:

1. **The *ea* digraph decodes as three sounds.**
2. **It most commonly decodes as long /ē/ as in h*ea*t.**
3. **It also decodes as short /ĕ/ as in br*ea*d.**
4. **In a few words it decodes as /ā/ as in st*ea*k.**

ie The *ie* digraph decodes as two sounds, long /ē/ and long /ī/. Excluding suffixed words, the most common sound is long /ē/. Only a few base words with *ie* decode as long /ī/. These are words such as p*ie*, t*ie*, l*ie*, and d*ie*. Words with suffix endings, however, often do decode as /ī/ as in tr*ied* (try + ed), dr*ied* (dry + ed), and suppl*ies* (supply + s). This is because the *y* is dropped and changed to *i*. There are, as stated, many examples of base words with *ie* decoding as long /ē/ such as the following:

***ie* as /ē/**	
bel*ie*ve	p*ie*ce
br*ie*f	sh*ie*ld
gr*ie*f	th*ie*f
n*ie*ce	y*ie*ld

We might generalize about the *ie* digraph as follows:

The *ie* vowel digraph decodes as two sounds, long /ē/ as in br*ie*f and long /ī/ as in p*ie*. Excluding suffixed words, the most common sound is long /ē/.

ei The *ei* digraph is highly irregular and difficult to classify except for its relationship to *c*. When *ei* follows a *c*, it always decodes as long /ē/. This digraph may also decode as long /ā/ in a few words. See the following:

A	***B***
ei* as /ē/ after *c	***ei* as /ā/**
rec*ei*ve	v*ei*n
conc*ei*ve	r*ei*gn
rec*ei*pt	v*ei*l

However, in addition to long /ē/ after *c* and the long /ā/ sound, this digraph shows considerable variability, as evidenced in the following words:

counterf*ei*t	/ĭ/	l*ei*sure	/ē/
*ei*ther	/ē/	s*ei*zed	/ē/
forf*ei*ted	/ĭ/	sover*ei*gn	/ə/
h*ei*fer	/ĕ/	prot*ei*n	/ē/

Teachers sometimes use nonsense sentences to help students recall these words: "Neither counterf*ei*ter s*ei*zed the sover*ei*gn. They wanted the h*ei*fer, prot*ei*n, and l*ei*sure."

We might generalize about the vowel digraph *ei* as follows:

The vowel digraph *ei* decodes as the sound of long /ē/ after *c*. It also decodes as the sound of /ā/ as in v*ei*n. Its vowel sound also varies in other words.

ey The vowel digraph *ey* usually decodes as the sound of long /ē/. In a few words it decodes as the sound of /ā/. See the following lists of words:

A	***B***
***ey* as /ē/**	***ey* as /ā/**
vall*ey*	th*ey*
k*ey*	pr*ey*
pull*ey*	conv*ey*
attorn*ey*	ob*ey*

We might generalize about the *ey* digraph as follows:

The *ey* digraph generally decodes as the long sound of /ē/. In a few words it decodes as /ā/.

We can now summarize all the generalizations of the *e* vowel digraphs as follows:

The digraph

1. ***ee* decodes as /ē/, as in sl*ee*p.**
2. ***ea* decodes most often as long /ē/, as in h*ea*t; as short /ĕ/, as in br*ea*d; and in a few words as long /ā/, as in st*ea*k.**
3. ***ie* usually decodes as /ē/, as in bel*ie*ve; as /ī/, as in t*ie*.**
4. ***ei* decodes as /ē/ after *c*, as in rec*ei*ve; as /ā/, as in v*ei*n; and its sound varies in other words.**
5. ***ey* decodes as /ē/, as in donk*ey*; as /ā/, as in ob*ey*.**

See Appendix B for example words to use in teaching digraphs with e.

To simplify all these generalizations, we may conclude that the *e* digraphs decode mainly as long /ē/ and sometimes as long /ā/.

Quick Self-Check 4

ee *ea* *ie* *ei* *ey*

1. Which digraph is fairly stable and encodes one sound?
2. Which digraph has the greatest variability?
3. Which digraph usually encodes /ē/ and /ĕ/ and /ā/?
4. Which digraph usually encodes /ē/ and /ā/?
5. Which digraph usually encodes /ē/ and /ī/?
6. What would be a simplified generalization for the digraphs with *e*?

Vowel Digraph with i

The letter *i* combines with *a* to form the vowel digraph *ai* that decodes as long /ā/. The letter *i* also combines with *e* in the vowel digraphs *ie* and *ei*.

The letter *i* will also combine with the consonant digraph *gh* mentioned under the unique *h* digraph. This three-letter combination *igh*, called a digraph by some, decodes as long /ī/ after a beginning sound. It is often referred to as "the three-letter i." Say the words below:

***igh* as /ī/**

bl*igh*t	r*igh*t
fl*igh*t	s*igh*

We might generalize about the letter *i* as follows:

The letter *i* combines with *gh* in the middle or end of some words and decodes as long /ī/.

See Appendix B for example words to use when teaching the three-letter *i*.

Vowel Digraphs and Diphthongs with o

The following digraph/diphthong classification beginning with *o* is based on an examination of basal readers.

oa The letter *o* combines with the letter *a* to form the *oa* vowel digraph and decodes as the long /o/ sound rather consistently. See the following examples:

***oa* as /ō/**

c*oa*ch	fl*oa*t
c*oa*st	gl*oa*t

We might generalize about the *oa* digraph as follows:

The *oa* digraph decodes as the sound of long /ō/.

oo The letter *o* combines with a second letter *o* to form the combination *oo*, and this combination, together with *ou*, *ow*, *oi*, and *oy*, is usually considered a diphthong. Examine the following two lists containing words with the *oo* diphthong:

A		*B*
***oo* as /o͞o/**		***oo* as /o͝o/**
bl*oo*m	s*oo*the	br*oo*k
br*oo*m	sp*oo*l	cr*oo*k
cr*oo*n	t*oo*th	sh*oo*k
sh*oo*t	tr*oo*p	st*oo*d

There are many more words with the long /o͞o/ sound than with the short /o͝o/ sound. Say the words in these two lists to yourself very slowly and hear the difference between the two sounds. Put a consonant such as *m* after the long /o͞o/ (o͞om) as in the word br*oo*m to hear the isolated long /o͞o/ sound. Put a consonant *k* after the /o͝o/ (o͝ok) as in the word cr*oo*k to hear the isolated short /o͝o/ sound.

We might generalize about the *oo* diphthong as follows:

The *oo* diphthong decodes as two sounds: long /o͞o/ as in br*oo*m and short /o͝o/ as in l*oo*k. The long /o͞o/ sound is the more common of the two.

ou The letter *o* also combines with the letter *u* and encodes several sounds. It is a very complex combination. Its two most common sounds are /*ow*/ as in cl*ou*d and /ŭ/ as in t*ou*ch. Additional words include:

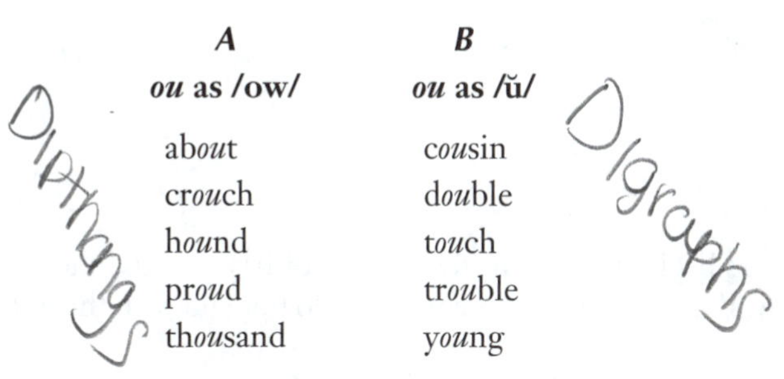

A	***B***
***ou* as /ow/**	***ou* as /ŭ/**
ab*ou*t	c*ou*sin
cr*ou*ch	d*ou*ble
h*ou*nd	t*ou*ch
pr*ou*d	tr*ou*ble
th*ou*sand	y*ou*ng

Say these words to hear the sounds.

Two additional sounds encoded by *ou* are /ō/ as in s*ou*l, and /o͞o/ as in gr*ou*p. Note these two lists:

A	***B***
***ou* as /ō/**	***ou* as /o͞o/**
s*ou*l	gr*ou*p
p*ou*ltry	r*ou*te
sh*ou*lder	w*ou*nd

Say these words to hear the sounds.

These last two sounds are not too common and are not always taught because together they represent only about 10 percent of the words containing *ou*.

We might generalize about the *ou* combination as follows:

1. **When *ou* is a diphthong, it most commonly decodes as /ow/ as in s*ou*nd.**
2. **Its second most common sound is /ŭ/ as in c*ou*sin.**
3. **In only a few words does it decode as /ō/ as in sh*ou*lder and /o͞o/ as in gr*ou*p.**

Now you can understand why it is so difficult to classify diphthongs and digraphs. Some vowel pairs as *ou* are diphthongs in one context, as in ab*ou*t, and digraphs in another, as in t*ou*ch.

ow The letter *o* combines with *w* to form both the /ow/ diphthong and the long /ō/ vowel sound.[6] Examine the following two lists:

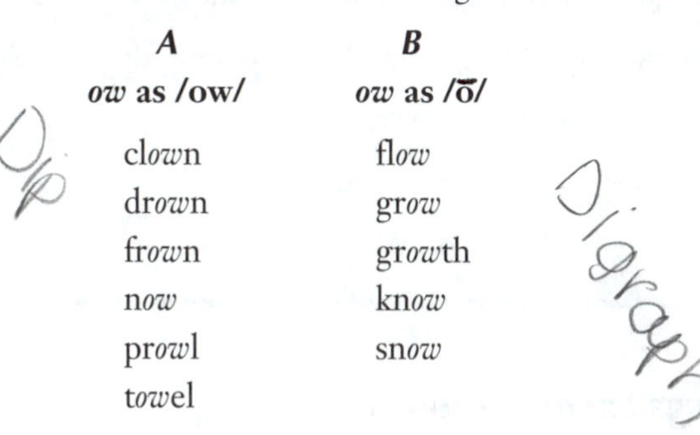

A	***B***
***ow* as /ow/**	***ow* as /ō/**
cl*ow*n	fl*ow*
dr*ow*n	gr*ow*
fr*ow*n	gr*ow*th
n*ow*	kn*ow*
pr*ow*l	sn*ow*
t*ow*el	

Repeat the words to hear these sounds.

In the first list, *ow* decodes as the sound of /ow/ as in t*ow*el. In the second list, *ow* decodes as the sound of long /ō/ in kn*ow*. Notice that most of the *B* list words are ending sounds.

We might generalize about the combination *ow* as follows:

The combination *ow* decodes as two sounds: /ow/ as in t*ow*el and long /ō/ as in gl*ow*.

[6] Many linguists consider all long vowels diphthongs.

oi and oy The letter *o* combines with *i* and also with *y* to form the two diphthongs *oi* and *oy*. Both encode the same sound of /oy/. Note the following lists:

A	*B*
***oi* as /oy/**	***oy* as /oy/**
o*i*l	t*oy*
so*i*l	empl*oy*
m*oi*st	destr*oy*

The *oi* is used at the beginning and in the middle of base words, and *oy* is used at the end, similar to *ai* and *ay*. English words, as mentioned, do not end with the letter *i* except for borrowed foreign words.

We might generalize about these two diphthongs as follows:

The two diphthongs *oi* and *oy* both decode as the /oy/ sound. *Oi* is used at the beginning and in the middle of base words, while *oy* is used at the end.

The letter *o* combines with other vowels to form digraphs and diphthongs. The combination(s) are as follows:

1. ***oa* decodes as /ō/ in c*oa*t.**
2. ***oo* decodes as /o͞o/ in m*oo*n and as /o͝o/ in b*oo*k.**
3. ***ou* usually decodes as /ow/ in cl*ou*d and as /ŭ/ in t*ou*ch; it also decodes in a few words as /ō/ in sh*ou*lder and as /o͞o/ in gr*ou*p.**
4. ***ow* decodes as /ow/ in c*ow*, and as /ō/ in l*ow*.**
5. ***oi* and *oy* decode as /oy/. The *oi* diphthong comes at the beginning and middle of words while *oy* is used at the end.**

See Appendix B for example words to use in teaching the *o* combinations.

Quick Self-Check 5

oa *oo* *ou* *ow* *oi* *oy*

1. Which combination may encode four different sounds? Identify the sounds and give key words. What are its two most common sounds?
2. Why do we have two diphthongs, *oi* and *oy*, encoding the same sound?
3. Which digraph encodes one sound? What is it?
4. List the two sounds encoded by *ow*. Write key words.
5. List the two sounds encoded by *oo*. Write key words.

Vowel Diphthongs Encoding /o͞o/

ui* and *ue The letter *u* combines with the letter *i* and also with the letter *e* to form diphthongs that decode as /o͞o/. Note the following two lists:

A	*B*
***ui* as /o͞o/**	***ue* as /o͞o/**
j*ui*ce	bl*ue*
j*ui*cy	d*ue*

sl*ui*ce	fl*ue*
s*ui*t	tr*ue*

Say the words to hear the sounds.

ew There is also another two-letter diphthong that begins with the letter *e* and decodes as /o͞o/. This combination *ew* could have been included with the vowel *e* combinations, but since it decodes as /o͞o/, it seemed more advantageous to place it here.

Examine this list of words:

ew as /o͞o/	
bl*ew*	dr*ew*
br*ew*	fl*ew*
ch*ew*	st*ew*
cr*ew*	str*ew*n

We might generalize about these diphthongs as follows:

The diphthongs *ui*, *ue*, and *ew* usually decode as the sound of /o͞o/ as in the words fr*ui*t, bl*ue*, and str*ew*.

During our discussion of the long vowel sound encoded by the letter *u*, we mentioned that there were actually two long vowel sounds: /yū/ and /o͞o/. This is also true of the vowel diphthongs *ew* and *ui*. While they usually decode as /o͞o/, when particular consonant sounds precede them, the sound will be /yū/. Examples: *few*, *hue*, *cue*, *mew*. Some phonics programs teach two sounds for these combinations; others teach only the most common sound /o͞o/.

Note again one of the difficulties encountered by children who are learning decoding strategies—too many ways of writing the same sound. For example, in addition to these three diphthongs that decode as /o͞o/, we also have *ou* as /o͞o/ in *group*; *oo* as /o͞o/ in *moon*; *o* as /o͞o/ in *prove*; *u* as /o͞o/ in *rude*.

The Letters *y* and *w*

The letters *y* and *w* have a unique position in our language and may function as either consonants or vowels. Also, *y* combines with other vowels to form digraphs such as *ay* in pl*ay* and *ey* in vall*ey*, and also forms the diphthong *oy* in empl*oy*.

y as a Consonant and Vowel

At the beginning of words, *y* is always a consonant letter as in the words *yacht*, *yard*, and *yellow*. However, *y* in the middle and at the end of words has a variety of vowel sounds.[7]

A	*B*	*C*	*D*
***y* as /ĭ/**	***y* as /ī/**	***y* as final /ī/**	***y* as final /ē/**
cr*y*stal	c*y*cle	appl*y*	cand*y*
g*y*m	tr*y*ing	fl*y*	hill*y*
m*y*sterious		m*y*	penn*y*.

Say these words to hear these sounds.

[7] One reason for this is that the letters *i* and *y* were used interchangeably during the Middle Ages, and even later. Note this sentence from an early New England account. "The pylgrims were pioneers in the land."

A word of caution. There are regional differences to be aware of with ending *y* words. Some people in various parts of the United States would pronounce the words in column *D* with a short /ĭ/ sound instead of the long /ē/ sound.

We might generalize about single letter *y* as follows:

1. **When single letter *y* is first in a word, it decodes as the consonant sound /y/ in words like *y*ard and *y*ellow.**
2. **When single letter *y* is in the middle or at the end of words, it decodes as a vowel. The vowel can be short /ĭ/ as in g*y*m, long /ī/ as in c*y*cle or repl*y*, or long /ē/ as in prett*y*.**

As mentioned during our discussion of the vowels, the letter *y* also combines with vowel letters. Recall *ay* as in pl*ay*, *ey*, as in vall*ey*, and *oy* as in empl*oy*. Putting all this together, we see a variety of possibilities with the letter *y*.

y as a consonant at the beginning:	/y/	*y*ard		
y as a vowel in the middle of words:	/ĭ/	g*y*m,	/ī/	c*y*cle
y as a vowel at the end of words:	/ē/	prett*y*,	/ī/	appl*y*
y as part of the vowel digraph *ay:*	/ā/	m*ay*		
y as part of the vowel digraph *ey:*	/e/	vall*ey*		
y as part of the diphthong *oy:*	/oy/	destr*oy*		

See Appendix B for example *y* words to use in teaching.

w as a Consonant and Vowel

The letter *w* also can be a consonant or vowel and the rules are similar to those for the letter *y*. When the letter *w* occurs before a vowel sound, it behaves like a consonant: *water, well*, and *work*. Unlike letter *y*, which may act like a vowel by itself (*gym, by*), *w* is not a stand-alone vowel. As a vowel, *w* does not represent a phoneme of its own. The letter *w* is only a vowel when it occurs after a vowel and connects with the vowel: *cow, draw*, and *now*.

We might generalize about single letter *w* as follows:

1. **When single letter *w* is first in a word it decodes as the consonant sound /w/ in words like *well* and *water*.**
2. **When *w* appears after a vowel, it may act like a vowel when paired with a "real" vowel in words such as *cow* and *draw*.**

Quick Self-Check 6

1. When does the letter *y* function as a consonant?
2. How does *y* function in the following words. *yes, cry, play, royal?*
3. When does the letter *w* function as a vowel?
4. Give some examples of *w* as a vowel and *w* as a consonant.

r-Controlled Vowels

r with Single Vowel Letters

er, ir, ur, and wor The letter *r*, often referred to as "bossy *r*." combines with certain single vowels and may condition the *preceding* vowel sound. Look at the following four columns of words:

A	*B*	*C*	*D*
***er* as /er/**	***ir* as /er/**	***ur* as /er/**	***wor* as /wer/**
p*er*t	s*ir*	h*ur*t	w*or*se
f*er*n	f*ir*st	ch*ur*n	w*or*thy
h*er*d	squ*ir*m	c*ur*l	w*or*ld
	ch*ir*p		

Pronounce all of these words and note that in each instance the vowel letter and following letter combine to encode the same sound of /er/.

In list *D* you will note that the sound of /w/ precedes the sound of /er/ as in *worse, worthy*, and *world*. The letters *or* decode as /er/ when the letter *w* precedes them.

Several questions might arise in teaching these sounds. A student might ask, "How about words like *here, fire*, and *pure*?" In these words *er, ir*, and *ur* do not decode as /er/. Notice what these three words have in common:

her*e* fir*e* pur*e*

All of them end in a final *e!* Remember that we discussed several reasons for final *e*, one of which was to change the preceding vowel sound. In words that end in *re*, the final *e* also conditions the preceding vowel sound; therefore it will not have the /er/ sound.

We might make the following generalization about the above *r* combinations.

1. **The combinations *er, ir*, and *ur* decode as /er/ when not followed by final *e*.**
2. **When the letter *w* precedes *or*, it decodes as /wer/.**

A word of caution about the letter *r* and the /r/ sound. *No other sound in the English language is pronounced in such a variety of ways.* For example: Easterners tend to omit a final /r/ altogether and then add an /r/ where none exists! Midwesterners tend to give *r* its full pronunciation regardless of placement in a word. African-American dialect speakers sometimes omit final /r/ unless the following sound is a vowel. In certain areas, many unaccented syllables that end with an *r* have a preceding schwa sound instead of a full vowel sound. Therefore, as a teacher you must *take into consideration the regional pronunciation of your area.*

ar The letter *r* with the single vowel *a*. See the following combinations:

A	*B*
***ar* as /är/**	***are* as /âr/**
f*ar*	f*are*
st*ar*	st*are*
m*ar*	m*are*

You will notice two different letter-sound combinations. In column *A*, the words, f*ar*, st*ar*, and m*ar* have the sound of /är/. In column *B* the words f*are*, st*are*, and m*are* have a different sound because of the final *e*. The sound is written /âr/. Say the words to hear the sounds.

We might make a second generalization.

The combination *ar* decodes as /är/ as in f*ar*. When *ar* is followed by an *e*, the sound changes to /âr/ as in f*are*.

or The letter *r* combines with the letter *o* to encode the sound /or/ as in f*or*. Sometimes *or* encodes the schwa vowel sound /ər/ in final unaccented syllables. Again, this has to do with regional variation. Examine the following groups of words and note the difference:

A	*B*
***or* as /ôr/**	***or* as ər**
c*or*k	fáct*or*
f*or*th	dóct*or*

po*r*ch	flávo*r*
sto*r*k	saílo*r*
tho*r*n	visito*r*

We might therefore make a third generalization about the letter *r*:

1. **The letter *r* combines with *o* to decode as the sound of /or/ as in sto*r*k.**
2. **Sometimes it decodes as /ər/ in final unaccented syllables as in words like flavo*r*.**

r with Vowel Digraphs

The letter *r* combines with the digraphs *ea*, *ai*, and *ee*. We will consider the *ea* digraph initially.

ea Note the following three columns:

A	*B*	*C*
***ear* as /ē-r/**	***ear* as /er/[8]**	***ear* as /âr/**
cl*ear*	*ear*n	b*ear*
d*ear*	h*ear*d	p*ear*
f*ear*	l*ear*n	t*ear*
h*ear*	s*ear*ch	w*ear*
9%	6%	2%

In list *A* the *ear* combination decodes as /ē-r/, its most common sound. In *B*, however, the *ear* combination decodes as /er/ while in *C*, *ear* decodes as /âr/. You will note from the percentages that only a few *ear* words (2%) have the /âr/ sound; therefore, words such as these are often taught as sight words. These percentages indicate the number of times such words are usually found in relation to the total number of words with the *ea* combination. About 83 percent of the time *ea* is followed by other consonants as in *mean*, *dread*, and *break*.

ai When *r* combines with the digraph *ai*, there is also a controlling of the vowel sound to /âr/ as in *stair*. Note the following group of words:

***air* as /âr/**

f*air*
p*air*
st*air*
pr*air*ie

About 15 percent of all *ai* words have a following *r* and therefore have this sound.

ee The digraph *ee* is also controlled by a following *r*. The sound becomes /ē-r/. See examples below:

***eer* as /ē-r/**

p*eer*
st*eer*
qu*eer*
ch*eer*

[8] Sometimes the *ear* combination decoding as /er/ is included with *er*, *ir*, *ur*, and *wor*.

Taking into consideration that there are regional differences, we might generalize about the letter *r* with vowel digraphs *ea*, *ai*, and *ee* as follows:

1. **When the letter *r* follows the vowel digraph *ea*, it usually decodes as /ē-r/ as in cl*ear*. It may also decode as /ẽr/ as in l*ear*n. In only a few words does it decode as /âr/ as in b*ear*.**
2. **The vowel digraph *ai* when followed by *r* decodes as /âr/ as in ch*air*.**
3. **The vowel digraph *ee* when followed by *r* decodes as /ē-r/ as in ch*eer*.**

Examination of the following lists will show more clearly the relationship of *r* with single vowels and with vowel digraphs.[9]

/er/	/âr/	/ôr/	/ē-r/	/är/
p*er*t	c*are*	f*or*k	h*ear*	f*ar*
f*ir*st	b*ear*	st*or*k	ch*eer*	p*ar*k
p*ur*se	ch*air*	m*ore*	r*ear*	b*ar*gain
w*or*se				
*ear*n				

We can now put together all of the generalizations for *r*.

The letter *r* controls the *preceding* vowel sound in the same syllable.

1. **Combinations of *er* (p*er*t), *ir* (f*ir*st), and *ur* (h*ur*t) decode as /er/. When *w* precedes *or*, the cluster decodes as /wer/ as in *wor*th.**
2. **The combination *ar* decodes as /är/ as in f*ar*. When followed by an *e*, it decodes as /âr/ as in f*are*.**
3. **The combination *or* decodes as /ôr/ as in st*or*k. Sometimes it decodes as /ər/ as in visit*or*.**
4. **The combination *ear* decodes as /ē-r/ as in h*ear*; as /er/ as in l*ear*n; and as /âr/ as in b*ear*.**
5. **The combination *air* decodes as /âr/ as in p*air*.**
6. **The combination *eer* decodes as /ē-r/ as in ch*eer*.**
7. **Regional differences must be considered with the highly variable sound of /r/.**

See Appendix B for example *r* words to use in teaching.

Quick Self-Check 7

1. What do these *r*-combinations have in common?
   her fur stir
2. How is *wor* like the above three words?
3. Examine the following words:
   fear search pear
   What conclusion can be drawn about the *ear* combination?
4. What other vowel digraphs combine with the letter *r?* What sounds do they encode?

[9] The letter *r* controls the vowel when it appears *in the same syllable* and *follows that vowel*. In a word such as *arise* the *r* does not change the *a* to /ä/ because it is not in the same syllable. It does not affect the sound of /ī/ in any way since it *precedes i* in the syllable.

Special Combinations That Decode as /sh/

Certain combinations in addition to *sh* as in ship decode as /sh/. Recall that the vowel consonant *ch* was shown to have three sounds, one of which was the /sh/ sound as in *ch*ampagne. There are three other common combinations that decode as /sh/ in addition to the two mentioned above.

Note the following words:

A	*B*	*C*
***ci* as /sh/**	***ti* as /sh/**	***si* as /sh/**
so*ci*al	cau*ti*ous	man*si*on
deli*ci*ous	men*ti*on	mis*si*on
spe*ci*al	sta*ti*on	ten*si*on
gra*ci*ous	fic*ti*on	permis*si*on

In each instance the *ci*, *ti*, and *si* all decode as the /sh/ sound. There was a period when these words were pronounced exactly as they are spelled, but this sound change took place several hundred years ago. The three combinations above are only found in the *middle* of words and are often taught as part of affixed endings.

We might generalize as follows about these three combinations.

The letters *ci*, *ti*, and *si* often decode as /sh/ as in such words as pre*ci*ous, fic*ti*on, and mis*si*on.

Quick Self-Check 8

1. Can ghoti be pronounced as fish?
2. What do we know about ti that helps provides the answer to question 1?

Six Major Syllable Patterns

How can a student tell if a vowel is long or short? Determining the sound a vowel makes (long or short) can be accomplished using some basic information about syllable patterns. Although few rules work 100% of the time, understanding the six basic syllable patterns will provide a starting point in determining whether the vowel sound is likely to be long or short.

Two beginning concepts include open and closed syllables. Open syllables end with a vowel having a long sound (paper, open). A closed syllable ends with at least one consonant. In a closed syllable, the vowel sound is short (hot, hog).

A third common syllable pattern is the consonant-*le* pattern. Consonant-*le* syllables are found at the end of a word and are divided before the consonant that comes before the *le*. Generally speaking, if there is one consonant before the *le*, then the vowel is long (rifle, stable, bridle). If there are two consonants before the *le*, then the vowel is generally short: apple, snuggle, battle.

The fourth type of syllable pattern is the double vowel (sometimes called the vowel team) syllable. Double vowels such as *ea*, *ai*, or *oa* are not divided and the first vowel has a long sound.

Remember that syllables have only one vowel sound, regardless of the number of letters used to make the one sound. Vowel digraphs or diphthongs such as *ai, ay, ea, ee, oa, ow, oo, oi, oy, ou, ie,* and *ei* should not be separated. When syllables have double vowels that do not usually appear together, they can be divided between the two vowels, as in the words *dial* or *museum.*

The fifth type of syllable is the final *e* or silent *e* syllable. This syllable is characterized by a vowel, then a consonant, then a final *e*, which is silent. This combination may appear in the middle of a word, but is most often found at the end of a word. The vowel preceding the silent *e* generally has a long sound. Examples include *rage, make, and rude.* The exception, as was discussed earlier, is with the letter *v*. Since English words do not end with the letter *v*, the *e* at the end of the word may or may not impact the vowel before the *v* (pen/sive, hive).

The final syllable type is the *r*-controlled syllable. *R*-controlled syllables have a vowel followed by an *r* and can be found in any syllable. The vowel sound is neither long nor short. When the vowels *e, l,* and *u* are followed by an *r*, they can be pronounced /er/. Examples are ord*er*, furth*er*, s*ir*, and f*ur*. What sound is represented by the *a* in the words *car* and *market?* What sound is represented by the *o* in *for* and *rigor?*

Students may be taught to use the mnemonic COLVER to help them remember the six basic syllable types: Closed, Open, Le, Vowel pair, final *E*, and *R*-controlled. The chart summarizes the syllable types.

Six Major Syllable Patterns (COLVER Mnemonic)	
Closed Syllable	• one vowel sound per syllable • one or more consonants end the syllable • the vowel has a short sound • *example*: fun, rag, shrimp
Open Syllable	• one vowel sound per syllable • the vowel ends the syllable • the vowel has a long sound • *example*: open, hobo, unit, paper
Consonant-**Le** Syllable (c-le)	• three letters: a consonant, the letter *l*, and the vowel *e* • the vowel *e* is silent • the consonant and the *l* are blended • *example*: battle, table, riddle
Double **V**owel Syllable	• two vowels together making one sound • the first vowel is usually long • the second vowel is generally silent • *example*: maid, treat, sleep
Vowel-consonant-**E** Syllable (vce)	• a single vowel, followed by a consonant, then the vowel *e* • the first vowel has a long sound • the *e* is silent • *example*: brake, shape, like, gene, rope
R-controlled Syllable	• one vowel, followed by an *r* • the vowel sound is neither short or long because the vowel sound is controlled by the *r* • *example*: fir, car, per, sugar

SUMMARY

The vowels may be more easily understood by dividing them into groups: short vowels, long vowels, third vowel sounds, schwa, digraphs, and diphthongs. Additionally, the letters *y* and *w* have unique positions, sometimes functioning as consonants and other times functioning as vowels. The letter *r* may control the preceding vowel sound when it is encoded by a single vowel or a vowel digraph. Table 3.1 identifies and divides the major areas of the English writing system related to vowels.

It is not the intent here that preservice and inservice teachers teach children all the information contained in this chapter. Preservice and inservice teachers do need a comprehensive understanding of how our sound system works prior to teaching its basic elements to school children.

TABLE 3.1 Overview of English Orthography—Vowels

Vowels	Single - Short	Schwa ə In Unaccented Syllables	Digraphs/ Diphthongs With *a*	Digraphs With *e*
a e i o u ə	ă act ĕ end ĭ it ŏ olive ŭ upon Single - Long ā able ē even ī icy ō omen ū and unit o͞o rude Single- 3rd Sound a ä always o o͞o do u o͝o push	a əbout e tickət i pencəl o aprən	ai as /ā/ maid ay as /ā/ stay au as /aw/ vault aw as /aw/ draw	ee as /ē/ sleep ea as /ē/ leaf /ĕ/ head /ā/ great ie as /ē/ relief /ī/ lie ei as /ē/ (after c) receive /ā/ vein ey as /ē/ donkey /ā/ prey

Cluster With i	Digraphs and Diphthongs With o	Diphthongs That Encode /oo/
igh as /ī/ sight	oa as /ō/ coat oi as /oy/ oil oy as /oy/ boy oo as /o͞o/ moon /o͝o/ look ou as /ow/ around /ŭ/ young /ō/ soul /o͞o/ group ow as /ow/ cow /ō/ low	ui fruit ue blue ew stew

r With Single Vowels	*r* With *a*	*r* With *o*	*r* With *o* Digraph *ae*	*r* With Digraphs
her fir purse worse /er/ /er/ /er/ /er/	fär câre	stôre doctər	hear learn bear /e-r/ /er/ /ar/	ai hair /âr/ ee peer /ē-r/

Review Questions

1. The vowel sounds contribute significantly to differences in dialect. Why do you suppose this is true? What do you know about vowels that would help explain this notion?

2. Considering all that you have learned in this chapter, in what order would you teach vowels? Short, then long, then silent *e*, the schwa, then digraphs, then *r*-controlled, then diphthongs? What factors should be considered when determining the sequence of teaching vowels?

3. Think of a way to adapt a commercially produced game into a classroom game for reinforcing vowel instruction.

Chapter 4

Prerequisites to Phonics Instruction

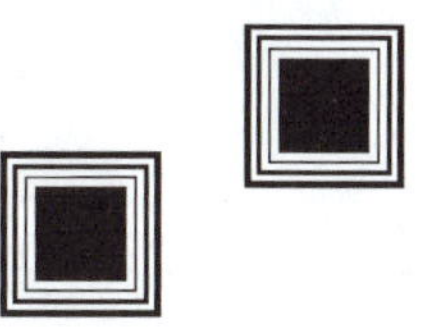

Research consistently indicates that alphabet knowledge and phonological awareness are highly correlated with success in beginning reading. Moats (1994) reports that research has "consistently demonstrated that many beginning readers, and nearly all reading-disabled children, have difficulty on phonological awareness tasks" (p. 83). According to the National Reading Panel, "Correlational studies have identified phonemic awareness and letter knowledge as the two best school-entry predictors of how well children will learn to read during the first 2 years of instruction" (NICHHD, 2000, p. 2-1).

Alphabet Knowledge

Most educators recognize and accept that knowing the graphic symbols of the alphabet is essential to learning to read (Adams, 1990; Blevins, 1998; Chall, 1967; Learning First Alliance, 1998; NICHHD 2000; Snow, Burns & Griffin, 1998). Researchers also acknowledge that knowledge of the alphabet is one of the strongest predictors of early reading success. This makes intuitive sense given that reading is the process of translating visual symbols into meaningful language. Alphabet knowledge then includes visual recognition of the letters, knowledge of the letter names given, and knowledge of the sounds represented by the letters. Blevins (1998) indicates that children must be able to name four sets of letters (uppercase manuscript, lowercase manuscript, uppercase cursive, lowercase cursive) with both accuracy and speed as this makes learning about the sounds associated with letters easier. Burns and Snow (1999) concur: "By the end of kindergarten, children should be able to name most of the letters of the alphabet, no matter what order they come in, no matter if they are uppercase or lowercase. And they should do it quickly and effortlessly" (p. 78). Children who demonstrate automaticity with letters are able to spend more time focusing on the sound-spelling relationships.

Alphabet Knowledge Instruction

There are many strategies and techniques for teaching children the letters of the alphabet. Primarily, children must be able to identify the letters of the alphabet as stand-alones (isolated letters with upper and lower case) and in the context of words. Bear, Invernizzi, Templeton, and Johnston (2004) recommend that children be provided with opportunities to actively explore the relationships between letter names and sounds, the way they look, and the motor movement necessary to write the letters. One way for children to actively explore is to provide them with letters for play. There are block letters, magnetic letters, beanbag letters, sponge letters, noodle letters, and a host of other forms in which the letters of the alphabet appear. Children should be encouraged to play with and manipulate the letters of the alphabet.

Using language that is familiar to children is another way to help them learn their letters. Children enjoy learning to read and write their names. Environmental print may also provide students with meaningful opportunities to explore letters and their sounds, shapes, sizes, and other characteristics. Children can be asked to sort letters and to match letters of different sizes, shapes, fonts, etc. Numerous activities can provide children with opportunities to explore letters, including the traditional alphabet song.

Reading to children also provides opportunities for them to learn letters. Books used frequently for teaching the alphabet include *Alphabet Under Construction* (Fleming, 2003), *Chicka Chicka Boom Boom* (Martin & Archambault, 1989), *Animalia* (Base, 1986). Jerry Pallotta, nicknamed the alphabet man, has written many special interest alphabet books including icky bugs, ocean, frogs, flowers, military, furry animals, and dinosaurs. Using alphabet books and other activities that pair letters and sounds (flashcards, word walls) assists in the development of the phoneme-grapheme relationship. Alphabet books generally contain brightly colored pictures, the letter (upper and lower case), and a word to associate with the letter (*a* is for apple; *k* is for key). Blevins (1998) recommends that teachers read the book several times with different goals in mind. The first time, Blevins says the alphabet book should be read in its entirety simply to enjoy the language and the pictures. The second time through the book, discussions could occur about interesting items in the pictures. The third reading could associate the words and pictures. Finally, Blevins recommends that children create their own alphabet books. Children could also personalize alphabet books by making their own with words that are familiar to them from their school and home settings. Children could also identify their own key words to represent the sounds that letters make.

Some students may require a more direct approach to learning letters and sounds. If this is the case, more direct instruction will be needed. Teachers can focus on a systematic procedure for teaching the letters and sounds by following a simple procedure: name the letter, have students repeat the letter name, then ask the students the name of the letter. A similar procedure can be followed for uppercase and lowercase as well as for the sounds of the letters. Once the letter has been taught by direct instruction, there should be direct application to real words and real reading.

Another teacher-directed procedure for introducing beginning sound-symbol relationships can be conducted in the following four-step sequence:

1. Students identify the capital and small letter that encode a particular sound, presented by the teacher in a novel way that emphasizes the relationship (step 1).
2. Students next select words containing the specific sound from words containing related sounds. Students suggest words with the specific sound (step 2).
3. Students write the capital and lowercase letters that represent the specific sound (step 3).
4. Students participate in purposeful activities applying the knowledge of the relationship between the letter and sound (step 4).

Step 1. The teacher begins with an activity in which students identify the sound-symbol under consideration such as *l* /l/. For example, s/he might ask them to watch his/her mouth because s/he is going to look like a singer. (Teacher says the words *let, like, love, lend,* and *land*, exaggerating the /l/). At the same time s/he writes these words on the board, making one word part of a short sentence such as *Let me go* to use a capital letter. (The words are written on the board so the written word will emphasize the symbol associated with the sound.)

Step 2. The teacher helps students notice how they open their mouths when they say this sound at the *beginning* of words. Then s/he reads a list of words, such as *lion, lazy, maze, left, Brian, lift*, and has them identify the ones that begin with /l/. Sometimes pictures with distractors are used, such as a picture of a lamp, a pencil, a lightbulb, a crayon, or a lemon. The teacher helps students think of words beginning with /l/ by asking riddles such as "What can you draw with a ruler?" (line).

Step 3. Prior to writing them without a clue, students often trace the letter over dotted lines, with arrows indicating the direction of each stroke. This is so the lines and circles they make are drawn from left to right, or in the same direction as they read.

Step 4. The teacher passes out "little lollipops" for them to "lick," and enjoy. Students are to find and think of other words beginning with /l/. Meanwhile, words used by the teacher and students throughout the day that emphasize the /l/ sound are written on a list and displayed. Children may write a simple sentence such as "I love . . ." and take their choice of words from those they may know, illustrate the word, or use one supplied by the teacher.

Assessing Alphabet Knowledge

Children's knowledge of the alphabet should be evaluated as to the recognition of the letters as well as their ability to produce the letters. Letters are randomly placed on a page, which is given to the student. The teacher then points to the letters and asks the student to identify them. Children could also be asked to say the letters of the alphabet. Some teachers may want to assess whether students are able to match the uppercase letter with the lowercase letter. A deck of alphabet cards could be purchased for this type of assessment, or they could be generated from the internet.

Quick Self-Check 1

1. Children must learn uppercase and lowercase cursive letters as well as uppercase and lowercase manuscript letters. Can you think of another complication students face when learning letters?
2. Using alphabet books is an authentic way of teaching children to recognize letters. What are some advantages to having students create their own alphabet books?

Phonological Awareness

Johns, Lenski, and Elish-Piper (1999) explain that as children are exposed to language and use language, they become aware of two additional concepts related to the alphabet: phonological awareness and phonemic awareness. Phonological awareness is the awareness that language is made of units of sound. It refers to the ability to identify and manipulate spoken language features (rhymes, words, syllables, onsets and rimes, and phonemes) that may be taken apart, put together, deleted, and substituted to form new words. Lane and Pullen (2004) define phonological awareness as the "conscious sensitivity to the sound structure of language" (p. 1). Heilman (2005) explains that early in a child's development, phonological awareness occurs subconsciously; however, as the child becomes more phonologically aware, s/he learns that words (a) can rhyme, (b) can have one or more syllables, (c) are in sentences, (d) can begin and end with the same sounds, and (e) are made of small sounds called phonemes. Phonological awareness involves only the auditory and oral manipulation of sounds.

Phonological awareness is important because it is necessary for children to understand that sounds in speech can be broken apart and blended together, which enables them to make connections between speech and print. Investigations have repeatedly demonstrated the importance of phonological awareness as the foundation for word recognition and fluent reading. Phonological awareness is also essential as the precursor for phonics instruction; if children are to benefit from phonics instruction, then they must have a clear understanding of the sounds of the language. Performance on phonological awareness tasks has been shown to be a strong predictor of later reading ability or disability; further, many children with significant reading problems also have a deficit in phonological processing. Goswami (2000) reports that many correlation and training studies support the existence of a causal link between a child's phonological awareness and his or her progress in learning to read. With underdeveloped phonological awareness skills, children are unlikely to benefit from phonics instruction and unlikely to become skilled at decoding words, which will impact their ability to become fluent readers.

Lane and Pullen (2004) have drawn several conclusions from their synthesis of phonological awareness research:

1. Phonological awareness is directly related to reading ability.
2. Phonological awareness is a reliable predictor of later reading ability.
3. Although the relationship is reciprocal, phonological awareness precedes skilled decoding.
4. Deficits in phonological awareness are usually associated with deficits in reading.
5. Early language experiences play an important role in the development of phonological awareness.
6. Early intervention can promote the development of phonological awareness.
7. Improvements in phonological awareness can and usually do result in improvements in reading ability. (p. 3).

Phonological Awareness Tasks

Ehri (1989) suggests that phonological awareness includes the abilities to detect, isolate, manipulate, blend, or segment units of sound, which include words, syllables, onsets and rimes, and phonemes. Chard and Dickson (1999) explain that phonological awareness skills lie on a continuum. It begins with the less complex activities of rhyming and sentence segmentation, both of which demonstrate the child's understanding that speech can be broken into individual words. Next on the continuum is segmenting words into syllables and blending syllables into words. These behaviors demonstrate that a child is able to take words (at the syllable level) apart and put them back together. Increasing in complexity, the next most difficult is segmenting words into onsets and rimes (dividing words into chunks) and blending onsets and rimes into words. The most complex phonological awareness task is *phonemic awareness*, an understanding that words are made of individual phonemes and that phonemes can be manipulated by segmenting, blending, deleting, or substituting. Chard and Dickson, as well as Kame'enui (1996), are very clear that the complexity of phonological awareness

FIGURE 4.1 Continuum of Phonological Awareness Skills

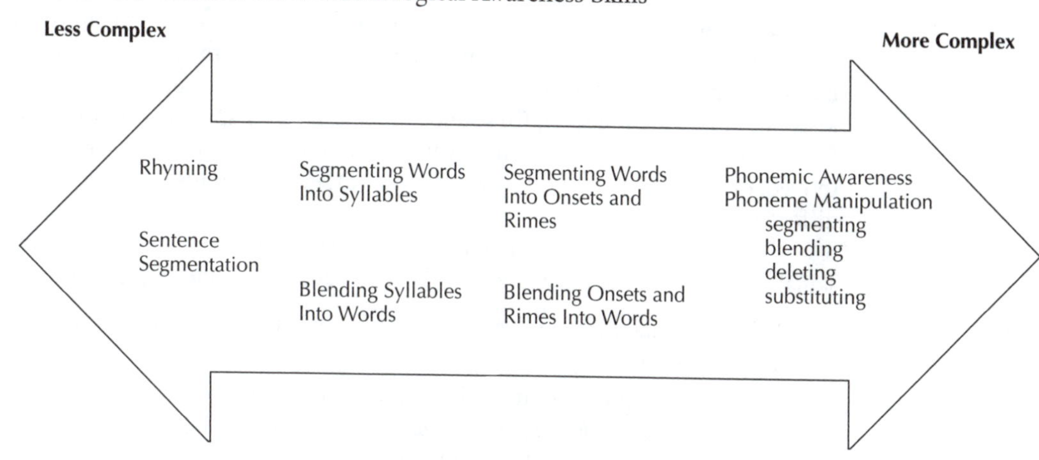

moves from the simple (sentences to words to syllables to onsets and rimes) to the complex (phonemic awareness).Figure 4.1 demonstrates this relationship.

Johnston (2004) reports that children do not generally come to school with well-developed phonological awareness because "... it is not something that parents understand well enough to directly teach their children before school because it is an oral skill and much more abstract than the very concrete and well-defined task of naming or writing letters" (p. 2). Since many children come to school at a disadvantage due to limited early experiences with print, it becomes the classroom teacher's responsibility to provide phonological awareness experiences.

Phonemic Awareness

Phonemic awareness, the most complex phonological awareness task, is the knowledge that speech consists of a series of sounds and that individual words can be divided into phonemes. Phonemes are the smallest units of spoken language, generally classified into two major categories: consonants and vowels. There are approximately 25 consonant sounds (most represented by a single letter) and 18 vowel sounds (5 letters represent these sounds) in English. To distinguish between phonological awareness, discussed earlier, and phonemic awareness, the National Research Council Report on Reading (Snow, Burns, & Griffin, 1998) explains:

> The term phonological awareness refers to a general appreciation of the sounds of speech as distinct from their meaning. When that insight includes an understanding that words can be divided into a sequence of phonemes, this finer-grained sensitivity is termed phonemic awareness. (p. 51)

Phonemic awareness is concerned only with the spoken word, with all instruction conducted orally and aurally. When letters and writing become involved, it is phonics instruction. In some textbooks, phonemic awareness is referred to as pre-phonics. In repeated studies, phonemic awareness has been shown to be a strong predictor of success in learning to read and has been shown to facilitate children's ability to benefit from phonics instruction. Stanovich (1994) stated that the ability to perform phonemic awareness tasks is the best predictor of early reading acquisition: "better than anything else that we know of, including IQ" (p. 284). The International Reading Association (1998) explained:

> First, it is critical that teachers are familiar with the concept of phonemic awareness and that they know that there is a body of evidence pointing to a significant relation between phonemic awareness and reading acquisition. This cannot be ignored. (p. 6)

The National Reading Panel (NICHHD, 2000) reported that instruction can improve phonemic awareness and these improvements lead to improvements in reading.

Heilman (2005) explains that phonemic awareness is the ability to identify and manipulate phonemes. Children understand that (a) words have small sounds that can be pulled apart and put back together, (b) sounds in words have a specific order (initial, medial, final), (c) the number of sounds in words can be counted, (d) sounds in words can be moved, removed, or replaced to make new words, and (e) several sounds can be represented with many different letters.

There appears to be some disagreement, however, on what constitutes phonemic awareness skills. According to the Learning First Alliance (2000), the phonemic awareness skills include

1. Phoneme matching: ability to identify words that begin with the same sound. *Which words sound alike?*
2. Phoneme isolation: ability to isolate a single sound from within a word. *What's the first sound in the word? What's the last sound in the word? What's the middle sound in the word?*
3. Phoneme blending: ability to blend individual sounds into a word. *What word do these sounds make?*
4. Phoneme segmentation: ability to break a word into individual sounds. *What sounds do you hear in the word?*
5. Phoneme manipulation: ability to modify, change, or move the individual sounds in a word. *Say mat without the /m/ sound. Say mat without the /t/ sound. Say mat; now, change the /m/ in mat to /f/.*

The National Reading Panel (NICHHD, 2000) identifies the phonemic awareness tasks as:

1. Phoneme isolation: recognizing individual sounds in words. *What is the first sound in the word?*
2. Phoneme identity: recognizing the common sound in different words. *What sound is the same in the following words?*
3. Phoneme categorization: recognizing the word with the odd sound in a sequence of three or four words. *Which word does not belong?*
4. Phoneme blending: listening to a sequence of spoken sounds and combining them to form a recognizable word. *What word is /m/, /a/, /t/?*
5. Phoneme segmentation: breaking a word into its individual sounds. *How many phonemes are in the word?*
6. Phoneme deletion: recognizing what word remains when a phoneme is removed. *What is mat without the /m/?*

Regardless of which scheme is selected for use, there is one point that Pressley (2002) makes about phonemic awareness: "Phonemic awareness can be developed through systematic practice in categorizing words on the basis of common beginning, middle, and end sounds" (p. 109). Some recommended strategies include using nursery rhymes, riddles, songs, poems, and read-aloud books (IRA, 1998). Figure 4.2 helps to clarify the relationship between phonological awareness and phonemic awareness.

Phonological Awareness Instruction

Blachman (2000) stated that, ". . . research evidence from a variety of disciplines provides unequivocal support for the critical role of phonological processes in learning to read" (p. 483). Moreover, Blachman (2000) indicated that many studies have demonstrated that a

FIGURE 4.2 Clarifying Phonological and Phonemic Awareness

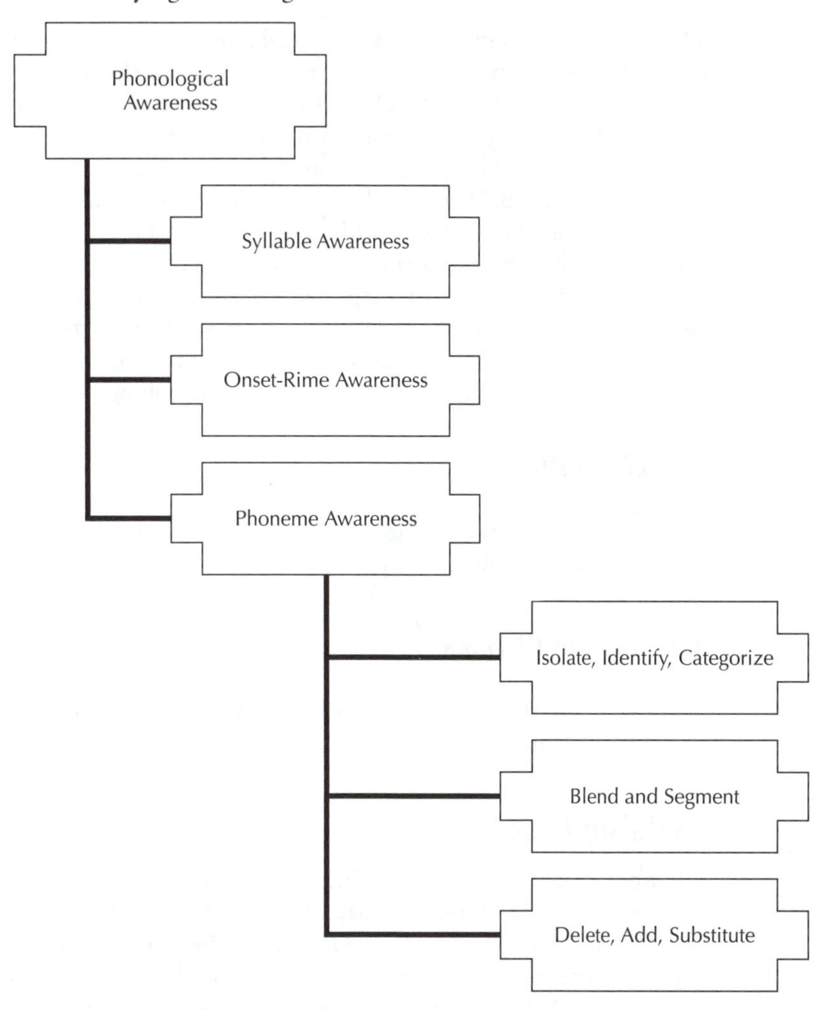

Adapted from Tolman, C. (2005). Working smarter, not harder: What teachers of reading need to know and be able to teach. *The International Dyslexia Association, 31* (4), 15–23.

child's phonological awareness could be improved by direct instructional activities. Yopp and Yopp (2000) also believe that phonemic awareness can be taught and recommend the following sequence: activities that focus on rhyme, then syllable units, then onsets and rimes, then phonemes. They recommended three basic rules for phonemic awareness instruction: child appropriate, deliberate and purposeful, and viewed as ONE part of a broader literacy program.

Sentence Level

Most children segment sentences into words with minimal instruction. They are able to hear when words stop and when they begin. One strategy that can be used is similar to the old "telephone" game or "rumor" game. The teacher can say a sentence aloud. Then each student repeats the sentence, replacing one of the words with a word of his/her choice. This should be repeated until every child has had an opportunity to change the sentence. Reading aloud to children will also help them practice dividing sentences into words.

Word Level

One of the phonological skills at the word level is rhyming. Children must not only be able to recognize rhymes, they must also be able to generate rhymes and match rhymes. Recognizing rhyming words involves identifying whether or not words rhyme whereas generating rhymes requires students to produce words that rhyme. Matching rhyming words requires that children identify words that rhyme from among words provided to them. Recognizing rhyming words can be practiced quickly and easily in whole class settings if all-respond strategies are used. Read-alouds could also be conducted with students identifying rhyming words in the story being read. Generating rhyming words could be easily accomplished by using poetry such as couplets, limericks, and other words. Matching rhyming words could also be set up as whole-class activities, or could be accomplished as individual activities. The keys to phonological awareness activities are that (a) they should not take up a great deal of time, (b) they should be fun, and (c) the skills learned or practiced should be transferred to real reading as soon as possible.

Matching Rhymes

Teacher: On the board is the word *mouse.* I am going to read some words and you tell me if they rhyme with mouse.

Generating Rhymes

Teacher: I'm thinking of words that rhyme with the word *cat.* Can you think of words that rhyme with cat?

Syllable Level

Children usually develop the ability to segment syllables before they develop the ability to segment phonemes; thus, they are able to listen to words and hear the syllables with minimal instruction. According to Adams (1990), the ability to detect, segment, and count syllables is more important to reading acquisition than the ability to manipulate and transpose them.

Teachers have used various strategies to teach this concept. Some use terms like the beats in a word or the rhythm of the word. Clapping or tapping the number of syllables heard is a common strategy used to develop syllable awareness. Chants and rhymes provide an enjoyable experience for children while introducing them to poetry. Children may also respond favorably to identifying the number of syllables heard in their names. Making instruction personal is naturally appealing to the learner.

Using the notion of everyone responses (response cards, standing up, thumbs up, hands up), teachers can engage in whole class activities to teach and practice understanding syllables. The teacher can say words, and children can raise their hands or cards to indicate whether the word has one, two, three, or more syllables. Games can be played. "I am thinking of a one-syllable color word that rhymes with bread."

Hink Pinks are also a fun way to work with syllables. Hink Pinks are rhyming words with one syllable. Hinky Pinky words are rhyming words with two syllables, whereas hinkity pinkity words have three syllables.

Examples: What do you call an angry father? A mad dad
What do you call a large pig? A big pig

What do you call an amusing hare? A funny bunny
What do you call a magical woman who milks cows? A dairy fairy

What do you call two drums talking? A percussion discussion
What do you call the White House? The president's residence

Onset and Rime Level

Syllables can be broken into two smaller units called onsets and rimes. Adams (1990) identified onsets and rimes as an intermediate and instructionally useful level of analysis between the syllable and the phoneme. The onset is the part of the syllable that precedes the vowel. The rime is the rest of the syllable. Because the rime is the part of the syllable that contains the vowel, all syllables must have a rime, but not all syllables have an onset. Onset-rime segmentation is an essential component of phonological awareness development.

Rimes are also known as phonogram patterns (see Appendix C), which are the rhyming portion of word families. In 1998, Fry identified 38 of the most common word families and claimed that 654 single syllable words could be made with those phonograms, rimes, or word families. The word families include the following:

ab	ed	ick	ob	uck	y
ack	eed	ight	ock	ug	
ag	ell	ill	op	um	
ake	est	im	ore	unk	
ain	ew	in	ot		
ail		ine	out		
am		ing	ow		
an		ink			
ank		ip			
ap					
at					
ay					

Again, poetry would be an excellent way to help students identify onsets and rimes.

Phoneme Level

Phonemic awareness is the knowledge that speech consists of a sequence of sounds (phonemes) and that these sounds can be manipulated in various ways. Yopp (1992) believes that phonemic awareness instruction should be playful, engaging, interactive, and social. Phonemic awareness instruction should stimulate curiosity about language and should encourage experimentation with language. Above all, phonemic awareness instruction should be deliberate and purposeful. Ehri and Nunes (2002) reported that segmenting and blending are especially effective contributors to reading and spelling. They provide some guidelines to consider for phonemic awareness instruction: (a) pretesting is advised to assess who needs what type of instruction; (b) phonemic awareness instruction is not a complete reading program, but a foundational piece; and (c) phonemic awareness is not an end but rather a means to use the alphabetic system in reading and writing.

After its extensive meta-analysis of previous research investigations, the National Reading Panel (NICHHD, 2000) drew some very specific conclusions regarding phonemic awareness instruction:

1. Phonemic awareness can be taught (p. 2-5).
2. Phonemic awareness instruction is effective under a variety of teaching conditions with a variety of learners (p. 2-5).
3. Teaching children to manipulate the sounds in language helps them learn to read (p. 2-5).
4. Phonemic awareness instruction helped all types of children improve their reading. (p. 2-5).
5. Phonemic awareness instruction may be most effective when children are taught to manipulate phonemes with letters, when the instruction is explicitly focused on one or two

types of phonemic manipulations rather than multiple types, and when children are taught in small groups (p. 2-6).

6. Phonemic awareness instruction is more effective when it makes explicit how children are to apply phonemic awareness skills in reading and writing tasks (p. 2-6).
7. Phonemic awareness instruction does not need to consume long periods of time to be effective (p. 2-6).

In addition to providing some guidance and direction regarding phonemic awareness instruction, the National Reading Panel (NICHHD, 2000) also issued several cautionary notes to teachers:

1. Phonemic awareness instruction is a means rather than an end (p. 2-43).
2. Some children will need more instruction than others (p. 2-43).
3. Phonemic awareness training does not constitute a complete reading program (p. 2-43).
4. Motivation needs to be considered for teachers as well as their students when designing instruction and selecting materials for instruction (p. 2-43).
5. More instruction is not necessarily better (p. 2-7).
6. Early phonemic awareness instruction cannot guarantee later literacy success (p. 2-7).

The International Reading Association (1998) suggests that, with respect to teaching phonemic awareness, teachers engage children in language activities that focus on the form and content of spoken language, and provide explicit explanations in support of students' discovery of the alphabetic principle.

Kame'enui (1995) suggests that it is best to begin phonemic awareness instruction with easier words and then move on to more difficult ones. He has identified five characteristics that make a word easier or more difficult. According to Kame'enui

1. The size of the phonological unit affects the level of difficulty. It is easier to break sentences into words and words into syllables than it is to break syllables into phonemes.
2. The number of phonemes in the word contributes to the difficulty of the task. It is easier to break phonemically short words.
3. The positioning of phonemes in words impacts the level of difficulty. Initial consonants are easiest, followed by final consonants, with middle consonants being the most difficult.
4. The phonological properties of words make them easy or difficult. As elongated consonant sound such as /s/ and /m/ is easier than brief consonant sounds such as /t/).
5. The type of phonological awareness task determines the difficulty. Rhyming and initial phoneme identification are easier than blending and segmenting.

Yopp (1995) believes that "the most accessible, practical, and useful vehicles to enhance students' sensitivity to the phonological basis of their language are children's books that deal playfully with speech sounds . . ." (p. 3). She also provides several brief rules for using the books: (1) read and reread the story aloud to students, (2) comment on the language use, (3) encourage predictions, (4) examine language use, and (5) create additional verses or make another version of the story. Yopp cautions, however, that while these books are useful for teaching, they should not constitute the entire classroom library.

Blending

Blending requires students to combine separate sounds into words, onsets and rimes into words, or syllables into words. If a child is given individual phonemes, he or she should practice blending (or putting together) the phonemes into a word. Similar procedures could be used for blending onsets and rimes and for blending syllables into words. Since blending is a skill that is used frequently while reading, it is an essential skill that should be taught.

Perhaps the easiest way to begin instruction in blending is to start with onsets and rimes. This amounts to blending a beginning (onset) with a chunk of letters (rimes). Starting with *at*, children could then blend onsets to form the following: bat, cat, fat, hat, mat, pat, rat, sat, tat, vat. For blending purposes, nonsense words or pseudowords could also be created: dat, gat, jat, kat, lat, nat, yat, and zat. Teachers should be reminded that the goal is to work with the words created by blending the onset with the rime. Once children have mastered the initial concepts of blending, then blending phonemes into words could be accomplished; however, it will take some time for children to master blending sounds together to form words.

Segmenting

Segmenting requires students to divide sentences into words, words into syllables, syllables into onsets and rimes, and syllables/words into phonemic parts. Initially, children must be able to distinguish the words that make up a sentence. Therefore, they must learn to break a sentence into its individual word parts. From there, they learn to break words into syllables, syllables into onsets and rimes, and syllables into individual phonemes. Children can understand taking apart compound words quite rapidly; therefore, classroom teachers may want to teach segmenting with compound words first and then move to single words and separating phonemes. Another part of segmenting is identifying the number of syllables in a word. Clapping or tapping syllables is a very common strategy.

Addition, Deletion, and Substitution

Another phonemic awareness task is adding, deleting (also called elision), and substituting sounds at the beginning, middle, or end of sentences, syllables, onsets and rimes, and words. Adding, deleting, and substituting words in sentences will help reinforce the notion that sentences are composed of individual words. Similarly, adding, deleting and substituting syllables will also help students. For example, the teacher could ask the students to say *football*. Then, the teacher could ask the students to say *football* without the *foot*. Then, the teacher could ask the students to say *ball* and add *base* to the beginning; so students would say *baseball*. A similar pattern would follow with onsets and rimes as well as with individual phonemes in words. Teachers should be reminded that working with sounds in the medial position is much more difficult for students than working with additions and substitutions at the beginning or end of a word.

Elkonin Boxes

Numerous research investigations point to Elkonin Boxes (Elkonin, 1963) as a successful way to help children hear the sounds in words and to make connections between the words they hear and the number of sounds in the words. Using Elkonin Boxes to teach phonemic awareness helps children to analyze the segmenting and blending of phonemes and to better understand the alphabetic principle in decoding.

Teachers should begin by creating boxes containing 2, 3, 4, or more cells. Since they may want to use them for words with up to 4 phonemes, each student might make a box with 4 cells, rather than multiple boxes with a different number of cells in each box. Students may even be asked to design their own boxes to add their personal touch to the teaching and learning of phonemic awareness. It is recommended that the boxes be laminated so they can be used repeatedly. Teachers also need to have enough colored circles, cubes, or markers for all the students to have 2, 3, or 4, so they can mark the number of sounds they hear by putting the manipulatives (circles, cubes, markers, pennies, etc.) onto the Elkonin Box.

Once the boxes are prepared, the teacher pronounces words from a high-frequency word list or a list of commonly misspelled words. The students repeat the word said by the teacher and count the number of phonemes in the word. For example, the teacher would say the word *so*. Students would repeat the word *so* and count the number of phonemes. Since the word *so* has two phonemes, the students would need to place markers in two boxes (one for each phoneme). If only one set of boxes is made (with 4 or 5 cells), then the student would have used only the first boxes for *so*. The students are directed to slide one marker into each cell of the Elkonin box as he or she repeats the word. The goal is for students to listen carefully to the word being pronounced and to place the correct number of markers onto the Elkonin Boxes to indicate the number of sounds heard in the word. The boxes could also be used with

FIGURE 4.3 Demonstration of Elkonin Boxes

so (a two-cell box and a four cell box)

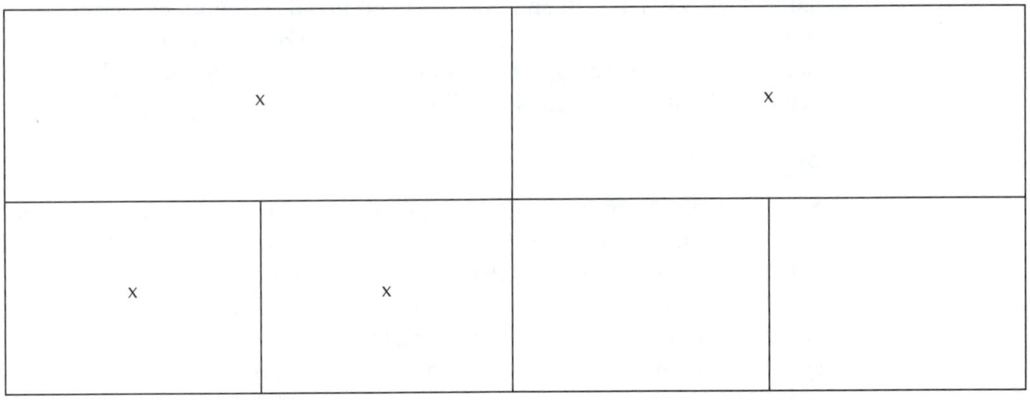

<table>
<tr><td colspan="2">x</td><td colspan="2">x</td></tr>
<tr><td>x</td><td>x</td><td></td><td></td></tr>
</table>

dad (students would use same type of marker for each d in dad), and only use three of the 4 boxes if a 4-box design is used)

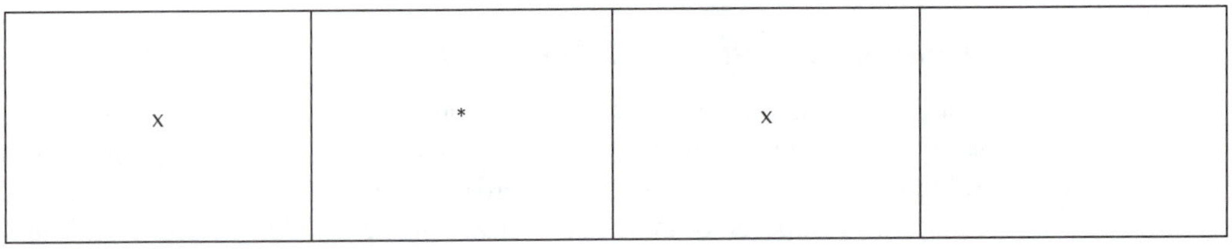

x	*	x	

pictures, rather than with teachers providing the words orally. Figure 4.3 shows the use of Elkonin Boxes using the words *so* and *dad*.

Picture Files

Teachers can collect pictures from a variety of sources to create picture files or card files. To facilitate instruction, picture cards could be created and organized into categories, such as pictures for rhyming games, pictures for syllable games, and pictures for phoneme games. Additional picture files could be created for alphabet words. Pictures for rhyming games could be sorted by sounds and pictures for syllable games by the number of syllables represented in each picture. The pictures could be obtained though a variety of resources including the Internet.

Picture Sorts

Picture sorts appear to be an excellent way for children to learn sounds. Magazines, clip art, food labels, newspapers, catalogs, and other materials are great sources of pictures. Sorting pictures by initial sounds, rhyming sounds, or number of syllables all contribute to active engagement with basic phonological skills.

Quick Self-Check 2

1. What is the relationship between phonological awareness and phonemic awareness?
2. What are the basic phonemic awareness tasks identified by the National Reading Panel?
3. In the word *chat*, what is the onset and what is the rime?
4. Define the following terms: blending, segmenting, addition, deletion, and substitution.

Implicit or Explicit Instruction

Both implicit (indirect instruction) and explicit (direct instruction) strategies may be used to teach phonological awareness (Lane & Pullen, 2004). Which of these is used depends on the individual child. Ideally, phonological awareness teaching would be implicit, concurrently imbedded within the context of meaningful reading or writing. However, for children who are struggling, explicit strategies may be more effective. If direct instruction is designed appropriately and effectively, it should be clear what the child is supposed to learn/achieve. According to the National Reading Panel (NICHHD, 2000), instruction should be in small groups for short periods of time. It should also focus on one or two phonological skills and provide opportunities for immediate application to text. Benchmarks for success should be identified so the child, as well as the teacher, knows when he/she has achieved the objectives.

Teaching English Language Learners

Some students come to class without knowing any English. As these students leave the early primary grades, the cognitive and linguistic demands they face in reading become increasingly challenging. These readers, as all readers, must bring to the text decoding skills and the conceptual framework needed to understand the text message. Thus, decoding skills are critical for the limited English speaker. All the skills and strategies employed in teaching native English-speaking children must be used. In addition, teaching strategies must be further refined, creative activities that speak to the students imagination must be employed, and instruction must be individualized. Sutton (1989) suggests the following key points for the teacher:

1. Know the grapheme/phoneme connection between Standard English (SE) and the primary language. You will be able to anticipate difficulties and avoid them as much as possible.
2. When particular phonemic distinctions do not exist in their native language, students will be unable to profit from certain types of discrete phonics instruction. Also, if they are in the early stages of acquiring English, it will be difficult for them to pronounce words whose sounds do not appear in their native language.
3. As much as possible integrate the phonics instruction with actual reading.
4. Focus on contextualized language. Students know many words they see in their extended environment (e.g., *Burger King, EXIT, cinema*). Build on this ability to recognize words in a context by integrating print into the classroom environment as well. Label items, locations, and activities in the room, on bulletin boards, and on display tables.
5. Write down or photocopy familiar dialogues and stories; have students practice reading them as creative dramatics, choral reading, role plays, and interviews.
6. Have students identify words they would like to know in print. This key word approach to the development of a sight word vocabulary has been quite effective with English Language Learners (ELL).
7. Provide students with a place (notebook or word cards) to keep track of important words. The student can use a combination of clues for meaning: an illustration, their own language definition.
8. Use folktales, as their stories and plots are universal and easy to identify with.

In other words, teaching ELL students should consist of "saturation in print," carried out by many different reading, speaking, and writing activities conducted in a warm supportive environment.

Reading tests in word recognition often penalize dialect/ELL speakers because their "sounding out" ability to discriminate between words such as *sole* and *sold* and *walk* and *walked* are not the same as the SE speaker. When these words are in the context of a phrase or sentence, they do not cause the same difficulty; differentiation for dialect speakers is easier.

SUMMARY

Teachers should keep these critical issues in mind when they work with students for whom English is not the native language.

It is clear that alphabet knowledge and phonological awareness are highly correlated with successful beginning reading experiences. Learning the letters of the alphabet involves at least four sets of letters (uppercase and lowercase manuscript, and uppercase and lowercase cursive). Providing enjoyable activities and games will motivate children. Applying learning to reading situations makes learning both authentic and contextual. Alphabet books are another way for students to make connections with the letters of the alphabet.

Phonological awareness is the knowledge that language is made of units of sound. Various taxonomies of phonological awareness tasks have been developed. Determining which taxonomy to use is generally impacted by the teaching materials available. Phonemic awareness is the knowledge that speech consists of a series of sounds and that individual words can be divided into phonemes.

Simple activities, such as nursery rhymes, chants, songs, and listening stations can be set up in a classroom to help students develop their phonological and phonemic awareness. Reading aloud, finger plays, picture counting, clapping, and tapping can all be used to teach the oral and aural skills needed to experience success with phonics instruction. The importance of phonemic awareness in reading instruction could not be made more clear: phonemic awareness is the "most important core and causal factor separating normal and disabled readers" (Adams, 1990, p. 305).

Review Questions

1. Why do you think that knowing the letters of the alphabet plays such a significant role in learning to read?
2. What are some other ways to teach letters of the alphabet in ways that are enjoyable and meaningful to students?
3. Why do you think there is disagreement on what constitutes phonological tasks?
4. Briefly explain the following: blending, segmenting, addition, deletion, and substitution as it relates to phonemic awareness.

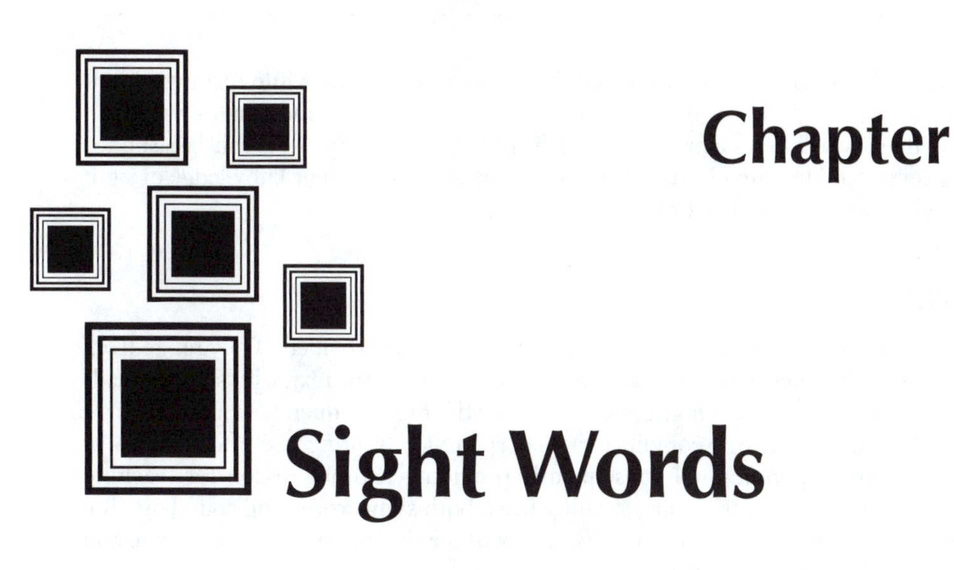

Chapter 5

Sight Words

In reading, a group of "heavy duty" words, such as *at*, *the*, *be*, *of*, are referred to as sight words. They must be recognized instantly on sight, so the term *sight words* is used when discussing them. Because they are encountered with great frequency, they are also known as high-frequency words. It would be difficult to read any extended passage without meeting a large number of them. Crawley and Merritt (2004) identify sight words as words that can be recognized instantly and pronounced instantly without using word analysis skills. Ehri's (1994) definition of sight words is more specific: For a word to be a sight word, the reader must instantly access his/her mental dictionary and identify the word's meaning, spelling, pronunciation, and grammatical role in the sentence. Antonacci and O'Callaghan (2004) explain that the term *sight word* has many meanings:

> At times it is used to refer to the high-frequency words whose spellings defy decoding . . . Sight words may refer to words that children remember because of a special visual cue . . . Sight words also refers to any word that a reader recognizes instantly . . . (p. 337)

Organizing Sight Words

To eliminate confusion over what does or does not constitute a sight word, Block (2003) has defined three general categories of sight words: basic sight words, content-specific sight words, and signal sight words. Basic sight words, according to Block, are words that appear frequently in print. This includes basic words that students know on sight and do not need to decode (yellow, green, yes) and high frequency words (of, in, on, the). Block also includes words that children recognize on sight because of configuration clues (the word shape such as elephant, monkey).

There are three basic reasons for focusing on sight words. First, the more words that students know on sight, the less time they have to spend decoding and the more time they can spend on comprehension. Another reason for sight vocabulary instruction is that some words simply cannot be decoded; therefore, recognizing these words instantly, rather than trying to decode them, will save students significant amounts of time while reading. Pikulski and Templeton (2004) remarked, "If a reader is to have at least a modicum of fluency, it is critical that these words be taught systematically and effectively" (p. 3). A third reason for emphasizing sight word learning is that students may be able to use their knowledge of sight words, through analogy, to decode other unknown words.

Basic Sight Words

For high-frequency words, percentages of occurrence are often provided. They range from 50% to 66%. The difference in occurrence is due to the nature of the text, with simpler reading materials usually containing a higher percentage of the high-frequency words.

Many high-frequency words contain irregular spellings, limiting the effectiveness of teaching them through phonics and consequently providing another reason for teaching them as sight words. As students in early reading learn both sight words and sound-symbol relationships as part of word recognition skills, they will see them in proper perspective and will avoid relying completely on either one.

Two of the most popular high-frequency sight word lists are the Dolch list, which contains a total of 220 words, and the Fry Instant Word List (1980), which contains 300 of the most frequently used words in print. There are a number of others, including the Harris-Jacobson, the Dale Johnson, and the Durr.

Dolch

The Dolch list, first developed by E. W. Dolch in 1952 and widely adapted, has four levels with the words arranged in increasing levels of difficulty. However, these divisions are somewhat arbitrary (see Table 5.1). There have been many attempts to update this list since Dolch first compiled it in 1936, but it nevertheless retains its original popularity. Johns (1978) later revised this list; however, 189 of the Dolch words were retained, while changes were made to the rest of the list.

In a later study, Palmer (1985) checked the Dolch list against four basal series—Ginn's Reading 720; Holt, Reinhart, & Winston; Houghton Mifflin; and Scott Foresman. She found that the Dolch words made up between 57% and 82% of the vocabulary in the passages and levels, with the average being 60%.

There are no nouns in Table 5.1 because the nouns used in any passage are determined by the subject matter and vary a great deal. In contrast, most of the words included in this list occur repeatedly in reading materials, regardless of the reading level.

Fry

The Fry Instant Word List (1980) consists of the 300 most frequently used words, which account for 65% of all print material. Only the first 100 words are presented here. These 100 words are said to account for 50% of the words in printed material (see Table 5.2).

Harris-Jacobson

The Harris-Jacobson core list (1972) (Table 5.3), which is quite a bit longer, includes some very common nouns. Students who do not experience reading problems will have learned most of these words by the end of the second grade. However, many problem readers, including some junior and senior high school students, will not have mastered them.

TABLE 5.1 Dolch Basic Sight Word List

Preprimer	Primer	First Grade	Second Grade	Third Grade
1. a	1. all	1. after	1. always	1. about
2. and	2. am	2. again	2. around	2. better
3. away	3. are	3. an	3. because	3. bring
4. big	4. at	4. any	4. been	4. carry
5. blue	5. ate	5. as	5. before	5. clean
6. can	6. be	6. ask	6. best	6. cut
7. come	7. black	7. by	7. both	7. done
8. down	8. brown	8. could	8. buy	8. draw
9. find	9. but	9. every	9. call	9. drink
10. for	10. came	10. fly	10. cold	10. eight
11. funny	11. did	11. from	11. does	11. fall
12. go	12. do	12. give	12. don't	12. far
13. help	13. eat	13. going	13. fast	13. full
14. here	14. four	14. had	14. first	14. got
15. I	15. get	15. has	15. five	15. grow
16. in	16. good	16. her	16. found	16. hold
17. is	17. have	17. him	17. gave	17. hot
18. it	18. he	18. his	18. goes	18. hurt
19. jump	19. into	19. how	19. green	19. if
20. little	20. like	20. just	20. its	20. keep
21. look	21. must	21. know	21. made	21. kind
22. make	22. new	22. let	22. many	22. laugh
23. me	23. no	23. live	23. off	23. light
24. my	24. now	24. may	24. or	24. long
25. not	25. on	25. of	25. pull	25. much
26. one	26. our	26. old	26. read	26. myself
27. play	27. out	27. once	27. right	27. never
28. red	28. please	28. open	28. sing	28. only
29. run	29. pretty	29. over	29. sit	29. own
30. said	30. ran	30. put	30. sleep	30. pick
31. see	31. ride	31. round	31. tell	31. seven
32. the	32. saw	32. some	32. their	32. shall
33. three	33. say	33. stop	33. these	33. show
34. to	34. she	34. take	34. those	34. six
35. two	35. so	35. thank	35. upon	35. small
36. up	36. soon	36. them	36. us	36. start
37. we	37. that	37. then	37. use	37. ten
38. where	38. there	38. think	38. very	38. today
39. yellow	39. they	39. walk	39. wash	39. together
40. you	40. this	40. were	40. which	40. try
	41. too	41. when	41. why	41. warm
	42. under		42. wish	
	43. want		43. work	
	44. was		44. would	
	45. well		45. write	
	46. went		46. your	
	47. what			
	48. white			
	49. who			
	50. will			
	51. with			
	52. yes			

TABLE 5.2 Fry Instant Word List

First 25 Group 1a	Second 25 Group 1b	Third 25 Group 1c	Fourth 25 Group 1d
the	or	will	number
of	one	up	no
and	had	other	way
a	by	about	could
to	word	out	people
in	but	many	my
is	not	then	than
you	what	them	first
that	all	these	water
it	were	so	been
he	we	some	call
was	when	her	who
for	your	would	oil
on	can	make	now
are	said	like	find
as	there	him	long
with	use	into	down
his	an	time	day
they	each	has	did
I	which	look	get
at	she	two	come
be	do	more	made
this	how	write	may
have	their	go	part
from	if	see	over

Several authors have developed sight word lists specifically for older readers. An example of this type of list is one developed by Johns (1971):

more	might	war	white
than	great	until	last
other	year	something	number
such	since	fact	course
even	against	though	later
most	used	less	knew
also	states	public	same
through	himself	almost	another
years	few	enough	united
should	during	took	left
each	without	yet	eyes
people	place	government	asked
Mr.	American	system	being
state	however	set	high
world	Mrs.	told	didn't
still	thought	nothing	
between	part	end	
life	general	called	

Appendix E includes a list of basic sight words for the older reader that incorporates frequently used words at the upper levels and a list of adult survival words for working with older readers.

TABLE 5.3 Harris-Jacobson Core Words for First Grade

CORE PREPRIMER LIST							
a	come	get	is	not	stop	who	
and	daddy*	go	it	play	the	will	
are	did	green	little	ran	this	work	
ar	do	have	look	red	to	you	
ball*	dog*	he	make	ride	up		
blue	down	help	me	said	want		
call	fun*	here	mother*	see	we		
can	funny	in	my	something*	what		
CORE PRIMER LIST							
about	cake*	him	may	run	thank	yellow	
all	car*	his	new	saw	then	yes	
around	eat	home*	now	say	they	your	
ask	fast	house*	of	she	too		
away	father*	into	on	show	train*		
bike*	fish*	jump	one	sit	tree*		
birthday*	from	know	out	so	two		
boat*	goat*	let	paint*	some	us		
book*	good	like	pet*	soon	want		
but	has	man*	put	take	word*		
CORE FIRST READER							
after	build*	find	hen*	more*	read	these	window*
again	bus*	fire*	her	morning*	ready*	thing*	wish
airplane*	by	first	hill*	must	right	think	won't*
along*	cage*	five	hold	name*	road*	those	would
am	came	fly	hop*	never	rocket*	three	zoo*
an	can't*	food*	horse*	next*	sang*	time*	
animal*	cat*	found	how	night*	sat*	told*	
another*	catch*	four	hurry*	nothing*	school*	tomorrow*	
any	children*	fox*	I'll*	off	seen*	took*	
as	coat*	friend*	ice*	on	shoe*	town*	
baby*	cold	game*	if	old	should*	toy*	
back*	color*	gave	it's*	or	sing	truck*	
bag*	could	girl*	just	other*	sister*	try	
balloon*	crow*	give	kind	our	sleep	turtle*	
bark*	cry*	gone*	kitten*	over	sound*	TV*	
barn*	cut	good-bye*	last*	own	stay	under	
be	dark*	got	laugh	pan*	step*	very	
bear*	day*	grass*	leg*	party*	still*	wagon*	
bed*	didn't*	had	letter*	peanut*	stopped*	walk	
bee*	does	hair*	light	penny*	store*	was	
before	don't	hand*	live	picnic*	story*	water*	
began*	dress*	hear*	long	picture*	street*	way*	
behind*	drop*	hello*	lost*	pig*	sun*	were	
better	duck*	hand*	made	please	surprise*	wet*	
bird*	fall	happy*	many	pocket*	talk*	when	
black	far	hard*	maybe*	pony*	tea	where	
box*	farm*	hat*	men*	prize*	than*	which	
boy*	fat*	head*	met*	rabbit*	their	white	
bring	feet*	hear*	miss*	race*	them	why	
brown	fight*	hello*	money*	rain*	there	window	

*Words that are not on the Dolch Basic Sight Word List.

TABLE 5.4 Examples of Content-Specific Sight Words

Math	Science	Language Arts	Social Studies
angle	atmosphere	analogy	allegiance
area	atom	adjective	altitude
average	axis	adverb	amendment
congruent	cell	antonym	anarchy
consecutive	classification	autobiography	bipartisan
cube	climate	biography	campaign
diameter	conservation	character	census
denominator	density	compare	citizenship
equation	ecosystem	contrast	civil
fraction	epicenter	definition	colony
horizontal	erosion	dialogue	constitution
inequality	extinction	expository	continent
inverse	force	drama	democracy
mean	friction	genre	domestic
median	fungi	literary	economic
numerators	galaxy	metaphor	federal
octagon	habitat	myth	foreign
parallel	magnitude	narrative	geography
perimeter	motion	novel	global
percent	nucleus	organization	inflation
planes	organ	persuasive	latitude
probability	planet	poetry	migration
radius	solution	prefix	national
ratio	stars	pronoun	population
rounding	temperature	prose	propaganda
sample	tundra	revision	racism
sphere	velocity	rhyme	regulation
square	vibration	simile	segregation
variables	voltage	theme	treaty

Content-Specific Sight Words

The second type of sight words described by Block (2003) is content-specific sight words. Because sight-word instruction is designed to minimize the amount of time children spend decoding, and maximize the amount of time children spend comprehending, it makes sense to consider words within each content area that should be known on sight. Having a core set of content-specific sight words would increase students' comprehension of basic concepts. Table 5.4 provides a brief sampling of content vocabulary words that should be sight words at the older grade levels.

Other content-specific sight words that appear to be transitioning to regular sight words due to our technological environment are words for the computer age. Today's children need to familiarize themselves with words used in the computer environment. Table 5.5 represents a core of major procedural and feedback words common to our technological age (Dreyer, Futtersak & Boehm, 1985). These words should be introduced early during computer classroom instruction and in the context of phrases or sentences in which they actually occur in programs.

Signal Sight Words

A third set of sight words identified by Block is signal sight words. According to Block (2003), these words

> . . . clue, or send a signal, that (1) cause-effect relationships are being described; (2) a specific ordering of ideas is important; (3) a summation, more of the same, or

TABLE 5.5 Essential Words for Computer-Assisted Instruction in the Elementary Grades, Based on a Sample of 35 Programs

activity	different	lesson	ready
adjust	directions	letter	regular
again	disk	level	remove
another	diskette	list	repeat
answer	display	load	return*
any	document	loading*	rules
arrow*	down	match	save
audio	drive	memory	score
bar	edit	menu*	screen
before	effects	monitor	select
begin	end	move	selection
bold	enter*	name*	sound*
button	erase	need	spacebar*
catalog	escape or <esc>*	no	speed
change	exit	number*	start
choice	find	off	team
choose*	finished	on	text
colors	follow	options	then
column	format	paddle	try
compete	game*	password	turn
complete	good	picture	type*
command	help	play	up
computer	hit	player	use
continue*	hold	please	video
control or <ctrl>	incorrect	point	wait
copy	incorrectly	practice	want
correct	indicate	press*	which
correctly	insert	print	win
cursor	instructions	problems	word
delete	joystick	program*	work
demonstration	key*	quit	yes
description	keyboard	rate	your

*Words present in at least 10 of the 35 programs.

something different is coming; or (4) changes in thoughts or new thoughts are about to occur. (p. 275)

Knowing signal words on sight and knowing what the signal words mean and do will also facilitate comprehension, which is the ultimate goal of any reading instruction (see Table 5.6 for a brief sample of the words Block calls signal words).

Selecting Sight Words

Based on Block's (2003) notion of three distinctly different types of sight words, it becomes clear that some distinction needs to be made between words that should be taught as sight words and words that should be taught as vocabulary words.

The first group that should be taught as sight words are those that occur frequently in print: high-frequency words. They may be taken from a variety of sources including basal series materials, content textbooks, and high-frequency word lists. Another group that should be taught as sight words are those that are in the reader's oral vocabulary and for which the reader should have meaning. A third set of words from which sight words may be selected are those that cannot be recognized or pronounced by applying phonic generalizations: irregular words.

TABLE 5.6 Signal Words

Cause / Effect	Contrast	Time Order	Conclusion
as	but	before	and
similarly	on the other hand	after	too
at the same time	in spite of	now	i, ii, iii
like	conversely	previously	finally
as well as	despite	last	furthermore
likewise	however	next	first, second
both	nonetheless	then	1, 2, 3
all	on the contrary	when	in brief
because	instead	even though	in the end
accordingly	rather	immediately	in summary
since	though	formerly	to reiterate
thus	yet	later	in conclusion
consequently	regardless	meanwhile	to sum up
hence	whereas	presently	finally
so	although	initially	therefore
then	in contrast	ultimately	thus
	unlike		

Finally, sight words may come from words the reader can identify by using picture clues. Heilman (1998) states, "It is true that pictures may provide clues to unknown words. . . . Pictures may suggest words. . . . Pictures help focus attention on meaning . . . where only a limited number of words are known, pictures supplement" (p. 27). The pictures help identify words in the text; therefore it makes sense to convert words that students can identify with pictures into sight words that are recognized without pictures.

Quick Self-Check 1

1. How does Block define basic sight words, content-specific sight words, and signal sight words?
2. What three reasons are given for focusing on sight words?
3. How should sight words be selected for teaching?

Strategies for Teaching Sight Words

Mastery of a core vocabulary such as the Dolch list is necessary for children to become fluent readers. Teachers sometimes check students individually on their ability to recognize these words, with mastery defined as the "instant" recognition of 90% to 95% of the words in any list. Reading words in a list, however, is always more demanding for poor readers than reading these same words in a story (Krieger, 1981).

To master many of these words, some students learn them in context by merely reading a variety of interesting stories and articles (the best way). Other students need simple introduction to the words followed by a little practice, engaging in some of the following activities for learning these words. There are others who need a more structured program. Each word must be carefully introduced by perhaps placing it in a pocket chart and asking such questions as:

1. How many letters are in the word?
2. With what letter does the word begin?
3. What is/are the letter/s at the end of the word?
4. Read the word.
5. Read the word in this phrase. Now read the word in this sentence.

With a more structured program, the introduction of each word is followed by lots of review and practice as suggested in some of the following activities. Before describing them, it is important to sound a note of caution. When learning any word recognition strategy, children need to know that words spoken in isolation are frequently stressed differently than when they are spoken in sentences. Sight words are particularly vulnerable in this respect. For example, the word *an* would be pronounced and accented as /án/ in situations in which it is spoken in isolation, but it would be unaccented as /ən/ when spoken in the context of a phrase as /ən ápl/. For this reason, whenever possible, present these words as parts of phrases and sentences. Remember, too, that most of these words have a variety of meanings depending on the context in which they are used. For example, notice the various meanings of up in these phrases: *add up*, *shape up*, *dress up*, *eat up*, *clam up*, *slip up*, *fold up*, *mess up*, and *frame up*.

Eldredge (2005) recommends that sight-word instruction should not take up more than 10 minutes of classroom time. Further, he provides some guidelines for sight-word instruction:

1. Children are more likely to remember words that are meaningful to them.
2. Children will more likely retain words if they focus on the letter sequences in the word, along with the sounds represented by the letters.
3. Children's memory for the word will be enhanced if they see the word at least six times during the lesson.
4. Children will more likely remember words if any unusual letter-sound relationships are explicitly emphasized.
5. Children will more likely retain words if they see them in context.
6. Teachers will increase the likelihood that children will remember words if their teaching involves the use of touch, sight, and sound while learning the word's letter-sound sequences.

Explicit Instruction

Crawley and Merrit (2004) developed an explicit method of teaching sight words. They recommend the following steps:

1. To begin, present only five words that the children will read or use to write.
2. Give students letters that they can manipulate to practice spelling the words.
3. Point to the words you are teaching while saying the word. Point to each letter and spell the word aloud.
4. Use the word aloud in a sentence so the students can hear the word in context.
5. Instruct the students to say the word aloud while they spell/write the word in the air.
6. Have the students manipulate the letters at their desks to spell the word.
7. Select a student to go to the board to rearrange the letters and spell the word.
8. Instruct all the students to say and spell the word aloud.

9. After all five words have been learned, show students riddles and have them write the answers to the riddles with the new words.
10. Post these words on word walls or elsewhere in the room.
11. Read a story aloud that contains the newly learned words.

Whole-Part-Whole Approach

Gunning (2001) believes that sight words can be taught through a whole-part-whole approach where students are introduced to new words in the context of a story. This approach, he believes, may be more appropriate for children who are reading short passages. The four steps to the whole-part-whole approach include the following:

1. Familiarize students with the selection. This includes selecting a short story, rhyme, poem, or song that the students will enjoy hearing over and over again. The teacher should choose four or five words that are important for students to learn as sight words (words they will encounter in their reading and writing). The teacher should preview the selection with the students, allowing time for predicting what the story will be about. The teacher should read the selection and point to the words as s/he reads the story.
2. Reread the text with students. The teacher should reread the text, inviting students to join in wherever they feel comfortable. After several re-readings, students should read the story on their own.
3. Reread the story on their own. Children should read the story independently (if possible). Children should also be instructed to focus on the words in the story and not on the pictures.
4. Reassemble the story. Copy sentences from the story and allow the students to reassemble the story. Teachers should consider selecting sentences with the sight words in them. Students could also cut the sentences into words and the words into letters, if necessary.

Part-Whole Approach

Gunning (2001) also suggests that sight words may be taught through a part-whole approach. In this approach, students learn the words before they encounter them in the story. Gunning suggests this approach might be better for longer selections. The steps of the part-whole procedure include the following:

1. Discuss the meanings of the words. This step only needs to be completed if students do not know the meanings of the sight words.
2. Present the words in isolation. The teacher should write out the new words and then check to see if the students can read them. Words known on sight by the students should be discarded and attention should be focused on the unknown words. If the word includes phonics elements, students should be encouraged to try the word. As the words are being shown, teachers should point out interesting and unique features of the word that might help students remember the word. During this step, students should also spell the word so that they attend to the letters. After students have examined the word carefully, they should read it chorally. Additional words should be added and practice should continue until students recognize the words immediately.
3. Present the words in context. After recognizing the words rapidly in isolation, students should be presented with the words in context (short phrases or sentences). Present the phrases and sentences until students can read them rapidly.

4. Apply the new words. Introduce the book from which the words were drawn. Predict what the story will be about. The story then should be read to assess predictions.
5. Review the words. After the reading, the sight words should be reviewed. Multiple opportunities for practice with the new sight words should be included.

Associative Learning Strategy

Johns, Lenski, and Elish-Piper (1999) explain that the associative learning strategy is designed for use with children who have difficulty learning the high-frequency words that lack meaning clues. They believe the associative learning technique helps children develop concrete associations for highly abstract words, such as *for, of,* and *the*. The steps to the strategy include the following:

1. Selecting words for teaching.
2. Presenting the targeted word in a phrase accompanied by an illustration (e.g., a plate of cookies) with the targeted word underlined and written in a different color ink to draw the students' attention to the word.
3. Ask students to brainstorm other uses of the word. Students should create their own picture card and label following the same procedure of using a different ink color and underlining the word.
4. Provide time for children to share their work. They should place picture cards in their word bank or on their personal word wall.

This procedure should be repeated to teach additional sight words.

Word Walls

Rasinski and Padak (2001) describe a word wall as a working bulletin board with words as the focus, but serving as a combination word bank and graffiti wall. Large sheets of paper are affixed to the wall, or individual index cards or larger paper can be used for individual words. Cunningham (2005) recommends "doing" word walls to learn sight vocabulary. According to Cunningham, doing a word wall is not the same as having a word wall. Cunningham explains that doing a word wall means:

1. Limiting the words on the word wall to those that children frequently use in their writing.
2. Adding words gradually, approximately five new words per week.
3. Making words accessible by mounting them so everyone can see them; writing them in big, thick, black letters; cutting around the words to provide configuration clues; and using a variety of colors for the background so words that are confusing have different-colored backgrounds.
4. Practicing the words using a variety of strategies such as chanting and writing them, so those who are not visual learners have multiple opportunities to learn the words.
5. Engaging in many review activities to provide practice in reading and writing the words instantly and automatically.
6. Ensuring that word wall words are spelled correctly in students' writing.

Using the word wall regularly and daily with children keeps the word wall alive. Cunningham adds that words for the wall may include words that students need in their reading and writing that they confuse with other words, words from their reading or high-frequency lists, name, words commonly confused or misspelled, and words with patterns. Content-area word walls may be generated based on units of study in any of the various content areas. Variations of the word wall can be used, such as a take-home wall (manila file folder), seasonal walls, monthly walls, and thematic walls.

Word walls are an excellent way to provide additional assistance for English Language Learners. Not only can difficult words be posted, but they can (and should) be posted in both languages. In the case of Spanish, the cognates (words that are similar in both languages) can be posted on the word wall along with the English term. Illustrations may also be helpful for ELLs.

Guidelines for creating the word wall include making the words large, legible, and accessible to everyone in the class. Generally, the words should be lowercase unless they are proper nouns. Cutting the words to shape, mounting them on colored paper, and categorizing words using special patterns can serve as reminders to students to help them differentiate one word from another.

Flashcards

One traditional way of teaching sight words to students is by the "flashcard method." Nicholson (2000) believes that the negative reputation of flashcard learning is undeserved. The use of flashcards is a very direct way to teach children sight words. According to Nicholson, "Flashcards can help them to build knowledge of these high-frequency words, which have to be known if children are to bootstrap themselves into reading of text" (p. 37). If children do not have a command of sight words, then they spend way too much time decoding and not nearly enough time comprehending.

Flashcards help children achieve the goal of recognizing many words instantly, which allows children to begin reading independently. One way to work with children on automatic recognition of sight words is to use a timer regular. Timing how quickly students recognize a set of sight words could be turned into a game. Teachers could record the time for students as they work to increase the speed at which they recognize the sight words.

In addition to using flashcards for teaching high-frequency words, flashcards can also be used for pre-teaching words that will appear frequently in the text to be read. This scaffolding strategy allows the students to learn the words before reading so they can recognize the words automatically during reading, thereby eliminating interference with comprehension (Nicholson, 2000). After a brief practice period, children should be moved into the text to facilitate transfer between the sight words and application to an authentic reading situation.

Nicholson (2000) also uses flashcards similar to sentence strips. This allows children to see the word in context. A sentence (not from the material to be read) is generated with the sight word. That sentence is then transferred to a flashcard/sentence strip with the word highlighted in some way (bigger print, different color, etc.) to draw attention to it. Once the practice is over (Nicholson recommends that it not exceed 20 minutes), the students should be directed to the story so they can transfer the knowledge to authentic reading situations. Nicholson reports, "The key to success is to use flashcards sensibly, in small doses, for fun, and with pizzazz!" (p. 43).

Word Banks

Word banks consist of words that a student knows in isolation or by sight. They may also contain words the child is in the process of learning. The words for the word bank can come from anywhere and may include words from reading or words of interest (Barr, Blachowicz, Katz, & Kaufman, 2002). When a new word is encountered through text or identified as a word to be learned, it is printed on an index card for each student. Older readers may make their own cards, but teachers of young children may want to print the word for them. As students learn new words, the cards accumulate. They can be punched and stored on rings, or they can be stored in index boxes. Other creative ways can be used to individualize the word banks for students.

Students should be encouraged to keep their words in alphabetical order, which allows them an opportunity to practice alphabetizing. When too many words have been added, students can be instructed to only include selected words. It might also be time to stop the word bank. These word banks provide incentive for children, because they serve as a record of how many words a student has learned. They can also be referenced during writing and spelling.

Word Sorts

Word sorts (Bear, Invernizzi, Templeton, & Johnston, 2004) enable students to sort letters, syllables, and words into categories thereby providing opportunities for hands-on experiences with letters, syllables, and words. Through the sorting process, students not only learn the words, but also learn additional information about the words. They should be on individual index cards to make it easier for sorting. They should also be connected to the students' lives through personal interaction, or through books, common sight words, or Spanish cognates.

Words can be sorted in a variety of ways, such as by beginning sounds, ending sounds, or medial sounds. They can be sorted by rhyming words, number of syllables, or how the words appear. They can be sorted by suffixes, prefixes, or inflected endings. If content words are used, they can be sorted by content area.

Word Ladders

Rasinski (2005) suggests a fun format designed to enable students to practice working with words. This format works well focusing on sight words. This activity is called word ladders. To begin, students are given a ladder with a word on the bottom rung. Teachers may also want to include a word on the top rung until students are familiar with the activity. Beside the ladder, the teacher provides directions for the student, along with a definition of the new word to be formed. Students climb the ladder by reading the clues and the definitions to add the next word (see Figure 5.1). While the directions in this example are limited to "change one letter," teachers may also wish to add other directions such as add a letter, rearrange the letters, or add two letters. This activity can be helpful for students learning to write sight words as well as learning the meanings of the words.

Games

Many favorite games of the students can be modified into games designed to provide practice with sight words. Both Candyland and Chutes and Ladders can be modified to be used as sight-word practice. Jenga is also a fun game for children to play and practice sight words at the same time. The game is played according to the standard directions; however, the blocks have sight words written on them. Before the child can keep the block taken from the pile, s/he must correctly pronounce the sight word on the colored block.

Bingo is another game that can be modified for classroom use to practice sight words. Children get a game board and are instructed to put sight words on the game board. Then, the game is played just like Bingo. The teacher may want to focus the game on 75 Dolch words, or 75 other words that the students should know on sight. The card game, Go Fish, is a favorite for pre-service teachers to adapt. Sight words are written on the playing cards and children try to collect sight words. The game is played as it normally is except that sight words are used to make matches. A similar adaptation can be made for Old Maid. Another popular game adaptation is Concentration. Students work in pairs or teams with their sight words while trying to remember where the match to the sight word was located in the grid.

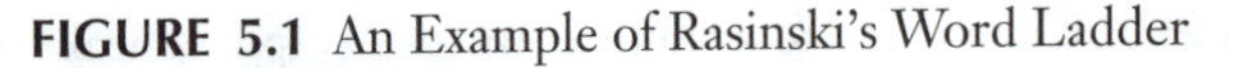

FIGURE 5.1 An Example of Rasinski's Word Ladder

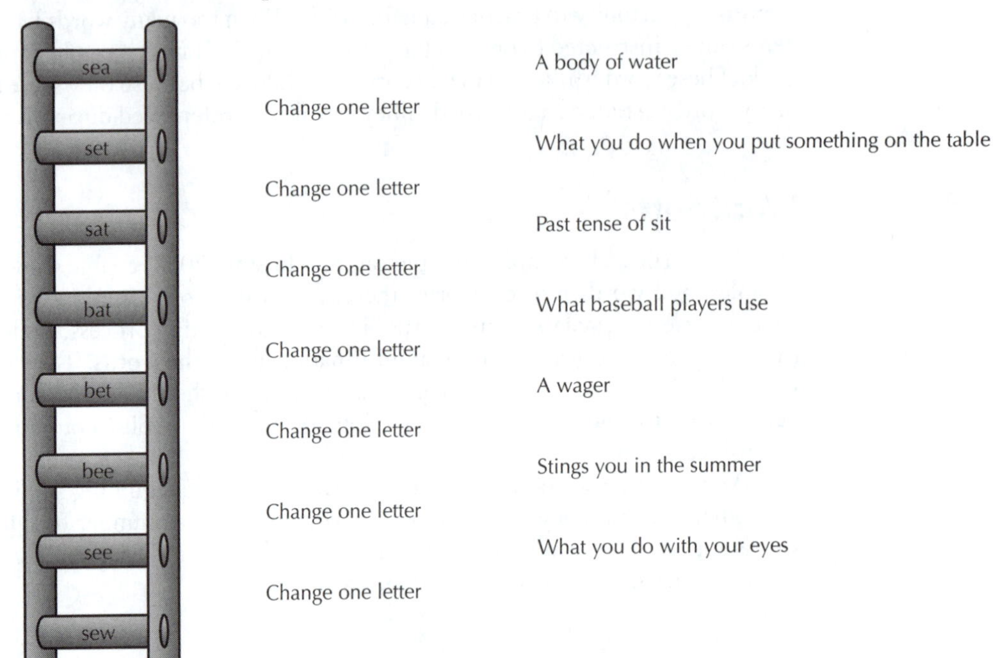

Adapted from Rasinski, T. (2005). Daily word ladders: Grades 2-3. New York: Scholastic.

Technology

Technology can also assist in developing games and activities to facilitate the review of newly learned and previously learned sight words. For example, PowerPoint can be used to practice automaticity with sight words or newly learned words. Each word can be typed on a slide. Then, using the timing function, the words can be flashed as the child works to recognize the new word on sight. Various computer games and online resources are available to help. Discovery's puzzle maker provides teachers with a valuable resource to use when developing crossword puzzles, word searches, cryptograms, and letter tiles (http://puzzlemaker.school.discovery.com). Another similar resource is Kid Crosswords (http://www.kidcrosswords.com/puzzle). Interesting and enjoyable word puzzles are also available on the Game House website (http://gamehouse.com). Mindfun (http://www.mindfun.com) contains many exciting and fun games including word scrambles, word webs, Build-A-Word, and Drop Quotes. Each of these games can be used to enhance sight word development.

Quick Activities for Reinforcement

There are many quick and easy activities that teachers could use to reinforce sight-word learning. The first three activities are designed to help students who experience difficulty with particular sight words.

1. With easily confused words such as *on* and *one*, have students identify the letter that causes the difficulty. Place several students' names on the board that contain the letter, such as *e*—Jerry, Ted, Jan*e*. Ask the student to identify the difficult letter in the names. Practice with phrases that include the easily confused words.
2. Trace words in sand that are repeatedly missed and point out the salient feature. Have the student repeat the tracing, verbalizing the difficult letters as s/he does so.

3. Construct a slotted stand-up frame to hold "My Word for the Day." Insert words needed for practice.

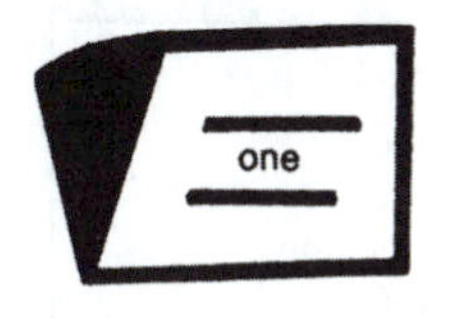

Sometimes quick activities are also needed to review and extend students' sight-word knowledge. The following activities are all aimed at reviewing and extending previous learning. While many of these activities are usual in nature, teachers should always practice and apply these newly learned words to authentic text.

1. Drill with phrase and sentence cards. (See Table 5.7)

jump up	He jumps up.
Example: Phrase Card	Example: Sentence Card

2. Prepare pairs of phrase or sentence cards. Start with about 5 pairs, or 10 cards, turning them upside down. Students must read the word or phrase card as they turn it over and attempt to find the matching pair.
3. Cards (phrases or sentences) may be passed out. The teacher says such things as, "Whoever has the phrase *will do*, stand up, get in line, or whistle."
4. Have about a dozen pairs of phrase cards ready. Take one set and distribute the remaining cards among a small group of students. Place one card in the pocket chart and say, "All those who have this same word or phrase card may place it in the pocket chart with mine." Continue with the rest of the cards.
5. Have each student develop a "word bank" that includes a file of words that are known and a file of words that need to be learned. These may be kept in alphabetical order.
6. Use the ever-popular bingo format with words or phrases as shown in these examples.

and	must	see
big	FREE	he
what	yes	play

I can	for me	is it
to run	FREE	what went
my new	to him	come down

7. Use a muffin pan or plastic egg carton. Write sight words on the bottom of each section with a felt pen. Make copies of these sight words on cards. Students sort and place them in the appropriate section, reading the word.
8. Use well-known short nursery rhymes, such as *Humpty Dumpty*, that contain lots of sight words. Write the words on the chalkboard or on a chart. Read them aloud. Ask students to read them along with you several times until the words are well known.

TABLE 5.7 Phrase Unit, Based on the Dolch Basic Sight Vocabulary

PHRASE	PHRASE	PHRASE
about it	he went	of their own
are big now	help me	one or two
as I do	here is an	only one
ask him	his green one	our yellow one
at the	how much	out came three
ate his		out came two
	I am	
be good	I can	please let
be just right	I do	pretty while
before long	I have	pull us out
best of all	I like	
but I do	I want	ran fast
	I will	ran to stop
came because	if he goes	read and write
can always see	into the	run away
can buy	is cold	
can find	is full	saw her
can fly	is going	see how small
can laugh	is not black	see my green
can use	it came from	shall both talk
carry her	it is	shall know soon
come and play	it is going	she gave eight
could not grow		she has five
	jump up	sit down
did not	jump upon	so am I
do not	just then	
do you		take hold
does not	keep him	talk at once
don't you	know which	tell me
draw a green	know why	tell them
		thank you
for a walk	let me	that big yellow
four little yellow	let us	the first one
	like to ride	the funny one
get on	like to show	the hot
give up	live in	the kind of
go to	long, long drink	the light
go together	look after	their brown
	look at	there are
had not been	look for	there are ten
had to clean	look under	they called
have found	look up	they said
he could see		this is
he got	made a blue	to cut some
he looked around	made him white	to drink
he never saw	may I sing	to eat
he put new	must be warm	to keep those
he ran	my big	to make
he said	my red one	to play
he saw		to play with
	not very far	to sleep
		to work

Then make word cards for each sight word you want them to retain from the rhyme. Shuffle the cards and spread them face down. Taking turns, the children choose a card and read the word. The card is then kept if read correctly. If a player misreads the card, s/he must keep it until the next round and then read it correctly.

9. Use predictable books for reading aloud to children. Predictable books repeat words, phrases, and sentences over and over. This repetition, while fun and enjoyable, is also necessary for children to convert new words to their sight-word list.
10. Word sorts may be used to teach and practice sight vocabulary.
11. Various word games can also be played to reinforce learned sight vocabulary words.

Troublesome Sight Words

Cunningham (1980) described sight words as "four-letter" words because of the connotation of "bad" and the fact that many include four letters such as *were*, *with*, and *what*. She stated:

> Since sight words have no tangible meaning and their function is to connect other words, children are often unaware of their existence as separate words. The word *what* is often used in "Whatcha doing?" *Them* is just pronounced "m." Some children do not even realize these are separate words such as *big*, *truck* and *elephant*, nor are they clear as to their function (p. 160).

Wiesendanger and Bader (1987) concluded that most problems are created by those sight words of low visual imagery that are easily confused, such as *their* and *then*, *what* and *when*. To remediate, they suggest teachers should subdivide the task, first teaching each word as a separate unit. Only after the words are learned separately, should they be presented together in order to discriminate between them. If a comparison between "easily confused words" is done too early, they believe children will become confused.

For students needing lots of practice, Higdon (1987) creates "sticker" books from stickers donated by parents. Each book contains about eight pages with a sticker on each one and a predictable sentence written about the sticker that includes sight words. Each book follows a format and uses a specific problem sight word, such as "I *want* a banana, an apple, a peach, etc." Smelly stickers add an extra sensory experience. (Many concepts can be taught using this method, such as toys, food, numbers, and insects.)

One final suggestion: Some teachers construct sight-word rings. They place six to twelve unknown sight words, written on index cards, on a ring. When a child can read the sight word correctly three times, cut off one edge of the index card. When a child can spell it correctly, cut off another edge. When a child uses it correctly in a sentence, cut off a third edge.

Sight-Word Storehouse

The sight words listed and discussed previously differ from the sight words acquired weekly, monthly, and yearly by students as they progress through the grades. By repeatedly encountering words (the number of times varying for different students), words are recognized immediately without any form of analysis. The goal in reading should be that words read are all part of a growing, expanding sight vocabulary. The vast storehouse of sight words accumulated by expert readers makes it possible for them not only to read rapidly, but also to pay full attention to thinking about what they are reading.

Quick Self-Check 2

1. What is recommended as the best way to master sight words?
2. What one word is the key to teaching sight words?
3. What determines whether a word is a sight word or whether it is decoded?

SUMMARY

Sight words can refer to words memorized as whole units (without learning the word through decoding) such as *brown*, *stop*, and *frog*, or to words that do not adhere to phonics principles so they are memorized such as *of*, *on*, and *the*. A large cache of sight vocabulary words allows students to spend more time comprehending and less time decoding. Many types of sight word lists exist with the Dolch list being the most popular. Block (2003) adds other types of sight word lists: *content-word lists* and *signal word lists*. The size of a child's sight vocabulary does impact his/her reading performance, as proficient readers tend to have larger, more extensive sight vocabularies than do poorer readers. While an extensive sight vocabulary is desirable, children also need to use other word recognition skills to determine the meanings of unknown words that do not occur frequently enough to warrant memorization.

Review Questions

1. What is your definition of a sight word? With what definition do you agree?
2. Which of the sight-word lists do you think is most appropriate for beginning readers?
3. Explain the similarities and differences between explicit instruction, whole-part-whole approach, part-whole approach, and associative Learning Strategy.

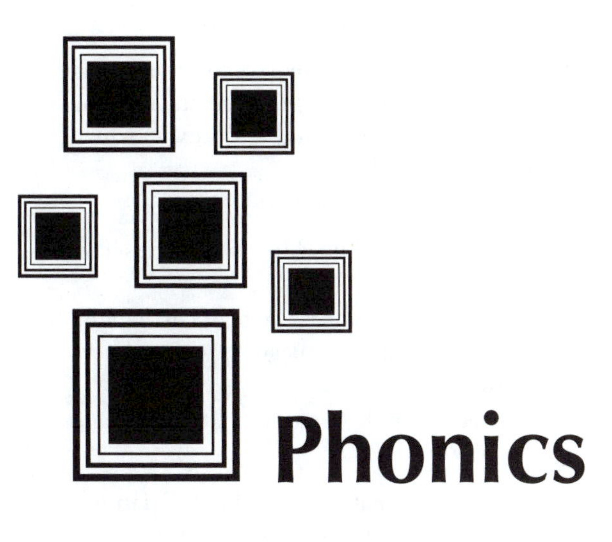

Chapter 6

Phonics

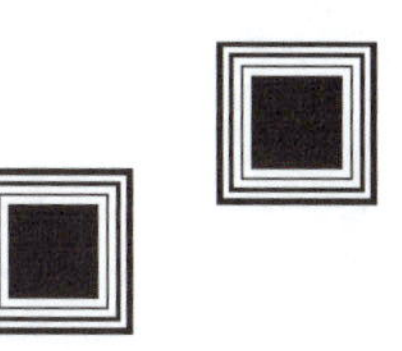

What phonics is and why we should teach phonics has been of great concern to reading researchers and educators for decades. Harris and Hodges (1995) define phonics as "a way of teaching reading and spelling that stresses symbol-sound relationships, used especially in beginning instruction" (p. 186). The National Reading Panel (NICHHD, 2000) explains that phonics instruction may be provided systematically or incidentally. Systematic phonics is a pre-determined, highly sequential set of discrete phonics elements taught at various levels of explicitness depending on the type of phonics method employed. With incidental phonics instruction, on the other hand, the teacher does not teach by following a planned sequence of phonics elements. Instead, the focus is on teaching the elements as needed or required by the text being read.

Based on their meta-analysis of phonics research, the National Reading Panel (NICHHD, 2000) concluded the following:

- Specific systematic phonics programs were all more effective than non-phonics programs, and they did not appear to differ significantly from one another in their effectiveness (p. 2–132).
- Systematic phonics instruction was effective when delivered through tutoring, through small groups, and through teaching classes of students (p. 2–132).
- To be effective, systematic phonics instruction introduced in kindergarten must be appropriately designed for learners and must begin with foundational knowledge involving letters and phonemic awareness (p. 2–133).
- Systematic phonics instruction was significantly more effective than unsystematic or no phonics instruction in helping prevent reading difficulties among at-risk students and in helping to remediate reading difficulties in disabled readers (p. 2–133).

Understanding Phonics

Logan, Rupley, and Erickson (1995) explain that the basic reason for phonics instruction is to teach students the alphabetic principle. Once they learn the grapheme/phoneme (letter sound) correspondences, students can approximate the pronunciation of unknown words and determine if their pronunciation makes sense in the context of the sentence or story.

The purpose of phonics, however, is ***not*** to enable students to derive the correct pronunciation of every unknown word they encounter: "Phonics is intended to aid in approximating the identification of the unknown word and using this in conjunction with the context in which the unknown word appears" (Logan, Rupley, & Erickson, 1995, p. 9).

Classroom teachers may choose among several options for teaching phonics:

1. A program that uses a basal reading series as the core curriculum. Most basal series have a built-in decoding strand.
2. A balanced whole language program using children's literature as the core curriculum. Many of the word recognition skills are developed through language activities. There may or may not be a sequential decoding strand.
3. A commercial reading program with its own materials, trade books, and literature, and with an intensive phonics program.

Most of the phonics programs available provide similar information with slight variations. The variations in programs arise because some strive to cover all the possible letter combinations, but others classify only the most regular writing features of English.

The National Reading Panel (NICHHD, 2000) explains that phonics instruction may differ in the following ways: (a) how many letter-sound relations are taught, how they are sequenced, whether phonics generalizations are taught, whether special marks are added to letters to indicate their sounds; (b) the size of the unit taught (graphemes and phonemes, phonograms); (c) whether the sounds associated with letters are pronounced in isolation (synthetic phonics) or only in the context of words (analytic phonics); (d) the amount and type of phonemic awareness taught (examples include blending or segmenting sounds orally in words); (e) whether instruction is sequenced according to a hierarchical view of learning with the steps regarded as a series of prerequisites (letters, letter-sound relations, words, sentences) or whether multiple skills are learned together; (f) pace of instruction; (g) word reading operations that children are taught (sounding out and blending letters or using larger letter subunits to read words by analogy to known words); (h) involvement of spelling instruction; (i) whether learning activities include extensive oral drill-and-practice, reciting phonics rules, or filling out worksheets; (j) type of vocabulary control provided in text; (k) whether phonics instruction is embedded in or segregated from literacy curriculum; (l) the teaching approach (direct instruction, constructivist approach); and (m) how interesting and motivating the instructional activities are for teachers and for students (pp. 2–103–104).

Additionally, certain programs organize and group their sound-symbol relationships differently. Most programs, however, place the basic division between the consonants and vowels, and these two basic groups may be further divided. In the consonant group are:

1. single consonant letters with a single sound.
2. single consonant letters with more than one sound.
3. digraphs—two consonant letters with only a single sound.
4. blends—two or three consonant letters with sounds blended rapidly together.
5. special consonant combinations.

In the vowel group are:

1. single vowels (long, short, and special vowel sounds).
2. schwa—a "reduced" vowel sound, neither short nor long.
3. vowel digraphs—two vowels together with only a single vowel sound.
4. vowel diphthongs—two vowels with a "gliding" sound between them.

The letters *Y* and *W* have unique positions, sometimes operating as consonants and sometimes operating as vowels. In addition, there is a special group of *r-controlled* vowels. See Table 6.1 for a model overview.

TABLE 6.1 Basic Division of a Phonics Program

Consonant Group with Examples	Vowel Group with Examples	*y, w*	The Letter *r*
Single: b, m, p Variant consonants: c, g Blends: cr, gl, st Digraphs: ch, th, ng Special combination: dge, tch	Single: a, e, i, o, u (long, short, special sound) Schwa: ə Digraphs: ai, oa, ee Diphthongs: ou, ow, oo	May be a consonant and vowel: yes, cry cow, law	Conditions the preceding vowel sound: ar, ur

Writers of phonics programs often find themselves in a dilemma. If they try to give attention to all letter combinations, their classifications become too cumbersome. If they strive for simplicity, they often omit combinations that deserve explanations. *Since teachers need more background in sound-symbol relationships than their students do*, a rather extensive phonics program will be presented for the teachers. This does not mean, however, that all students will need this kind of background to master reading. When the occasion arises, however, for letter-sound relationships to be discussed, it is important that teachers possess the knowledge to explain why a word decodes (recognizing letters and sounds) or encodes (writing the word or sound) as it does.

Such explanations show word groups and patterns and not only satisfy the curiosity of students but also help reinforce learning. When explanations begin by showing a generalization for one example, such as *dge* in the word *bridge*, and then include other words that "behave" in a similar fashion, such as *dodge, edge*, and *fudge*, difficult reading-writing combinations are clarified.

Once sound-symbol relationships are introduced, students must learn to blend the sounds together, a crucial stage in beginning reading. The idea of letters representing sounds that must be glided together quickly represents an abstraction; this becomes a difficult concept for some children to understand. Once they have mastered blending together a few sound-symbol relationships and can apply the principle, they progress far more rapidly.

Rosenshine and Stevens (1984) found that time spent in blending activities at the first and second grades resulted in higher scores on achievement tests. The Commission on Reading's report (Anderson, Hiebert, Scott, & Wilkinson, 1985) corroborates this: "Teachers who spend more than average amounts of time on blending produce larger than average gains on reading achievement tests."

A major disagreement exists in the area of blending as to the presentation of the combined sounds that make up words. Many reading educators believe that sounds must never be presented in isolation; that is, to have the teacher say /c-c-c-a-a-a-t-t-t/ and then blend this to *cat* is tantamount to dooming children to life-long remediation! They think that children will blend combinations together by noting when words begin and end the same and noting that a one-letter change in a word makes a different word.

Part of this blending controversy comes from particular consonant phonemes known as "stops," /p/ /b/ /t/ /d/ /k/ /g/ /ch/ and /j/, that cannot be said in isolation. An /uh/ sound always follows when saying these sounds alone. They argue that children would sound a word such as ball as /b-u-all/ and that blending isolated phonemes distorts the true sound of the word.

Other educators argue that this is the only way some children will learn to read new words in the early stages; that is, the teacher saying the sounds in isolation as /c-c-c-a-a-a-t-t-t/, then blending them together, and showing students the combinations that "make" such a word. After sounding the isolated phonemes, teachers have students say them faster and faster until they approximate the spoken word.

Some educators adopt a middle-of-the-road attitude about blending and suggest a procedure such as follows: With the word mat, they have students pronounce the vowel sound alone /a/; add the consonant sound /m/, blended together as /ma/; and then add the /t/ to form /mat/. Others suggest that when blending, students identify the ending sounds /at/ first, and then add the /m/ to form /mat/. In these latter methods the movement is from right to left and can interfere with directional eye sweep, since reading is from left to right. Nevertheless, these methods are still used quite successfully, as are the two blending methods previously mentioned.

A method that differs from all of those just mentioned introduces the abstraction of blending by combining compound word parts. Children are shown parts of compound words such as *base* and *ball*, *side* and *walk*. They are asked to blend the two parts together to form the words *baseball* and *sidewalk*. Many other compound word parts are used to encourage understanding of the blending concept.

A summary of ways to blend sounds follows:

1. No sounds are isolated. Children reason that changing one phoneme changes the word. *Mat* becomes *sat*.
2. Individual phonemes are pronounced, then blended together. Teacher pronounces each phoneme separately as m-m-m-a-a-a-t-t-t, repeating the sounds faster and faster until they approximate the word.
3. The vowel is pronounced first, followed by the first consonant sound, then the final sound.
   ă mă mat
4. The ending phonogram is pronounced first, then the beginning consonant sound.
   ăt mat
5. Compound words are broken into their respective parts and blended together.

As with other reading issues, this one is far from settled. Children can profit from some formal instruction in blending—the method used is not as important as the children's ability to apply the skill to new vocabulary. To teach initial consonant blending, teachers can use common household products, such as *Sc*ope, *Gl*ad, and *Pr*ide, and cereal boxes, such as *Fr*uit Loops and *Fr*osted *Fl*akes.

Quick Self-Check 1

1. Why do phonics programs differ between and among types of texts?
2. Generally speaking, how is consonant instruction divided?
3. What are the typical divisions for teaching vowels?

Teaching Approaches

When working with sound-symbol relationships, the teacher may follow one of several procedures: (1) guiding the lesson by *telling* the sound-symbol relationships, and requiring students to memorize certain rules (explicit phonics); (2) guiding the lesson so that students *conclude* what the sound-symbol relationship is after studying particular known words (implicit phonics); (3) presenting words with regular spelling patterns such as man, tan, fan, ran, can (analogy phonics); (4) embedding phonics instruction into authentic reading by extracting phonics lessons from the story; and (5) modifying previous strategies to fit the needs of the students.

Explicit Approach (Synthetic, Deductive)

The explicit approach or synthetic approach is defined by Harris and Hodges (1995) as a part-to-whole approach whereby the student learns the sounds represented by letters and letter combinations, and blends these sounds to pronounce words. This approach is characterized by early, direct, and explicit emphasis on learning letter-sound relationships and blending or synthesizing these elements into whole words.

The explicit or synthetic approach generally begins with the teacher telling students that this is the letter *d*, and it makes the *duh* sound. This approach, telling students the sounds and letters, is also referred to as the deductive approach or code-emphasis approach. Students learn the letters and sounds, and then are expected to use their sounding out and blending strategies to pronounce a new word. With explicit phonics, the skills to be learned are clearly identified and sequenced. Blending is important to synthetic phonics, because students learn to put sounds together to form words through the blending. An example of an explicit (synthetic, deductive, part-to-whole) phonics lesson follows.

Teacher: Today, we are going to learn about a new letter combination. (Teacher holds up a card with *ph* printed on it.) This letter combination is *ph* and it stands for the sound of /f/. Here are three words you have probably seen with this combination: Phil, telephone, and graph. (Teacher writes them on the board or has them on transparencies.) Note that this combination may come at the beginning (points to Phil); middle (points to telephone); or end of the word (points to graph). (Teacher stresses the /f/ sound in the words.) (With children who have poorer skills, the teacher might want to show only the combination in the initial position.)

Students: (Teacher calls on different students to read the three words.)

Teacher: I have another group of words here. (Words are as follows:)

dolphin	elephant
phonograph	Daphne
photograph	pictograph

Will someone underline in each word the two-letter combination that stands for the /f/ sound?

Students: (One or more may underline the *ph* combination.)

Teacher: Let's read these words together, and then see if there are any that you want to talk about. (Continues.) Who thinks they know what a pictograph is? (Discuss the word and its parts, the word's meaning, and that the word refers to picture writing used in some countries.) Let's try these words in sentences to make sure that they are in your meaning vocabulary.

Students: (Offer sentences using the words.)

Teacher: (May call attention for review to other known phonics elements.) What three words do you notice with the *gr* blend? (Continues.) Let's compare these words (points to words on the board) with words that have the consonant *p* alone. Let's read these words. (Stress the differences between the two sounds as follows:)

pill	Phil
pant	phantom
peasant	pheasant

(If necessary, the teacher might decide to review the *ea* digraph as in peasant and pheasant.)

Students: (Read words and place them in sentences orally.)

Teacher: On a piece of paper, number from 1 to 12. I will read several words to you, all beginning with the letter *p*. You know some of these words from previous lessons.

Tell me whether the first sound should be written as just *p* or as *ph*. (Reads *pantry, posture, phonograph, phase, protest, phantom, photograph*.) (Continues discussing words and sounds, assigning some follow-up work if needed.)

Critics of the explicit approach cite the following:

1. Students rely on the letter-sound relationships too much, paying no attention to context and meaning; hence, the term *code-emphasis*.
2. Memorizing rules does not mean they will be applied.
3. Many readers discover the rules and relationships themselves, and class instruction about these rules and sounds can be wasteful.
4. Prolonged work with phonics diverts students from getting meaning.

Advocates of the explicit approach are adamant that:

1. Children see very early that there is a relationship between letters and sounds, and quickly decode words instead of depending on surrounding context.
2. Children become independent readers, decoding many difficult words on their own and taking great pride in doing so.
3. Beginning readers can attend to meaning, since they are not frustrated by unknown words.
4. The method systematizes and teaches the needed sound-symbol relationships.

Therefore, the basic argument of advocates of this approach is that the explicit approach—structured, sequential, and comprehensive—will eliminate the students' floundering with unknown words and will therefore actually enhance meaning. They believe their approach not only helps to break the code, but also ensures that meaning (comprehension) will take place.

Implicit Approach (Analytic, Inductive)

Harris and Hodges (1995) identify the analytic approach as a whole-to-part approach to word recognition. The student is first taught a number of sight words and then relevant phonic generalizations that are tied to other words. Teaching focuses initially on text rather than on specific sound-symbol relationships. Children acquire phonics knowledge by analyzing words and larger language units encountered in text.

The implicit approach is also called the analytic approach, or the inductive approach. To learn a letter (such as the *d* mentioned previously), the teacher would pronounce words such as *door, Debbie, desk, dive*, and *dish*. Students would then apply this learning to produce their own words that begin with the letter *d*. Therefore, in a sense, the students discover the sound made by the letter without learning it in isolation. Following is a sample of an implicit (analytic, inductive) phonics lesson.

Teacher: I noticed yesterday that we had some difficulty reading words with the letter combination *ch*. One of the words is in this sentence: The scheme failed, and they left. (The sentence should not be read but may be either on the board or on a transparency.) Before we look at the sentence, let's look at these words that you do know. Teacher reads *chair, inches, beach*, emphasizing the known sound of /ch/.

Teacher: (Continues) What sound does the *ch* stand for in these three words?

Jane: The sound of /ch/.

Teacher: Good. Give me some examples of other words with this sound.

Tim: *Chip, champ*.

Mary: *Attach*.

Teacher: Good. (Teacher writes /ch/ next to the original three words to show the sound and underlines each of the *ch* combinations:

chair /ch/
inches /ch/
beach /ch/

Now, we'll read some other words that also have the letter combination *ch*, but in these words notice something different about the sound that *ch* stands for. (With more advanced students, one of them may know the words and be able to read them.) (On the board or on a transparency, the teacher displays another group of words):

character ache stomach

What sound do you hear as we read these words together?

John: Is it the /k/ sound?

Teacher: That's right. Will you read the words for us? again? (S/he may do this several times to reinforce the concept.)

Teacher: Who wants to try to read the sentences on the board now? The word we had trouble with was this one. (She points to the word *scheme*.)

Sue: Their scheme failed, and they left.

Teacher: Right. What other word can you think of? Where do you go everyday to learn?

All: School!

Teacher: Right. Most of the words with *ch* that stands for the /k/ sound come to us from the Greek language. Therefore, when we have such a word, we know it is of Greek origin. Let's look at this exercise, and use our dictionaries if we need to, and try to find the *ch* word with the /k/ sound that could complete each sentence.

The ______ on the car had rusted. (chrome)

The children sang in the ______. (chorus)

I smelled ______ in the swimming pool. (chlorine)

(Always apply what has just been learned.)

Like the explicit approach, the implicit approach also has a great deal of variety, but usually begins with words students are familiar with at sight. Sometimes consonant sounds are identified first in these words and then the vowel sounds. Often, there is a combination approach. Teachers note the parts of words that are similar and the parts that are different. Then a phonics analysis (hence the term *analytic*) of the words may be made, and principles deduced. A point of difference exists even among those favoring the implicit approach; that is, whether it should be systematic or incidental. Advocates of the latter argue that since there is not agreement as to the order in which the elements should be taught, instruction with phonics should take place only when the need arises and be strictly incidental. Advocates of the analytic method cite that students learn the sound-letter correspondences naturally with whole words, sentences, and stories; phonics is contextualized. Another advantage of analytic phonics is that students discover the relationship themselves, rather than sit passively while the teacher explains the letter-sound correspondences. One disadvantage is that this strategy may be too advanced for students who are inexperienced with language. Additionally, the apparent lack of explicit teaching may not work well with some students.

Analogy Approach (Linguistic, Word Family)

The analogy approach, also called linguistics phonics, is a highly structured patterned approach. This is primarily because research by linguists has shown that some patterns in

English appear with greater frequency than others. Basal readers that employ this method of teaching word recognition skills use a tightly controlled and systematic method of introducing phonics patterns. Emphasis is placed on learning many words quickly through word families. Children learn the word *can*, and then are taught the following words by inferring the relationship between the initial consonant sounds and the word-family ending *an: ban, Dan, fan, man, pan, ran, tan,* and *van*. Beginning readers read sentences such as *Dan ran to the tan van*. A basic criticism of this approach is that linguistic readers use a stilted, unnatural language because of the tight control of phonics patterns. In speech, a variety of sentence patterns are used, and if reading is "talk written down," then controlling the pattern creates an artificial language. Nevertheless, some teachers are quite successful in using these linguistic readers, especially with students who seem unable to learn to decode other ways.

The linguistic method, or word-family method, provides students with frequently used word families from which more than 500 words may be generated. This method also seems to be more exciting for students, and they attempt to create all the words they can, using the rime pattern. Spelling is also enhanced by the development of the word families. One major disadvantage is that students do not use their decoding skills to identify words they do not know. Since families of words are created, it requires little-to-no effort to identify new words. This may be detrimental to students later when they need to use decoding skills to identify unknown words.

Embedded Approach

The embedded phonics approach requires that phonics instruction be embedded into authentic reading experiences. With embedded phonics, students learn phonics as they encounter it in reading as opposed to learning a pre-established set of phonemic elements. Embedded phonics is different from other approaches in that it begins with a story. The elements taught come directly from the story to be read. Embedded phonics focuses on shared reading, guided reading, partner reading, and other approaches that place students in authentic reading situations.

An obvious criticism of the embedded approach is that the teaching of phonics may be left to chance, because there is no structure concerning which books should be used and which skills should be taught.

Modified Whole/Part/Whole Approach

In actual practice, the aforementioned approaches do not have to be, nor are they, mutually exclusive. An example follows of a modified approach that incorporates aspects of other approaches. Temple, Ogle, Crawford, and Freppon (2005) have identified a four-part approach, which is a more elaborate version of the whole/part/whole approach.

1. Demonstration and immersion: Seeing the acts of reading and writing carefully demonstrated to students as they are drawn into meaningful literacy activities. The teacher reads a book or shares a piece of writing, thereby showing the whole from which the part (the skill) will be taken. The purpose is to show the context in which the skill makes sense.
2. Attention to detail: Paying attention to detail and developing their knowledge of the structure of written language. The teacher highlights the skill—the part—and makes sure students understand what it is and how it works.
3. Guided practice: Guiding practice in meaningful reading and writing so that students, may internalize effective strategies. Students practice a skill under the teacher's supervision, with prompt correction and reteaching if needed.
4. Application and extensions: Carrying out independent activities in which students apply and extend their reading and writing abilities and develop lifelong habits of literacy. Students are encouraged and reminded to use the skill in context as they read and write independently. (pp. 23–24)

Quick Self-Check 2

1. What is the key characteristic of each of the following approaches to teaching phonics: explicit phonics, implicit phonics, analogy phonics, and embedded phonics?
2. What are the components to the modified whole/part/whole approach?

Teaching Activities

Teacher-Designed Materials

In addition to teacher instruction, discussion, and the student reading more extended language with these sound-symbol relationships (always the most important), there are many teacher-designed materials with phonics and many commercial materials used in teaching these skills. A number of different formats are used, and variations of these formats make up the myriad of activity books, workbooks, games, puzzles, and manipulatives that are used to extend and reinforce phonics principles. Following are listed some of these materials/activities in three broad categories. Because there is a good deal of overlapping and combining, the lists are somewhat arbitrary.

Game Activities	Puzzle Activities	Manipulatives
Open gameboards	Matching shapes	Foldovers with answers
Filling the correct slot/cup/box, etc.	Concentration activities	Plastic pockets with inserts
Pinning/sticking/taping on the correct response	Solving riddles	Wheels with spinners or windows
Line/group games	Cards	Tachistoscopes, single and double
	Bingo variations	Flipbooks
	Domino variations	
	Solving anagrams/crossword puzzles	

Some abbreviated suggestions for carrying out these activities or for constructing these materials follow. They are often extended to include more than one skill area. For example, instead of having an activity to identify just beginning consonants, the activity could be extended to include ending consonants, medial consonants, blends, digraphs, and vowels. These ideas should always be adapted to your own particular classroom situation and your own particular students.

Games

1. *Objective: To identify beginning sound-symbol relationships.* Give pupils index cards. Have them write the letter name you are introducing or reviewing (both capital and lowercase) on one side. The other side is to be blank. Call out words. If the word begins with the letter on the card, pupils turn the card toward you with the letter displayed. If the called word does not begin with the letter, pupils display the other side. Variations include (a) having pupils clap hands softly if the word is correct, (b) pretending they are jack-in-the-boxes and jumping up if the word is correct, and (c) showing a smiling or an unhappy face. (A smiling face denotes the word is correct.)

2. *Objective: To build and expand onset-rime relationships:* Set a timer. Students write as many rhyming words as they can from a given stimulus word. Starter words could be *man*, *pat*, or *tag*.
3. *Objective: Practice with digraphs.* Teacher or students construct "digraph-show" cards by dividing a paper into four sections, labeling each with a particular diagraph such as

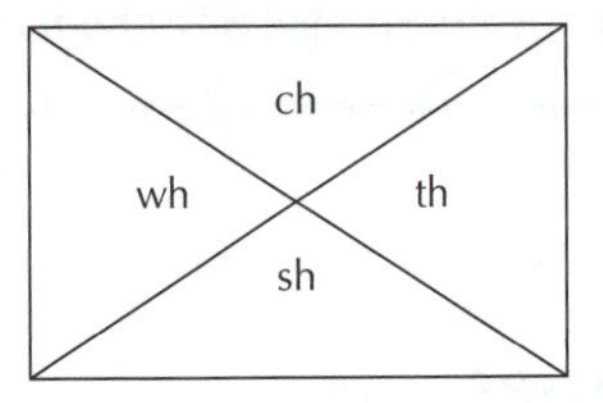

The teacher reads a word from a list. Each player holds up the card with the correct digraph at the top. Points are awarded for correct answers. (For children who are having difficulties, use four separate cards.)
4. *Objective: Review and reinforcement of the magic* e. Cut 40 cards. On 20 of these, write words such as *kit*, *pan*, and *shin* that change to other words with the addition of a final *e*. On 10 cards, write words that do not form a new word by adding *e*, such as *jam*, *stem*, and *slip*. On the remaining 10 cards write *magic e*. Place cards in a brown bag and shake. To play, each child draws a card and reads the word. When unable to read the word, it goes back into the bag. When a *magic e* card is drawn, it may be added to a word card to form a real word or saved to play later. Count each word/*magic e* combination as 5 points and other words as 1 point. *Magic e* by itself receives no points. Bags may be labeled and decorated.
5. *Objective: Review short vowels.* Using familiar names (and shortened names such as M*a*tt or P*a*t, P*e*g or M*e*g, L*i*l or W*i*ll, B*o*b or T*o*dd, and R*u*ss or G*u*s), rhyming sentences can be created such as those that follow. First, volunteers read the names (they have been written on the board) and either the teacher or the child underlines the vowel to be sounded. The teacher points again to the underlined letter and repeats the sound.

   Teacher: These letters stand for the short vowel sound in these names. Let's practice listening for these short vowel sounds. I'll say the words, and you can echo them back to me.

   Use rhythmical speech (some teachers use a "rap" style) or any "tune" with which you are comfortable.

   Teacher: Matt, Matt, Matt, lost his hat, hat, hat. (Emphasize the words with the short /ă/ sound.)

   Students repeat the sound. The teacher continues with other sounds and sentences:

   Teacher: Peg, Peg, Peg hurt her leg, leg, leg. Lil, Lil, Lil saw the hill, hill, hill.

   Follow-up may include having a volunteer recall the word that rhymed with a name and then having the teacher or student write that word under the appropriate name. Some of the more advanced students might erase a beginning consonant and substitute another, to make a new word that appears in the text just read or to be read. For example, removing *h* from hill and supplying the letters *m*, *p*, *s*, and *d* would lead to the words *mill*, *pill*, *sill*, and *dill*. You may ask students to infer and state the generalization based on the lesson that "a vowel letter between two consonants often has a short sound" or state the generalization yourself before further application in reading or reviewing part of a story.
6. *Objective: Review and practice blending.* A motivating blending game is "What is it?" The teacher shares with the class that she is thinking of an insect. (Use any category, even correlating with a current unit.) The teacher gives a clue—the separate sounds in the word. For example, for *ant*, she tells the class that the insect is an "/a/-/n/-/t/," articulating each

of the sounds separately. Children then must blend the sounds together to discover the insect the teacher is thinking about.

To increase motivation, use picture cards and face them away from the children. Give the segmented clues, then turn the picture around once the children have guessed. Or use a toy box or grab bag, peeking inside and saying, "I see a toy /p/-/l-/ā/-/n/ in here. Who knows what I see?"

Puzzles

1. *Objective: Recognizing long and short vowel sounds.* Cover bulletin board with light-colored paper. Use thick felt-tipped pens to draw three or four short shelves on the left side of the paper and three or four longer shelves on the right side. Students flip through old magazines cutting out pictures of objects whose names contain long or short vowel sounds. The pictures should be of items that would actually fit on a shelf. Then have the students paste their chosen objects on the appropriately labeled shelf (longer shelves are for long vowels and shorter shelves for short vowels). Print the name of each object by the picture.
2. *Objective: Practice in reading blends and digraphs.* Make flowers for the *r, l,* and *s* blends that the students have learned, such as *cr, gl,* and *sp.* Then make many bees with ending patterns on them, for example, __________ *ad,* __________ *ate,* __________ *ell.* Each child is instructed to place a bee and a flower together, using a correct blend to form a word. If the word is incorrect, the child gets "stung" by the bee. (This puzzle match has many variations.)
3. *Objective: Expanding vocabulary.* Create a grid similar to the one that follows. List various phonetic elements across the top of the grid. General categories are listed at the side of the grid. Duplicate a grid for each student. Have students fill in the grid with words that correspond to both categories. Allow students to consult books and dictionaries to find appropriate words. Have them share responses with the class. Students score one point for each word that correctly completes a square. Play individually or in groups. The sample shows two teacher-provided words and six words supplied by a student:

	ai	ay	ee	ea
Things	train	*clay*	*cheese*	*lead*
Action words	*sail*	play	*freeze*	*spread*

Manipulatives

1. *Objective: Reinforcing words through sensory experience.* Distribute individual letter cards to the students displaying such letters as *a, d, e, h, l, p, m, n, t, A, H, M, N.* Make word cards such as *am, man, mat, help, Nat, Ted,* and *Nan.* Place them face down in a stack. Choose and display word cards. Students with these letters are to stand next to each other to form a word. A student is then asked to read the word aloud. Continue until all the words are read.
2. *Objective: Practice with the final letter e.* Cut 16 slips of paper into 6-by-3-inch strips. Fold over about 1½ inches of one end of each slip. Copy a word with one short vowel onto the larger portion of each slip of paper. Write an *e* on the back of the folded portion. When the *e* is flipped back, only the short vowel word can be seen. When the *e* is flipped forward, it changes the short vowel sound of these kinds of words to a long

vowel sound. Suggested words: *cut, cap, tap, fat, hat, mat, past, rat, rod, tub, pan, man, sit, rob*, and *grip*.

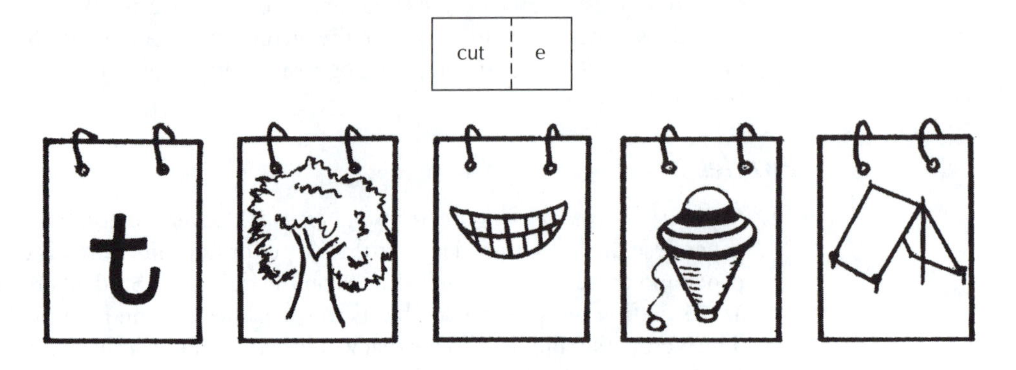

3. *Objective: Practice with letters or words using teacher-made or commercial flip books.* On the back of letters, place little pictures for self-checking. These flip books can also be made for CVC (consonant–vowel–consonant) words with beginning blends and digraphs, and for final *e* words.
4. *Objective: Increase rate of speed for learning words.* Using tachistoscopes (teacher-constructed of oaktag or cardboard, or purchased commercially), teachers can create a device to help isolate letters or words. For those that are teacher-constructed, a strip of paper is fed through the slits of a fun-type figure (see examples below). The student reads each word as it appears. The object is to increase the rate of speed and to learn the words as sight words. Sometimes two strips of paper are used to teach generalizations such as the final *e* changing the preceding vowel.

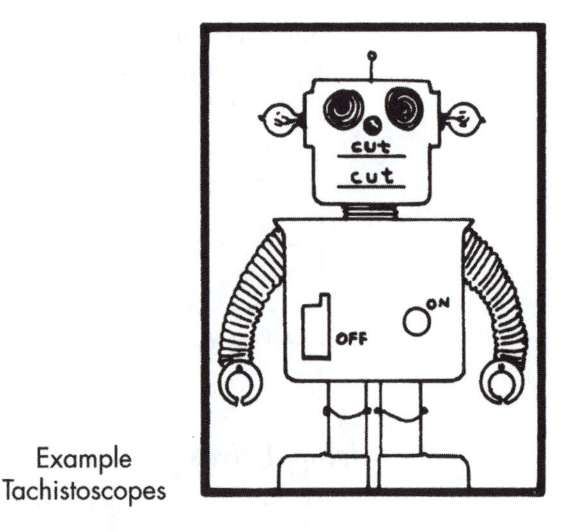

Example Tachistoscopes

5. *Objective: Practice with vowel sounds.* Vowels cause many problems. The following suggestion may help minimize some of them. Use a mirror to reinforce the sounds under study as students produce the sounds and watch the shape of their own mouths in the mirror. The visual sensation, plus the kinesthetic sensation—how the mouth, tongue, and cheeks feel while creating the sounds—help to underscore the differences. Instead of a mirror, students may place their hands on their mouths to sense the difference as they pronounce the sounds.

   Many vowels become more distinguishable through this visual or kinesthetic system. Long /ō/, /o͞o/, /ī/, /ē/, and /ā/ differ greatly in the mirror. Diphthongs *oi* and *ou* differ from each other and from other sounds because visually the mouth changes shape during production. The visual distinction among short vowels is slight but the tongue and teeth position can help discriminate (Ahmann, 1982).

Materials Inundation

On the market today are a variety of computers and software programs. There are *Controlled Readers* for increasing the eye sweep, with the line of print adjusted for rate of speed and size of type. Additionally, videos, films, filmstrips, cassettes, computer programs and records are available, all promising to teach word recognition skills. Kits combine cassettes, filmstrips, compact discs and books and programs with animal and cartoon cutouts, posters, and all manner of motivational gimmicks that purport to teach and improve word recognition skills. The Internet also provides a variety of games, activities, and electronic workbook pages.

Confronted with so many materials, activities, and ideas for teaching these sound-symbol associations (and many of these are suggested in teaching other word recognition skills too), teachers often engage students in these activities to the exclusion of actual reading. Phonics or skill instruction becomes the end, instead of the means to an end (Anderson & Fordham, 1991).

Spiegel (1990) examined many materials that purported to reinforce phonics skills, and found the following:

> There were many problems with the amount of reinforcement and transfer potential of the materials. Often several letters were introduced at one time. . . . In many cases the skill/strategy was practiced only with spelling and only with isolated letters. . . . Serious content validity problems were found. Pictures were often uninterpretable . . . inappropriate rules were introduced. . . . Other problems included visually cluttered pages, tasks beyond the level of the child, and activities requiring too much teacher direction.

See Appendix F for guidelines to evaluate phonics programs and websites.

Because phonics skills, in varying degrees of intensity, are usually emphasized in early reading, it is important to stop a moment to consider some guidelines that will help keep the teaching of phonics in proper perspective.

Guidelines for Teaching Phonics

Many researchers have suggested and recommended guidelines for teaching phonics. What follows is a compilation of those suggested by Anderson, Hiebert, Scott, and Wilkinson (1985); Stahl (1992); and Strickland (1998).

1. Phonics must be viewed as a means to an end, not an end in itself. It should be integrated into a total reading program, rather than BE the reading program as reading and phonics are not synonyms. The goal of phonics instruction should be to develop automatic word recognition skills so that students can devote their attention to comprehension.
2. Phonics instruction will not work for all children and will not manifest itself in each child in the same way. Too much instruction causes some students to become overanalytic, but too little leaves students with insufficient knowledge of phoneme-grapheme relationships.
3. Phonics should build on a child's concepts of print, as well as the foundation in phonological awareness that the child brings to the learning situation. Phonics is a skill that must be used in conjunction with the skills of contextual and structural analysis.

4. In learning phonics, children must have the opportunity to see, hear, and say the components they are asked to learn. Memorizing phonics rules will not ensure that students can apply the rules. Children need to be taught to use phonics, not taught about phonics, which requires immediate transfer of learning to their own reading and writing. The best context for learning and applying phonics is actual reading and writing.
5. Phonics can be taught by using synthetic (explicit) and/or analytic (implicit) approaches to instruction. Whichever method is used, memorizing rules should not be the focus of instruction.
6. Teachers should present well-designed phonics instruction that should be kept simple and should be completed by the end of second grade.
7. No phonics program will be successful unless children have alphabet knowledge, phonological awareness, and background knowledge. Phonics helps to decode an unknown word only if the unknown word is part of the reader's speaking-listening vocabulary.
8. Periodic evaluation of student's skill needs must be made through both informal and formal assessments.
9. A teacher must know the skills thoroughly so that what is taught is not only correct, but appropriate and necessary.
10. Teachers should ask themselves, "What is my objective in engaging in this activity? Is it necessary for all students? (Durkin, 1990) Would John, May, and Suzy, who seem to know and use these skills so effectively, need this exercise/activity?" Not only is it a waste of time for many students who already know and use the skill effectively, but many materials commonly used in classes are confusing and have no real reading transfer value!

Questions Teachers Ask Concerning Teaching Phonics

Because phonics is a controversial topic and teachers are concerned about best practices, they frequently have numerous questions about the teaching of phonics. We answer some of the most frequent questions here.

1. *How much phonics do children need?* Many educators flippantly say, "As little as possible." This answer is quite misleading. Initial reading can be frustrating and overwhelming if too many words are introduced too rapidly without considerable phonics review and reinforcement. On the other hand, too much phonics for competent readers is a waste of time. *Periodic careful assessment*, coupled with teacher observation to determine who needs what, is the key.
2. *Should the phonics lesson be taught before the reading lesson, after, or during a separate period?* In beginning reading it must be part of the lesson, but after children begin reading more fluently by the second grade, a separate period is necessary. This is because group reading should be primarily concerned with comprehension, interpretation, and enjoyment to foster a love of reading.
3. *What do I say when a generalization doesn't work?* Tell students that generalizations are merely starting points. Emphasize that they must remain flexible when decoding and that when letters combine in different ways, they sometimes encode different sounds.
4. *Should I try to induct generalizations?* It depends. What must be kept in mind is that the goal of phonics instruction is teaching children to learn to decode quickly. Sometimes inducting generalizations takes a long time.
5. *What is a reasonable skill sequence?* Because there is greater consistency between consonant letters and their respective sounds than there is between vowels and their respective sounds, most instructional programs begin using the consonants to initiate learning some sound-symbol associations. In general, a few letters are introduced (no two programs agree), together with the short *a*, followed by additional consonant letters, and

some of the other short vowels. Gradually a few blends and consonant digraphs are introduced, followed by the long and special third sounds of certain vowels. The more difficult *r*-controlled vowels, vowel diphthongs, and special combinations are taught later.

6. *Should I tell children to try the short vowel sound if they are undecided?* Yes, especially with troublesome words, because short vowel sounds occur more frequently than long vowel sounds do, except with the two sounds of /o͞o/ where the long sound predominates.
7. *What correspondences are worth teaching?* It all depends. To learn to read, some children need intensive instruction in almost all the correspondences, while others, through a kind of osmosis, seem to soak up these relationships without any explanation. Again the key is assessment.
8. *Should children state the rule?* The inability to state a phonics rule did not seem to hinder children's efforts to analyze unfamiliar words. They used the generalizations without being able to state them. (Rosso & Emans, 1981). The important thing, therefore, is their ability to *apply* the rule. The teacher, however, should be able to state a generalization *since s/he must verbalize it to the student.*
9. *Should students use the terms* blend *or* digraph? As in the previous example, this is not essential but depends on the teacher's philosophy and the type of class. Students need to understand that blends are pronounced very rapidly, while digraphs encode only one sound. Some programs use the term *phonogram* to apply to any two-letter combination. The teacher may use these terms as s/he is responsible for definitions.
10. *What should I do when children who are first learning to read continually ask for help in decoding words?* Help them begin to develop a word-pronunciation strategy and suggest they do something similar to the following:
    a. Try the first sound of the word, noting whether it is a single consonant letter, a letter combination (blend or digraph), or a vowel.
    b. Continue reading the sentence to see if further clues are within the sentence to help decode the word.
    c. Reread the sentence to see if the word as they have decoded it makes sense.
11. *Can I teach phonics well if I am not confident in my own phonics skills?* No. Teachers must understand phonics and the role phonics instruction plays in learning to read to avoid over-exposure or under-exposure of the importance of sound-symbol relationships.

As children mature, their strategy must expand. Initially they will profit from using the sound patterns and context, while later they will need to learn how to use the structure of words, context, and sound patterns. They must also learn to use the dictionary.

Assessing When the Decoding Process Breaks Down

Regardless of which reading approach is used, teachers will find that the development of some students' decoding skills is not progressing the way it should. Their goal must be for the students to develop independent word recognition skills. A consideration, therefore, is whether students already have the skill or whether they lack it at the text reading level, the word level, or the discrimination level (Wisconsin Department of Public Instruction, 1985).

- *Text reading level.* Student's oral reading gives the clues. If the student cannot use the skill at this level, check the skills at the word level.
- *Word level.* This can be observed quickly in oral reading or determined from a worksheet. If the student understands the skill at the word level, but fails to use it while reading, s/he needs help in applying the skill. Suggest (a) reading the rest of the sentence, (b) looking at the elements or parts of the word, (c) using the skill to see if the word s/he decoded makes sense.

- ❒ *Discrimination level.* If the student cannot recognize and use the skill at the word level, check the discrimination level. Can the student visually identify the letters or spelling pattern of the word? If so, s/he can receive instruction at the word level. If not, begin with the discrimination level.

In other words, see where the decoding process seems to break down for the student, and then take steps to address it.

Spelling: Its Relationship to Word Recognition

Reading and spelling are alike in that they both develop in stages, and to some extent both rely on phonics and other visual clues. They are, however, different processes. We know this because a few students in each class will be excellent readers but poor spellers, and conversely some excellent spellers will be poor readers. Why this is so continues to be a matter of debate. For some students who use the computer for writing, the spellcheck may not only help them to spell correctly but also teach them the importance of some of the patterns and visual clues they have not internalized.

The good speller, however, not only understands the patterns in the encoding of words, but also has a photographic imprint of the word so that it looks correct when it is spelled. This is the goal in teaching spelling—that students will have a rich storehouse of words as in reading, calling upon it in their writing and knowing how to spell the words correctly.

Teaching Spelling: A Balanced Approach

While it is true that immersion in reading and writing with many practice opportunities will result in some fine spellers, most students will profit when spelling patterns and generalizations are made more explicit for them (Adams, 1990; Clay, 1990; Routman, 1993). As with reading, the teaching of spelling is moving to a more balanced approach. As mentioned previously, invented spellings used by children in kindergarten and first grade are not supposed to mean that "anything goes" but are a useful way of freeing children's writing creativity.

After the beginning reading/writing stages, children need to be accountable for certain standards (Adams & Bruck, 1995; Novelli, 1993; Routman, 1993; Snowball, 1993). They should take pride in their work and, even in daily journal or story writing, be expected to use legible handwriting, correct spelling of frequently used words, and correct punctuation (capitals and periods). They should also be expected to reread their draft and check for spelling, punctuation, and meaning before asking a partner to read what they have written or before having a conference with their teacher.

The student should also be able to read the draft with ease. This puts greater responsibility on the student and makes him/her aware that the spelling, if not perfectly correct, should be reasonably so. For example, a child who spells *president* as *pt* needs to think through the word more carefully, listen to the sounds, and approximate it more closely (Snowball, 1993).

Direct Teaching

Young children profit from an introduction to certain consistent English spelling generalizations that reinforce their decoding skills. The generalizations can be taught as children write words the teacher is dictating. These generalizations should be reviewed and reinforced during the primary years, together with more advanced generalizations, along with much creative writing practice. Again, a *balance* is achieved. As the teacher dictates a group of words to children, the spelling patterns within the words are discussed so that the generalizations are internalized and understood, not merely memorized by rote. Questioning of the students by the teacher as they are writing helps them to think through the pattern. Some frequently taught spelling generalizations include the following:

1. The rules for long vowels.
2. The five reasons a word may end in a final long *e*.
3. The reasons *c* and *g* have two sounds.
4. The letter *y* can function as the long vowel *i* or *e* at the end of a word (*i* in a one-syllable word: *cry*) and *e* in a two-syllable word (*la dy*).
5. The /er/ sound can be written five ways.
6. *l*, *f*, and *s*, are often doubled at the end of a one-syllable word.
7. *av* is used to write long *a* at the end of a word.
8. *dge* is used to write /j/ at the end of a word.
9. *i* precedes *e* except after *c* or when *ei* "says" long *a*.
10. *ti*, *si*, and *ci* are used to write /sh/ at the beginning of a two- or three-syllable word.

Learning these generalizations reinforces the decoding of words as children write the words that exemplify these generalizations.

Activities to Reinforce Spelling

Finger Spelling

To help students master frequently occurring words of three to five letters, Foss (1995) uses a finger spelling procedure. The teacher begins by telling children that there are five (or three or four) letters in the word and holds up his/her hand, spreading the fingers. The left hand is used, the palm facing the students so that directionality is correct. The teacher points to the thumb and asks, "What is the first letter?" The children give the first sound as perhaps *t*. The teacher agrees, pointing to the thumb, and then pointing to the second finger. She asks, "What do you hear next?" If the children mention a letter in the word, but not in the sequence, the teacher shows them where in her hand the letter belongs, and then asks, "What else do you hear?" This helps some children begin to understand the sequencing of sounds. (An alternative method is to draw a hand on the chalkboard and place letters correctly as they are called.)

Making Words

Cunningham and Cunningham (1992) suggest a strategy called "Making Words" to enhance the spelling-decoding connection. In this 15-minute activity. children are individually given a combination of letters to use in making words. During the activity, children make 12 to 15 words beginning with two-letter words and continuing with three-, four-, or five-letter, and longer words until the final word is made. The final word, a six-, seven-, or eight-letter word always includes all the letters used that day in class. In this hands-on manipulative activity, children discover letter-sound relationships and learn how to look for patterns in words.

In a beginning lesson (abbreviated here), children have one vowel letter (always in red) and know they must use the vowel card in every word. Additionally, they would have the consonant letters *g*, *n*, *p*, *r*, and *s*. Here are some of the steps the teacher might use, although other combinations are possible:

1. Take two letters and make *in*.
2. Add a letter to make the three-letter word *pin*.
3. Change just one letter, and turn your *pin* into a *pig*.

4. Now change just one letter, and your *pig* can become a *rig*—sometimes we call a big truck a *rig*. (Other intermediate words with teacher instruction and explanation follow: *rip, rips, nips, spin, snip, pins, sing*.)
5. Now, change just one letter, and change *sing* to *ring*.
6. Now, we will make a five-letter word. Add a letter to change *ring* to *rings*.
7. Has anyone figured out what word we can make with six letters?
8. Take all six of your letters and make the word *spring*.

Many children are amazed to learn that more than one word can be made with the same letters and that you can make a different word simply by putting the same letters in different places.

"Making words" with two vowels offers children opportunities to work with vowel digraphs such as *ea*. It also may be used with intermediate children and older remedial readers.

"Making words" works well because of the endless possibilities it offers children to see how our alphabetic system works. (See the original article for many letter combinations to use, for words to be constructed, and for patterns to be learned.)

Classroom Spelling Explorations

One author recalls a spelling exploration in a sixth-grade class that did not provide the answer, but proved to be a rewarding learning experience for the students. The class was having trouble spelling words that ended in either *ant/ance* or *ent/ence* and decided to see if there was a rule for using the appropriate form. Actually there are some so-called "rules" for these endings, but they are quite complicated. While the students did not discover any definitive patterns, they did decide that the *ant/ance* form appeared much more frequently than the *ent/ence* form. In the meantime, they had learned to read and spell many words with these endings.

Additionally, they wrote letters to the various lexicographers of the most popular intermediate children's dictionaries and asked for their insights regarding these forms. The lexicographers then responded that it was a matter of discipline to learn them!

As Snowball (1993) advises, these spelling explorations should arise in the context of the children's writing so it is relevant to what they are learning. Here are some strategies that could be used to explore the long *e* sound with primary-grade children:

1. Select some of the words the students are trying to write that contain the long *e* sound. Write the students' attempts on a chart.
2. Read the words from the chart and discuss that all these words have this long *e* sound. Students may like to suggest various ways they think their words could be spelled.
3. Read from a story and ask the students to listen for words with the long *e* sound: *thief, queen, be, mean, he, donkey*.
4. List the words and identify the part of each word that represents the long *e* sound.
5. Ask the students if they know or can find any other words with the long *e* sound. Add these to the class list: *believe, sleep, scream, money*.
6. Have the students work in small groups with their word cards to see if they can find various ways to group the words. Share these ideas and eventually group the words according to their spelling patterns.

be	thief	queen	mean	donkey
he	believe	sleep	scream	money

Try to elicit from the students generalizations such as, the long *e* sound can be written in many ways. In spelling words with this sound, we need to attend to the letter(s) that encode(s) the long *e* sound.

With older students, it might be useful to explore a generalization such as how to add the suffix *ed* to a base word:

1. Choose a story the class has read. Ask the students to search for words ending in *ed*. Have them find many other words with this pattern.
2. Have students list the words with the base word and then group them according to their pattern. (This is an abbreviated list.)

claim/claim*ed*	paint/paint*ed*	play/play*ed*	relieve/reliev*ed*	nap/napp*ed*
mail/mail*ed*	treat/treat*ed*	journey/journey*ed*	change/chang*ed*	rob/robb*ed*
train/train*ed*	thread/thread*ed*	spray/spray*ed*	rule/rul*ed*	tug/tugg*ed*

Ask students what they noticed about the way the base word changed when *ed* was added. Did all the words change? Try to elicit from the students generalizations such as these:

1. For words such as *claim*, *mail*, and *train*, ending in *m*, *l*, and *n*, merely add *ed*.
2. Words ending in *t* and *d* add *ed*. *Ed* becomes an extra syllable when the word is pronounced: *paint-ed*, *treat-ed*, *thread-ed*.
3. Do not drop the letter *y* when adding *ed*: *played*, *enjoyed*.
4. With words ending in *e*, drop the *e*, and add the *ed* or *ing*: *rake*, *raked*, *raking*.
5. *One*-syllable words ending in *one* consonant, preceded by *one* short vowel, as in *rob*, doubled the final consonant when adding *ed*: *robbed*.

Spelling Dictionaries

Angeletti (1993) suggests two types of spelling dictionaries, one for the class, and a personal one that each student develops. The class spelling dictionary is divided into three sections. In the first section, a page is included for each letter of the alphabet. Students identify high-frequency words from their classroom lessons, then list them under the appropriate letter. In the second section, word lists are grouped according to selected patterns. For example, after a lesson on the *dge* pattern, the students enter newly learned words on the *dge* page. A third section can have word categories—animals, countries, cities, important people, etc.

The personal spelling dictionary is modeled after the class dictionary. It can be as simple as using a part of a page for each letter of the alphabet, with separate sections for word patterns and word categories.

Students should enter high-frequency words from their writing and reading into the alphabetized section. Do not expect young children to alphabetize correctly, but help them alphabetize to the second letter. At the end of the year or when they are ready, they can make new dictionaries with words alphabetized to the third letter, or even with appropriate guide words for each page.

Summary

This chapter began with a definition of what we mean by phonics as well as the goal and function of phonics instruction.

Teaching phonics can be done explicitly (directly taught); implicitly (letting students discover relationships); linguistically (using a patterned approach); embedded (learn phonics as it is encountered in text), or using a modified whole/part/whole approach (demonstration, detail, practice, application). The method used depends on student maturity and skill level.

Students' decoding skills may break down at three levels: the story level, the word level, or the discrimination level. Ways to correct these were detailed. Differing teacher approaches in teaching decoding skills were suggested.

Ways of teaching, extending, reinforcing, and reviewing sound-symbol relationships were presented. The inundation of materials on the market necessitates consideration before use. Care must be taken to ensure these materials do not take the place of actual reading. As students begin to learn to read, it is important to identify their skill strengths and weaknesses through formal and informal assessments and to plan appropriate lessons accordingly.

Most frequently asked questions about teaching phonics with were included along with suggested answers. Teachers must learn that purposeful phonics instruction helps children learn to decode words and read them on sight through meaningful activities. Teaching phonics has a definite place in today's classrooms.

A section on spelling and its relationship to phonics examined some creative ways to teach spelling generalizations to children. Twelve spelling rules were outlined that more traditional spelling programs include.

Research suggests that systematic phonics instruction increases accuracy in decoding and word recognition skills, which facilitates comprehension. Classroom teachers must understand that phonics skills are a necessary, but not sufficient, condition for reading and comprehending. Teachers must also understand that systematic phonics instruction is only one component of a total reading program and should be integrated to create a complete reading program.

Teachers must also understand that no one approach will work with all children. Teachers should consider the needs of their students in determining which type of program will be most effective for each individual reader. This notion is conveyed most eloquently in the International Reading Association position statement on using multiple methods of reading instruction:

> There is no single method or single combination of methods that can successfully teach all children to read. Therefore, teachers must have a strong knowledge of multiple methods for teaching reading and a strong knowledge of the children in their care so they can create the appropriate balance of methods needed for the children they teach.

Review Questions

1. In this chapter, some strengths and weaknesses of a variety of approaches to teaching phonics were explained. Can you identify additional strengths and weaknesses of each approach?

2. Would one approach be better than others for teaching some phonics lessons? Can you think of examples?

3. To review the approaches outlined in this chapter, it may help if you could select a phonics skill that you would like to teach, and then write a brief lesson plan for that skill using each of the approaches outlined in the chapter.

Chapter 7

Structural Analysis

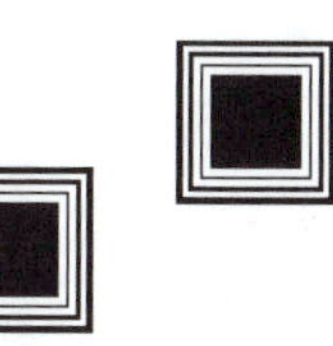

Structural analysis becomes an increasingly important word recognition strategy as children move through the grades and on through high school. Johnson and Baumann (1984) explain that structural analysis involves analyzing words and separating them into free morphemes (base words) and bound morphemes (affixes and inflected endings including plurals, possessives, comparatives, and tense morphemes), identifying the individual meanings, and recombining these parts into a meaningful word. Structural analysis may also consist of recognizing big word "chunks," such as compound words, and understanding certain principles of syllabication, thereby providing students with the ability to "break apart" words quickly (Blanchowicz, 1987; Peterson & Phelps, 1991; White, Sowell & Yanagihara, 1989). The rationale for teaching syllabication is based on the belief that decoding is facilitated for children who can segment unknown words into manageable parts.

Components of Structural Analysis

Children begin reading words with these structures as early as first grade when they are introduced to verb units such as *ing* and *ed* and plural endings such as *s* and *es*. Prefixes such as *re* and *un* are sometimes introduced as early as second grade. Work with more complex affixes (prefixes and suffixes) and roots usually begins in the middle grades and continues through high school. Structural analysis instruction typically involves teaching base words and common affixes, and inflected endings (plurals, possessives, comparatives, and tense morphemes). This chapter will focus on the common elements of structural analysis including compound words, contractions, affixed words, and syllabication.

Compound Words

Compound words are simply a combination of two base words and are fairly easy to decode. English abounds with compound words (seatbelt), and their number is increasing all the time. As a matter of fact, many new words that come into our language (*download*, *cranapple*, *software*, *cyperspace*) are compound.

Students may be informed that in most cases the meaning of the compound word is a combination of the two joined words. Sometimes, however, it is not, as in the case of the word *blackboard*, when it refers to a green chalkboard. Students should also know that because of wide usage some compound words are thought of as single words. Examples: *windshield* (shield from the wind) and *sidewalk* (walk by the side of the road).

Activities for Teaching Compound Words

1. *Objective: To practice combining two base words.* Write words on the board that can become part of a compound word, such as *dog, plane, thing, some, house, noon, man, air, after*. Ask children to choose two of the words to form a compound and write the word on a slip of paper, later sharing their word/words by using them in sentences. There are many variations of this activity.
2. *Objective: Review and extension.* Use a folder with pockets. On one side place the first part of almost a dozen compound words. On the other side place the second part of these words. Students combine these pieces. Answers are on the back of the folder for self-checking.

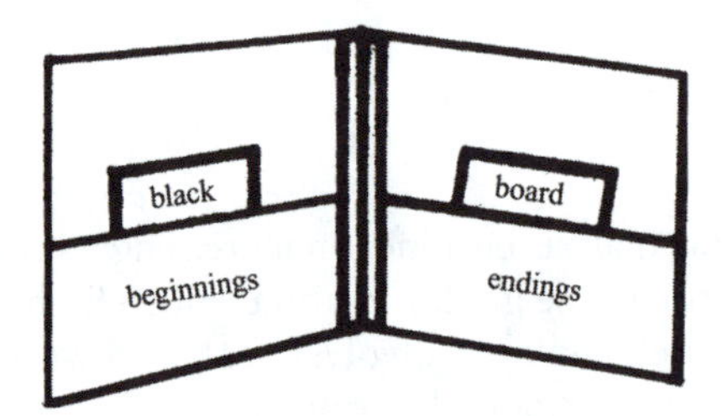

3. *Objective: Extending knowledge of compound words.* Construct a large wall chart with five headings such as *People, Places, Things, Animal Life*, and *Time* at the top. Ask students to find compound words that fit under the headings. The list can be quite extensive as the following chart indicates:

People	Places	Things	Animal Life	Time
anybody	anywhere	airplane	butterfly	afternoon
chairman	barnyard	broomstick	goldfish	bedtime
everyone	bedroom	birdhouse	horseshoe	birthday
fisherman	doorway	boxcar	starfish	daylight
grandmother	downstairs	baseball	watchdog	lifetime
grownup	downtown	basketball	wildlife	playtime
housewife	driveway	cardboard		springtime
milkman	farmhouse	campfire		
nobody	farmland	dollhouse		
policeman	fireplace	doghouse		
postman	highway	doorbell		
runaway	outside	firewood		
salesman	playground	eyesight		
shoemaker	roadside	football		
	schoolyard	footsteps		
	sidewalk	flashlight		

People	Places	Things	Animal Life	Time
	storeroom	greenhouse		
	upstairs	houseboat		
	workshop	moonlight		
		mousetrap		
		newspaper		
		raindrop		
		snowman		
		sunburn		
		sunlight		
		snowball		
		steamship		

Quick Self-Check 1

1. What generalizations about compound words can be drawn from the words *carseat* and *firewood?*
2. What are three compound words that have recently entered the English language?

Contractions

In discussing compound words, some instructors also introduce the concept of contractions. These forms are frequent in the conversation of characters in stories read by children. Confusion occurs because sometimes more than one letter of a contraction is omitted and also because some forms have similar sounds but differ in meaning. A list of some common contractions follows:

I am	I'm	I have	I've	I will	I'll
You are	You're	You have	You've	You will	You'll
He is	He's	She is	She's	It is	It's
We are	We're	We have	We've	We will	We'll
They are	They're	They have	They've	They will	They'll
cannot	can't	could not	couldn't	have not	haven't
would not	wouldn't				

One of the most common errors young students make (and also older students!) is in writing the phrase "would of." It should be written as *would have*, but because it sounds like a contracted form, students shorten the *have* to a *v* sound and write the word *of*, since this is what they hear. *Would of* is always incorrect.

Prefixes, Roots, and Suffixes

Prefixes: Definitions and Dilemmas

Defining a prefix for the teacher is not the same as defining it for the student. Linguists begin to define prefixes as morphemes. Simply defined, a morpheme is a minimal unit of meaning.

A morpheme differs from a syllable. (For example, the /t/ written as *ed* in *jumped* is a separate morpheme; therefore, the word *jumped* consists of one syllable, but two morphemes.)

By definition, prefixes, being bound, are *dependent meaning-bearing elements* attached at the beginning of independent words. Therefore *un* as in *unable* is a prefix, but *un* as in *until* is not (because *til* is not an independent word). By definition, therefore, *pre* as in *presume*, *in* as in *insult*, and *dis* as in *disturb* are not prefixes, again because they are not attached to independent or base words. Words such as *presume*, *insult*, and *disturb* have historical roots, but as the language changed, these words changed or they were taken directly into English as whole words from Latin or French. Some educators refer to these kinds of related prefix syllables, attached to nonwords, as "absorbed" prefixes.[1]

This information and definition is, of course, for the teacher and much older students. Certainly young children should not be burdened by such an explanation; instead, the teacher may proceed by instructing a third or fourth grade class with the following lessons as suggested by White, Sowell, and Yanagihara (1989). They believe in explicitly defining and teaching the concept of a prefix by presenting examples and nonexamples. Thus, after discussion, the teacher would write, "What is a prefix?" on chart paper and, below it, the following:

1. A prefix is a group of letters that go in front of a word.
2. The prefix changes the meaning of a word.
3. When you "peel off" the prefix, a word must be left. (This is demonstrated by contrasting genuine prefixed words such as *unkind* and *refill* with non-example words such as *uncle* and *reason*.)

They believe students taught in this way begin with a clear idea of what a prefix is.

Three prefixes taught early are *un*, *re*, and *dis*. Generally, exercises such as the following are used so that students can see the difference when the prefix is added. You will note that an independent base, a clearly recognizable whole English word, is used to minimize confusion.

re + pay repay
re + state restate
un + able unable
un + sure unsure
dis + like dislike
dis + trust distrust

Students encounter words such as *disdain*, *determine*, and *result* in which there is a decodable common beginning syllable. Should they use their phonics/syllabication skills to help decode these words if they are unknown? Certainly! Clues are important. But students should gradually be instructed about these absorbed "prefix" forms after first having exposure to the more traditional prefix plus whole word combination, as just shown. This does not mean that children cannot learn to read and understand words with absorbed prefixes while doing a lot of independent reading.

Roots and Suffixes

Since suffixes are attached to roots (or bases), defining *root* at this point for the teacher seems appropriate. A root is defined as a basic unit having a semantic connection with other words. For example, in the words *lighted*, *lightning*, and *enlightening*, *light* is the root word. More specifically, the root is that part of a word, neither prefix nor suffix, that conveys the major portion of the word's meaning. (Linguists use the term *base*.) Again, much of this information is provided for the benefit of the teacher and the older student. For the young student, a simple definition such as "a root carries the main meaning of a word" should be sufficient.

[1] While these absorbed prefixes do not change the word meaning, the prefix does affect the accent or stress pattern of the word. Absorbed prefixes are often unaccented syllables.

As with prefixes, defining a suffix can also present difficulty. A suffix (again, not necessarily a syllable) is a "meaningful" language unit or morpheme, bound, as with a prefix, and affixed to the end of a root or base word. While other aspects of meaning are involved, a primary function of a suffix is to indicate the part of speech of the word; that is, how it functions in a sentence. Although there are some cases in which the suffix does not change the part of speech (for example, *race* and *racist*), in general, there are four types of suffixes, and these may form nouns, verbs, adjectives, and adverbs. In addition to often changing the part of speech, some suffixes also change the lexical meaning of roots, such as *colorless* and *colorful* or *doubtless* and *doubtful*.

Suffixes are of two types: inflectional suffixes as defined in list *A* (the sum total) and derivational suffixes as exemplified in list *B* (only a few of the many that exist in the English language).

A

Total Inflectional Suffixes

s (es) plural	boys, brushes
's (s') apostrophe	boy's, boys'
s third person singular	sings
ed past tense	grabbed
ing present participle	singing
en past participle	(has, have) eaten
er comparative	taller
est superlative	tallest

B

A Few Derivational Suffixes

Root Word	Part of Speech	Suffix	Affixed Word	Part of Speech
base	n.	ic	bas*ic*	adj.
correct	adj.	ly	correct*ly*	adv.
fool	n.	ish	fool*ish*	adj.
allow	v.	ance	allow*ance*	n.
person	n.	al	person*al*	adj.
attract	v.	ive	attract*ive*	adj.
clever	adj.	ness	clever*ness*	n.
agree	v.	ment	agree*ment*	n.

The suffixes in list *A* (a closed group of only eight) do not usually change the part of speech of the word. These suffixes also represent some of the first ones taught to primary children. It is much easier to understand the word changes in list *A* than it is to understand those in list *B*. (There are many, many derivational suffixes.) Not only are there alterations in the meanings of the words in list *B*, but in addition, the parts of speech change.

A simple definition such as "a suffix is a letter or group of letters (a unit) that comes at the end of a word" would be sufficient for most students. With older students, you could add "and that often change the part of speech."

The concept of a suffix can be taught at upper elementary levels similarly to the prefix. After discussion and examples, the teacher would write, "What is a suffix?" and below it, the following:

1. A suffix is a group of letters that comes at the end of a word.
2. The suffix often changes the part of speech of a word. For example, verbs can be changed to adjectives, such as the word *accept* (a verb) + *able* (an "adjective" suffix) can become *acceptable* (an adjective).
3. When you "peel off" the suffix, a word is usually left.

Further Complexities of Affixed Words

It is not difficult to decode a suffix, provided that the student recognizes the letters or syllables as a unit. The difficulty arises when the suffix has changed the part of speech or changed the word concept to such a degree that students do not recognize the meaning of the affixed word. Being familiar with the noun *person* and then having to shift to a phrase such as a *personal matter* may take some understanding. Studies show that students do not always make these shifts in meaning. While the root word is known, the affixed form may not be understood until much later.

Added to the problem of a shift in the part of speech of the word, which affects syntax and meaning, the suffixed word sometimes undergoes shifts in spelling as in *prescribe/prescription*. The same suffix is often spelled differently, such as *tion/sion*, *ant/ent*, *ance/ence*, *ar/er*. These differences are of historical origin, but have nothing to do with meaning or pronunciation. There are also shifts in some of the vowel pronunciations as *cave/cavity*, *crime/criminal*, *supreme/supremacy*. Even more puzzling, some suffixes denote words as either adjectives or adverbs: *kindly* (adj.) and *quickly* (adv.). And then, there are words like *hardly*, which has nothing to do with *hard*. Since oral language has far fewer derived words than does written language, many children have not had exposure to these affixed forms. TV programs, which monopolize much of children's time today, have a paucity of these kinds of words.

Added to these complexities is the difficulty of understanding the meaning of many of the bound roots. Therefore, it is necessary that the teacher guide discussion in the classroom to clarify the decoding, the meaning, and the related vocabulary of these affixed forms. This is certainly time well spent and is perhaps the most important aspect of teaching these words.

Spelling and Suffixes

A direct link exists between spelling generalizations about suffixes and the reader's ability to mentally separate suffixes from roots to identify the total derived or inflected word. The following generalizations are worth knowing:

1. When adding a suffix beginning with a vowel to a word that ends with an *e*, the *e* is usually dropped: *believe* + *able* = *believable*; *secure* + *ity* = *security.*
2. When adding a suffix beginning with a vowel to a one-syllable word that ends in one single consonant with a short vowel before it, the last consonant is usually doubled: *run* + *er* = *runner; knot* + *ing* = *knotting*. (This permits us to differentiate between words such as *sloping* and *slopping*.). When analyzing two-syllable words, the accented syllable must be considered.
3. When adding a suffix to a word that ends with a *v* preceded by a consonant, the *y* is usually changed to an *i; greedy* + *ness* = *greediness; fancy* + *full* = *fanciful.* Exception: The letter *y* is never changed to an *i* when adding *ing; reply/replying; cry/crying.* This is because English does not permit two *i*'s together, and without the *y*, the words would be pronounced as /repling/ and /cring/.
4. When adding a suffix to a word that ends with a *y* preceded by a vowel, the *y* is *not* changed: *employ* + *ment* = *employment; play* + *er* = *player.*

Affix Lists

Although there is a difference of opinion as to which are the most common prefixes and suffixes, Table 7.1 includes many common prefixes and Table 7.2 includes common suffixes. Some common roots are listed in Table 7.3.

Much variety can be found in basals and in materials that purport to teach the prefixes and suffixes used in instruction. White, Sowell, and Yanagihara (1989) point out that there are nine common prefixes and ten common suffixes. The prefixes includes *un, re, (in, im, ir, il,* with a

TABLE 7.1 A List of Common Prefixes

Prefix	Meaning	Word Example
a	on, in, at, not	afoot, asleep, atypical
ab	from	absent, abstain
ad	to, toward	admit, adapt
an	not, without	anonymous, anaerobic
ante	before	anteroom
anti	against	antiwar
amphi	both, around	amphitheatre
auto	self	autobiography
be	make	befriend, belittle
bene	well, good	benefit
bi	two	bicycle
centi	one hundred	centipede
circum	around	circumnavigate
co	with, together	cooperate
con	with, jointly	concur
contra	against, opposite	contradict
de	from, away	deport
deca	ten	decade
*dis	apart from, not	disagree
en, em	in	encircle
equi	equal	equation
ex	out of	exit
extra	outside	extracurricular
fore	in front of, before	forecast
giga	billion	gigabyte
hemi	half	hemisphere
hetero	different	heteronym
hyper	excessive	hyperactive
*in, im, ir, il	not	incapable, impossible, illegible
inter	between	intermission
kilo	thousand	kilogram
mal	bad, badly	malfunction
mega	large, million	megaphone
micro	small	microphone
mid	middle	midnight
mis	bad, wrong	misplace
mono	one	monotone
neo	new	neoclassical
non	not	nonfiction
omni	all	omnificent
over	too much	overrate
para	almost	paralegal
per	throughout	permeate
peri	around	perimeter
phono	voice, sound	phonograph
poly	many	polygon
post	after	postdated
pre	before	prenatal
pseudo	false	pseudonym
*re	again	replay
retro	back	retroactive
semi	half	semi-monthly
sub	under	submarine
super	above	superman
trans	across	transworld
tri	three	trimester
ultra	beyond	ultrasuade
*un	not	untrue
under	below, less than	underestimate

*Four most common prefixes

TABLE 7.2 A List of Common Suffixes

Suffix	Meaning	Word Example
able	able to, worthy	breakable
ac, ic, al, an	characteristic of	cardiac, comical
ade	action, process	escapade, blockade
al	relating to	fictional, dismissal
an	one who does	veteran
ance, ancy	state or quality of	truancy, annoyance
ant	one who does	accountant
cide	to kill	homicide
cle, cule	small	particle, miniscule
crat	person of power	autocrat
ee, eer, or	one who	farmer, volunteer
en	to make	fasten
ence, ency	state of	absence, frequency
er	more	easier
est	most	easiest
ette	small	diskette
ful	full of	playful
fy	to make, cause to be	satisfy
ic	like, pertaining to	comic
ice	act of, quality of	justice
ide	chemical compound	fluoride
ion, tion	act or state of	champion
ism	state of, quality of	heroism
ity, ty	state of, quality of	necessity
ive, ative, itive	tending to, relating to	passive, negative
ize	to make	computerize
kin	little	munchkin
less	without	loveless
let	small	piglet
ling	small	duckling
logy, ology	study of	criminology
ly	having the quality of	fatherly
ment	state, quality, act	amazement
ness	state of being	sadness
or	one who	actor
ory, orium	place where	auditorium
ous, eous, ious	having, full of	generous
phobia	fear of	acrophobia
ry	state or quality of	bravery
s, es	plural	boys, boxes
ship	state of	friendship
tion	state or quality of	caution
ule	small	granule
ulent	full of	fraudulent
ure	action or process	procedure
ward	direction	forward
wise	manner, direction	clockwise
y	like a, full of	fruity
yer	one who	lawyer

meaning of *not*),[2] *dis*, *en*, *non*, (*in*, *im* with a meaning of *in* or *into*), *over*, *mis*. The suffixes are *-s/es*, *-ed*, *-ing* (these are the 3 most common inflected suffixes) and the derivational suffixes *-ly*, *-er*, *-ion*, *-able*, *-al*, *-y*, and *-ness*.

[2] The prefix *in* has different forms because the final letter assimilates to the root or word: *immature*, *irregular*, and *illegible*.

TABLE 7.3 A List of Common Roots

Common Roots (For Elementary)		
Root	**Meaning**	**Word Example**
cap	head	captain
cycle	ring, circle	bicycle
dent	tooth	dentist
form	shape	uniform
geo	earth	geography
gram	letter	telegram
graph	write	autograph
phone	sound	earphone
vis	see	television
Roots (For Upper Elementary and Junior High)		
Root	**Meaning**	**Word Example**
ambi, amphi	around	ambition, amphitheater
anthrop	man	anthropology
aster, astr	star	asterisk, astral
bio	life	biology
cav	hollow	cavity
chrom	color	chromosome
circum	around	circumstance
contra	against	contraband
demo	people	demonstration
derm	skin	dermatologist
dict	to speak	diction
duc	to lead	induction
epi	upon	epidermis
gam	marriage	polygamy
hetero	different	heterogeneous
homo	same	homonym
loc	place	location
mal	bad	malformed
manu	hand	manual
mar	sea	maritime
mort	death	mortician
port	to carry	porter
scrib, script	to write	transcribe
theo	god	theology
vid, vis	to see	vision
vinc, vict	to conquer	invincible, victim
vita	life	vitamins
viv	to live	vivacious
voc	to call	vocalize

While there is some disagreement over which specific affixes to teach, there is broad agreement in the research that emphasizes the importance of knowing how to decode and understand affixed words, especially as students move into more complex reading in the content areas of social studies and science. A proliferation of commercial materials to teach these skills has also flooded the market. While some of them may have a place in the classroom, we need to always remember the importance of teacher instruction, motivating activities that build interest in words, and, most importantly, the benefits that accrue to students who do wide and varied reading, thus learning many of these words through the context of varied selections.

Figure 7.1 includes an example of an abbreviated lesson for students who are in the early stages of learning structural skills and some example lessons for more advanced students.

FIGURE 7.1 Sample Lessons for Teaching Prefixes and Suffixes

EXAMPLE LESSON: YOUNGER CHILDREN

Begin by drawing a simple picture of a house, telling children that some words can be compared to a house; that just as you can add on to a house, you can add on to a word (add on to the house as in the example):

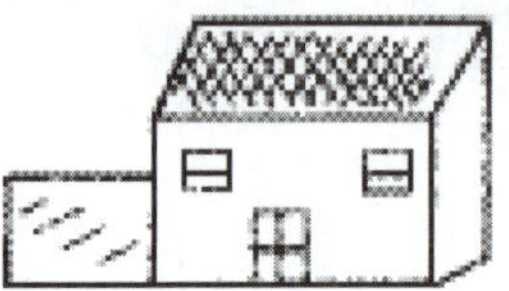

Write the words *happy* and *unhappy* on the board (under the house) and ask a student to underline the parts that are alike.

Teacher: What did we add to the beginning of the word *happy? (un)* We call this a prefix. Say prefix. A prefix is not a word by itself, but we add it to a word to make a new word.

Teacher: (writes the two parts under the house) What does *happy* mean?

Children: (respond)

Teacher: (Points out to children how *un* changed the meaning, or inducts the meaning from the children)

Follow Up: Offer additional exercises with *un* for words such as *untrue*, *unfair*, *unlike*, *unreal*, and *unable*. Children dictate sentences with these words as the teacher writes them on the board or on a transparency. Children underline the root word and draw a ring around the prefix. (The activity may be extended after sufficient practice, and an addition made to the house to introduce the idea of a suffix.)

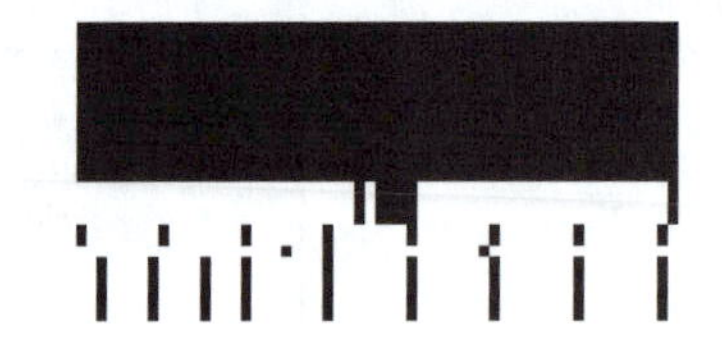

EXAMPLE LESSONS: ADVANCED STUDENTS

I. Recognizing Prefixes

Purpose:

Students will recognize certain common prefixes and learn to read them as part of a larger word unit.

Procedure:

1. Write the following roots on the board explaining to students that each is a base word to which a prefix may be added. Also impress upon students that our roots, sometimes referred to as stems, are very selective and will only accept particular prefixes. A stem often carries the lexical meaning of the extended word. Read the stems with the students.

agree	sight	sense	war
claim	pay	circle	merge
place	play	world	port

2. Now write each prefix on the board. These are commonly found in reading materials. Have the students pronounce these prefixes. You may want to explain that we have several prefixes that mean something similar to "not" such as *dis*, *mis*, *non*, and *anti*. You may want to discuss some of the meanings of other prefixes, although as mentioned, some of these are absorbed prefixes and carry no meaning in and of themselves.

dis	in	non	anti
pro	pre	semi	sub
mis	re	trans	ex

3. Now attach the prefixes to the roots or base words and have the student read the new words:

disagree	insight	nonsense	antiwar
proclaim	prepay	semicircle	submerge
misplace	replay	transworld	export

4. This lesson should be followed by practice. Place prefixed words on the board or a worksheet. Have students identify and pronounce the prefix, identify and pronounce the root or base word, and blend the two together to pronounce the affixed word.

unfit	overbid	antifreeze	pro-American
degrade	redraw	preschool	supervisor
misbehave	transport	forewarn	subterranean

5. Students will, when asked to offer prefixed words, give examples such as "pro/perty." Tell them these are not prefixes in the true sense of the word but knowing prefixes can aid in pronunciation. This is a good place to learn something about the fascinating history of the English language.
6. Have students verbalize that looking for a prefix can be a first step in decoding polysyllabic words and have them locate prefixed words in their reading materials, identifying the prefix and the base word or root.

II. Recognizing Suffixes

Purpose:

Students will recognize certain common suffixes and learn to read them as part of a larger word unit.

Procedure:

1. Write the following stems on the board explaining to students that each is a base word to which a suffix may be added. Again as with the first lesson on prefixes, impress upon students that our roots are very selective and will only accept certain suffixes. The suffix often changes the part of speech of a word, whereas the prefix usually does not.

block	dance	music	wise
employ	wool	fear	simple
poet	act	fool	alarm

2. Now write each suffix on the board. These are commonly found in reading materials. Have the students pronounce these suffixes. You may want to explain that suffixes may change the part of speech of the word and show them examples of these changes. Point out also that the spelling sometimes changes when suffixes are added to words but does not usually change when prefixes are added to words.

ade	er	ian	dom
ee	en	ful	fy
ic	tion	ish	ist

3. Attach the suffixes to the root and have the students read the new words.

blockade	dancer	musician	wisdom
employee	woolen	fearful	simplify
poetic	action	foolish	alarmist

4. Practice with other suffixed words. When students have confidence and show they understand the principle involved, have them locate suffixed words in their reading materials and identify the suffix and root.

III. Recognizing Words with Prefixes and Suffixes

Purpose:

Students will recognize that certain words are composed of a prefix, a stem, and a suffix. Half of the words with prefixes also have suffixes (White, Sowell, & Yanagihara, 1989).

(continued)

FIGURE 7.1 Continued

Procedure:

1. Write the following words on the board. Ask students to identify and pronounce the prefix and then to look at the rest of the word. If they cannot identify the root, have them check the suffix first and pronounce it, then return to the stem, pronounce it, and then blend all three parts together. Some students will be able to identify the word parts in order after they have had practice and will not need to always locate prefix, suffix, and then root.

repayment	exceeding	interchangeable	enrichment
enjoyment	unsinkable	unknowing	reboarded
undesirable	inaction	removable	preheated

2. Have students locate words in their materials with prefixes, suffixes, and roots. Practice with these word parts, trying to build other words with these structural parts.

Always remind students that after identifying the word parts of unfamiliar words as the prefix, suffix, and root, and blending them together, the next step is to place the word in context to see if it makes sense.

Turning Incorrect Answers into Learning Experiences

Often incorrect answers can be turned into learning experiences. Collins' (1987) suggestions have been adapted for working with affixes.

Think once again. If you believe a student has the background to answer correctly say something like, "Take just a little more time. I believe you do know the answer." (You have asked the question, "Name two prefixes that mean 'not'.")

Paraphrase the question. By rephrasing the question to, "Name two prefixes that mean 'not,' and that change the meaning of a word," you include a needed clue.

Help with a prompt. Offer a small piece of relevant information to help students such as, "If you understand something, it is clear. If you do not (pause for a moment to let students supply the answer), it is unclear," and let the student supply the word.

Expand the answer. Repeat the part of the answer that was correct as "Unclear, that's correct." Now add, "Now, what is the prefix?"

Asking for clues. In some classrooms you might call on other students to give clue words or suggest some yourself such as "unable, unbeaten, unusual." You may also ask a student who missed the question to call upon a classmate to help with clues. The student could offer words such as misprint, misconduct, inaction, invalid, dislike, disregard.

Making students accountable. If students give two incorrect answers to the same question, tell them you will ask the question again to give them the incentive to remember. Return to the students before the period ends and ask the same question.

Nonexamples. The writer once had a young student offer "dis-a-minute" as a word with a prefix. Giving a clue such as "Do you like candy?" (always receives a "yes" answer) "How about spinach? Do you like it or do you __________ it?" helps the student supply a correct word.

Wait time. If students do not raise their hands after a suitable time, tell them what the answer is not. This allows time for thinking and, at times, can introduce a little humor into the lesson.

Activities with Affixed Words

When teachers believe students would profit from drill activities with affixes and roots, some of these types of exercises might prove useful:

1. Showing change of meaning when prefixes are added.

dis	interest
dis	agree
dis	approve

2. Using roots to form new words and then discussing their meaning.

phone	phonograph, phonics, telephone
graph	graphics, telegraph, photograph
geo	geology, geologist, geography

3. Reviewing affixed words.
   a. Write two columns of words such as the following on the board. (This list should be more extensive, with review words from their texts.)

movement	believable
payment	excitement
usable	portable
readable	agreement
equipment	lovable

   b. Divide students into two teams.
   c. A student from the first team selects a word from the first column, reads it, and uses it in a sentence.
   d. If the second team agrees that the word is correct, both in pronunciation and meaning, team one erases the word. The procedure continues, and a member of the second team selects a word from the second column, reads it, and uses it in a sentence. The first team to erase all their words wins.
4. Creating visual-auditory links. Select roots such as *script* (to write) and *audi* (to hear). Locate a picture with which to associate the meaning of the word part. (Libraries have copies of reproducible artwork, or use magazines and cartoons.) Students or the teacher create a slogan that helps recall the root's meaning. For example, *Scriptus, the writer,* is the auditory link for the picture (the visual link) of a rabbit *writing* on a chalkboard. Transparencies can be used for reference. Worksheets for other roots can eventually become small booklets for students as they collect their words, finding and enlarging their word families. Always share and discuss the words (Peterson & Phelps, 1991).

Audi's all ears

Scriptus, the writer

5. Practicing reading words with a particular prefix. Use a tachistoscope with a strip of words.

6. Seeing the relationship between words with similar roots. Use word building whereby students begin with a word and build on this root to form as many new words as possible. With the root *graph*, a "tree" can be constructed with the word *graph* on the trunk, and the related words written on the leaves. Example words might include *geography, spectograph, telegraph, graphic, mimeograph, photograph, polygraph, phonograph, graphics*.

   Another method is to show the relatedness by drawing "bricks" of the meaningful word parts as:

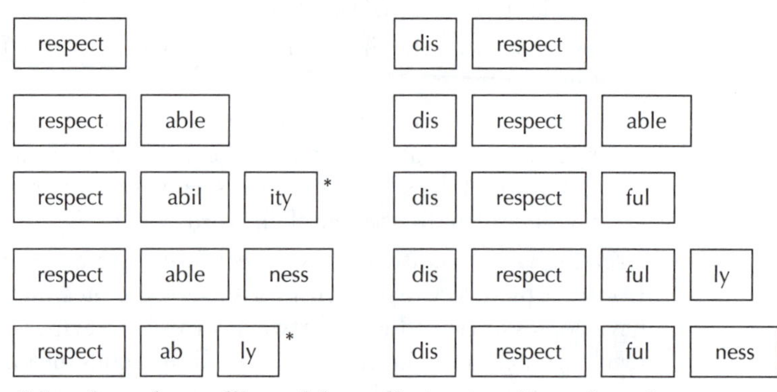

   *Note how the spelling of the suffix is sometimes altered.

7. Gaining an overview of vocabulary in a new unit.
   a. The teacher places a list of words on the board, a transparency, or worksheet. The words are discussed and read. In pairs, the students decide what words they will pantomime. These might be such words as *feudalism*, *nobleman*, or *conquistadors* from a social studies unit about the Middle Ages. (Use about a dozen words.)
   b. In pairs, students pantomime their word and then after a minute or so call on a classmate to spell the word, define it, and use it in a sentence.
8. Engaging in overall practice.
   a. Copy bingo cards so that there are a total of 25 blocks. From a list of words on the board or a worksheet, students make up their own cards, placing the words in whatever blocks they wish. The teacher (or a knowledgeable student) reads the definition of the word.
   b. Students with limited vocabulary skills may sit with a buddy, and the two-member team then plays with two cards. The caller states whether the winner must cover five spaces horizontally, vertically, or diagonally. The winner reads the words and may define particular ones. An example card is shown on the following page.
   c. Further variations include covering the four corners, the *B* row, the *I* row, etc.

B	I	N	G	O
certainly	dependable	vocalize	autograph	appliance
disagree	biology	respectful	television	electricity
transportation	countless	free	carefully	intensity
subscribe	believable	replacement	selfish	impossible
phonograph	agreement	extremely	misplace	submarine

Guidelines for Teaching Affixed Words

1. Teachers who use activity exercises to reinforce these skills should remember that difficult words with affixes encountered in reading should be *talked about*. Students should say the words aloud to one another and in groups. School language is more easily clarified and reinforced as it is learned initially by frequently meeting and hearing words in meaningful context (Eller, Pappas, & Brown, 1988).
2. Try to encourage students to be "word collectors" with their own personalized list. Set aside a time to share and discuss these words. Have bulletin board displays with particular kinds of words. Bring in books about words. Build *word consciousness* through meaningful language activities.
3. Be certain to schedule time in the curriculum for working with affixed words. Don't assume students will learn to decode and understand them on their own.
4. Emphasize to students that base words are very selective as to which prefixes and suffixes they will accept. For example, *nation*, *national*, *nationality*, but not *nationment*.

For extensive word lists of prefixes and suffixes, with a suggested grade level see Appendix B.

Questions Teachers Ask About Roots and Affixes

1. *Should students be taught to search for "little" words in "big" words?* Not really. This is a poor practice because it can lead to all kinds of misinformation. Example: In the word *father*, should it be *fat-her?* The only "little" words students should search for in "big" words are subunits of meaning. There is only one smaller word in *splashed: splash*, not *lash*, or *as*, since they do not represent a meaning unit within the word. Uncovering the root is therefore not the same as finding little words in big words.
2. *Should students be aware of problems in definition? Should they be told why affixed words can present difficulty?* It depends on many factors such as age and maturity. Teachers should understand structural analysis so they are in a position to answer questions, but avoid burdening pupils with more information about affixes than they can utilize.
3. *What should students focus on when they meet an unknown affixed word?* They should be taught to isolate letter combinations resembling affixes in unfamiliar words and to recognize what remains as a base word, subject to spelling changes *(debate/debatable)*. It is the underlying meaning units that should receive the focus. A strategy such as the following might be employed:
   a. Note the contextual clue. What kind of a word do you think it is?
   b. Separate or "peel off" the prefix and suffix (depending on the word) from the root.
   c. Put the word together. Think about related roots and other affixes for clues to meaning.
4. *Why is work with structural analysis considered so important?* First, because it is particularly useful in identifying word forms not previously encountered in print, such as *dentist/dental*. Second, fluent reading depends on the ability to quickly decode unknown

polysyllabic words, many of which are affixed. Third, many of the difficult words students meet in the content areas (social studies and science), beginning in the fourth grade, are often affixed words they have never met before.

5. *Are phonics skills important in using structural analysis?* Yes. This is because once the root is sorted out and recognized, sound-symbol relationships can help a reader arrive at the root's pronunciation. Of course, the ease with which students proceed through this structural reading skill stage depends as mentioned on their accumulated storehouse of a large sight vocabulary.

Quick Self-Check 2

1. What are the differences between a prefix and a suffix?
2. What is the relationship between a prefix, a suffix, and an affix?
3. Identify the two types of prefixes from the following list:

   recent insist dislike
   prepay uncertain impersonal
4. Identify the two types of suffixes from the following list:

   foolish singing called
   cleverness jumps safely
5. What are some of the generalizations students need to know when suffixes are added to words?
6. What is one of the best ways for students to learn to read and understand affixed words?
7. Why is structural analysis work so important?

Syllabication

Good readers tend to learn to divide words into syllables intuitively and to capitalize on this skill to help them decode words. Some students do not have this ability and need considerable practice with syllabication, as an aid to both reading and spelling. They need to understand that a syllable is a *unit of spech* that always contains one vowel sound, and has nothing to do with the number of letters. (*Oleo* has three syllables, while *squashed* has one.) This is because the focal unit of language is the stress given to vowel sounds, with consonant sounds being subordinate to this stress. Therefore, in teaching students to syllabicate to decode multisyllabic words, it is necessary to help them understand that the vowel sound is the key unit.

Dividing Words into Syllables

A review of the six basic syllable patterns is a prerequisite to formal instruction in syllabication. Using the mnemonic COLVER, students can review the basic syllable patterns.

Six Major Syllable Patterns (COLVER mnemonic)	
Closed Syllable	• one or more consonants end the syllable
Open Syllable	• one vowel ends the syllable
Consonant-**L**e Syllable (c-le)	• three letters: a consonant plus le
Double **V**owel Syllable	• two vowels together making one sound
Vowel-consonant-**E** Syllable (vce)	• one vowel, followed by a consonant, then the vowel *e*
R-controlled syllable	• one vowel, followed by an *r*

Teaching Syllabication

Young children do not have to know the precise rules of syllabication but after some reading instruction, they should have a general idea of how to break a word into smaller units, as aids to reading and spelling. Practice can take place by first working with words they know to get the concept of a syllable. They may engage in such activities as

1. saying words in syllables.
2. writing words in syllables.
3. sensing the syllables by placing their hands under their chins and saying the word. As their jaws drop, they can "feel" the syllable division.

To begin instruction in syllabication, teachers do not always start with a definition such as "every syllable contains a sounded vowel," but instead often begin in a game-like format. Children are asked to note columns of words in which the vowel sound rather than the number of vowel letters is the key to the word parts or syllables. For example:

Teacher: We are going to play a game. Look at these three lists of words. Let's read these words together. How many parts, or syllables, do you hear? Listen carefully.

A	*B*	*C*
mat	same	can dy
talk	spray	rob in
short	mail	catch er
scrap	coat	but ter
duck	tease	may be

How many vowels do you see in column *A?*

How many vowel sounds do you hear in column *A?*

How many vowels do you see in column *B?*

How many vowel sounds do you hear in column *B?*

How many vowels do you see in column *C?*

How many vowel sounds do you hear in column *C?*

The teacher draws conclusions from the students about the three groups of words.

Certain prerequisite knowledge and skills are necessary before beginning formal instruction in syllabication, such as long and short vowel sounds as well as a knowledge of affixes and root words. Vowels and affixes are critical to understanding syllabication. Students must learn two basic concepts during early syllabication instruction: the syllable is the basic unit of pronunciation, and each syllable contains one and only one vowel sound. That vowel sound may be by itself (a-bout), or combined with a consonant sound or consonant sounds (be-gin). Digraphs (examples: *ch, sh, th, wh, ng, nk, ng, ck*) cannot be divided into separate syllables.

When introducing more formal syllabication instruction, many teachers begin with the concept of the open and closed syllable. By definition, an open syllable has a long vowel sound, and a closed syllable has a short vowel sound followed by a consonant.

A	***B***
Open Syllables	**Closed Syllables**
po ny	fin ish
pa per	hab it
la bel	mod el
mu sic	riv er
mo tor	sig nal

The idea is that in list *A* the "open syllable" as the first syllable in *po/ny* has a long vowel sound, while in list *B* the second consonant sound has "closed" the syllable and the vowel sound is short. In working with syllabication, two-syllable words such as those in list *B* often follow the CVC rule: when you have one consonant, one vowel, and one final consonant (not *r*), you generally have a short vowel (m*a*t, b*e*d, f*i*g). This rule also holds in multisyllabic words such as *fin/ish*, *hab/it*, *mod/el*, *riv/er*, and *sig/nal* as above. In a word such as *power*, remember that *ow* is a diphthong, and therefore the letter *w* is not a consonant here but is part of a vowel combination and therefore not separated.

In an unknown two-syllable word, however, sometimes there is no way for the student to tell whether the syllable division should be before or after the second consonant. Students must often try both vowel sounds to see which one works. Some reading programs suggest that if there is not a double consonant in the middle of a word, it is divided after the first vowel, and it is long. Example: *sha/dy*, *me/ter*: Obviously, based on list *B* on the previous page this is not always the case.

After practice and instruction in syllabication with older students, it is a good idea to place categories of words on the board and to draw generalizations about how these words are usually divided, as an aid in decoding. For example:

Compound Words		**Affixes**		**Double Consonants**	
birdhouse	bird/house	kindness	kind/ness	dollar	dol/lar
outside	out/side	lovely	love/ly	happen	hap/pen
seatbelt	seat/belt	return	re/turn	rabbit	rab/bit

Different Consonants		***le* Preceded by a Consonant**	
envy	en/vy	icicle	ic/i/cle
picture	pic/ture	maple	ma/ple
silver	sil/ver	table	ta/ble

Once such a discussion has taken place, students may be encouraged to generalize some basic rules, such as those that follow.

1. If the word is a compound word, divide it between the two smaller words. If either or both of the two smaller words have more than one syllable, follow the general syllable rules as outlined in the chart. Examples include *bird/house*, *out/side*, and *seat/belt*.
2. Check the word for prefixes and suffixes. Separate prefixes *(un/like, pre/paid, re/vision)* and suffixes *(friend/ly, watch/ful, kind/ness)* from the word. Endings such as *ing*, *er*, *est*, and *ed* often form separate syllables. The remaining portion of the word is a root word, which should be decoded using the general syllable rules.
3. When two or more consonants appear in the middle of the word, divide the word between them (VC/CV). Try the short sound for the vowel in the first syllable. This rule does not apply if the two consonants form a blend or a digraph such as *ch*, *tch*, *ph*, *sh*, or *th*. Blends and digraphs should not be separated. Examples include *but/ter*, *mag/net*, *pic/nic*, *dol/lar*, and *den/tist*.
4. When only one consonant appears between two vowels, divide the word before the consonant (V/CV). Then try the long sound of the first vowel. If a recognizable word is not formed using the long sound, divide the word after the consonant (VC/V) and try the short sound for the first syllable. *O/pen*, *e/vil*, *ri/ver*, and *cab/in* illustrate this generalization.
5. When a two-syllable word ends in a consonant plus *le*, the consonant and *le* usually form the last syllable *(-ble, -cle, -ckle, -dle, -fle, -gle, -ple, -tle, -zle, -stle)*. If the preceding syllable ends in a consonant, try the short sound of the vowel *(han/dle)*. If the preceding syllable ends with a vowel, try the long sound of the vowel *(ri/fle)*.

6. Never break apart vowel digraphs or diphthongs such as *ai*, *ay*, *ea*, *ee*, *oa*, *ow*, *oo*, *oi*, *oy*, *ou*, *ie*, and *ei*.
7. Try the word in context. Does it make sense? If so, continue reading.
8. If the word does not make sense, then try the dictionary or ask for assistance.

Dividing words into syllables can be generalized by the following statements:

- ❒ Divide between words in a compound word or before/after the affixes (prefixes and suffixes).
- ❒ Divide between double consonant letters (do not divide blends or digraphs).
- ❒ When a VCV pattern is present, divide between the first vowel and see if that works. If not, divide after the consonant.
- ❒ If a word ends in *le*, divide before the consonant that precedes the *le*.

Accent is a key word in any discussion of syllabication. Some guidelines for determining accents in syllables include:

1. Each syllable contains one and only one vowel phoneme (sound).
2. In multisyllabic words, one syllable always receives more emphasis that the other syllables *(pur' chase, en'vy)*.
3. In multisyllabic words, there could be more than one syllable accented. One syllable has the primary accent, and another syllable has a secondary accent *(germ' i nate', prov' o ca' tion)*.
4. In words with affixes, the affixes usually form their own syllables and the accent is attached to the root word *(el' e va' tion, un' ac cept' ed)*.
5. In compound words, the accent is usually assigned to the first word *(light' house, bed'room)*.
6. In a word with double consonants, the accent usually falls on the syllable closest to the first letter of the double consonant *(pup' pet, swag' ger)*.

Activities for Teaching Syllabication

1. *Objective: To begin to recognize two-syllable words.* Write words with one and two syllables on the board. Have them read. Then let one pupil read a word, while others clap hands softly to indicate how many parts they hear in the word.
2. *Objective: To teach syllabication of words with medial consonant digraphs.* Write these words on the board: *bucket, washer, cricket, gather, bother, nephew, bishop, leather*.
   a. Ask pupils what the words have in common.
   b. Divide words with a slash mark for students.
   c. Ask pupils what they can deduce from your division.
   d. Elicit from them that a digraph is not to be divided.
3. *Objective: To decode words based on syllabication generalizations (as many as they have learned thus far).* Pass out a worksheet with a number of words as follows:

pattern	department	equipment
shallow	oatmeal	subject
exposed	cardboard	pinhole
thickness	complete	darkroom
maple	thimble	staple

On the board, write a word as shown that typifies a specific example of each rule.

Compound Words	***Prefixes and Suffixes***	***Double Letters***	***le Words***
sidewalk	largely	butter	angle

4. *Objective: Teaching syllabication.* Writing Haiku, or other forms of poetry that depend on counting syllables can be used as an effective, authentic means for teaching syllabication. Some examples include:
   a. *Haiku:* Japanese verse (traditionally about nature or seasons) with three unrhymed lines of five, seven, and five syllables
   b. *Senryu:* Japanese verse (traditionally treating human nature in an ironic or satiric fashion) with three unrhymed lines of five, seven, and five syllables
   c. *Tanka:* Japanese verse (may be on any topic) written in five lines with lines 1 and 3 each having five syllables, and lines 2, 4, and 5 having seven syllables each
   d. *Renga:* Similar to Haiku, renga is typically written by two or more people and contains three verses. The first verse contains three lines (5 syllables, 7 syllables, 5 syllables) about a season. The second writer composes the next verse of two lines (7 syllables in each line) linking with the first verse. The final verse is another three-line verse written by the first author, or a third author. This verse is linked to the second verse, but not the first verse. Each verse generally uses a word representing a season.
   e. *Cinquain:* This poem consists of five lines with the following number of syllables 2, 4, 6, 8, and 2—for a total of 22 syllables. Any topic is permissible.
   f. *Diamante:* This is a diamond-shaped poem with seven lines and a clearly established format involving word patterns. This poem format is appropriate for work with suffixes, but not with syllable counts. Line 1 contains a single noun, which is the subject of the poem. Line 2 consists of two adjectives that describe the noun in line 1. Line 3 has three verb participles ending in -ing or -ed that describe the noun in line 1. Line 4 contains four words in any order; two of the words relate to the noun in line one, and two relate to the noun in line 7. Line 5 consists of 3 participles ending in -ing or -ed and describes the noun in line 7. Line 6 has two adjectives that describe the noun in line 7. Line 7 is a single noun either the opposite of the noun in line 1, or related to it.

Quick Self-Check 3

1. What are the six major syllable patterns (COLVER)?
2. What two basic concepts are essential for syllabication instruction?

SUMMARY

The effectiveness of using structural analysis depends in large part on the extensiveness of a student's reading vocabulary. Students who have internalized the phoneme-grapheme relationships of English, and who also have a rich storehouse of sight words and word roots, are in the best position to profit from this kind of instruction. Structural analysis instruction generally includes base words, common affixes (prefixes, suffixes), and common inflected endings (plurals, possessives, comparatives, and tense morphemes). Syllabication is also generally included with structural analysis. The rationale for teaching syllabication is based on the belief that decoding will be facilitated if children learn to segment unknown words into more manageable parts.

Review Questions

1. What kind of a generalization would you make for students regarding formulating contractions?
2. Can you explain the difference between a morpheme and a syllable?
3. How would you explain to a student that the *dis* in the word *disturbed* is not a prefix?
4. Can you clarify the connection between affix, prefix, and suffix?
5. What key factors need to be considered when beginning syllabication instruction?

Chapter 8

Context Clues

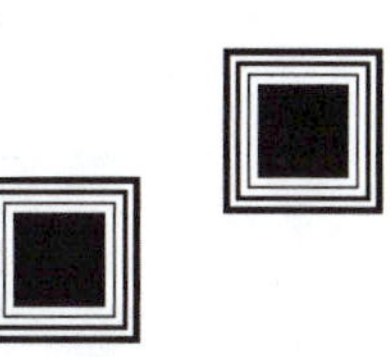

In addition to phonics and structural analysis, students should be taught additional strategies to help them unlock the pronunciation and meaning of unknown words that they encounter while reading. Beginning readers usually rely heavily on phonics clues to identify words because of a limited ability to use context. More advanced readers may be able to use context clues as an additional word recognition strategy. Context clues help readers approximate the pronunciation and meaning of unknown words they encounter as they read. The words, phrases, or sentences that appear on either side of a specific word are called the context. Rasinski and Padak (2001) define context as "the neighborhood where a word lives" (p. 108). Clues may be obtained from the context around an unfamiliar word provided the material is not too difficult for the student. This is one way to decode unfamiliar words and gain meaning, the result being a faster and more efficient word identification process than is available through any single technique.

Johnson and Baumann (1984) summarize research regarding children's use of context clues and find (a) that children do use contextual information in identifying words, (b) that there is a developmental trend in children's use of syntactic clues, (c) that developing and mature readers are able to use semantic clues, (d) that the use of context clues seems to be linked to the type of reading material, (e) that the word frequency and difficulty level of the material affects the power of context clues, and (f) that contextual clues are partially mediated by automaticity reading.

Johnson and Baumann (1984) include the following clues as context clues: pictorial and graphic aids (pictures, charts, graphics, diagrams), and typographical aids (quotation marks, parentheses, footnotes, bold print); however, they say that the most powerful context clues are syntactic clues and semantic clues. Syntactic clues provide grammatical information, and semantic clues provide lexical or meaning information. When readers understand the meaning of other words in the surrounding context, they use their semantic knowledge to help decode the unknown word. Their syntactic understanding or sense of the English sentence, which they must have to be able to speak, can help them deduce what type of word (noun, verb, adjective) would fit in a particular slot.

Since these two types of clues, semantic and syntactic, are interdependent, readers tend to use them together to anticipate and confirm what they believe the word will be. For this reason, most reading programs combine the two types under the umbrella term *context clues*.

Examples of Context Clues

Many teachers claim that students do not use context to its full advantage (Cunningham, 1979). They need help in judging whether context can be an aid to identifying and pronouncing unknown words. Few students are aware of the variety of ways context can help unlock unknown words and give them meaning. There is not one single taxonomy of context clues; many exist, and a variety of terms are used to identify the various clues. Various research articles and methodology texts suggest that there are from 4 to 15 different types of context clues. We have attempted to identify the most common ones using the least complicated language. Following are some examples of different context clues.

Direct Explanation or Definition Clue

Often authors realize students will not know a word so they provide an explanation to help them. Words such as *is* and *means* provide clues that indicate a meaning or explanation will follow. This information may be contained in one sentence or in a number of sentences. Examples include:

Tagliatelli is a type of pasta.

Lobbyists got their name because they used to stand in a lobby or hall outside the room where the laws were passed. They try to influence the laws that are made.

Experience Clue

A student's own experience can help unlock an unknown word. The student must consider an experience that s/he has had and relate it to the sentence to obtain the meaning. Examples include:

In any team, the members must *cooperate* by working together.

A *tintype* picture reminds me of an old black and white photograph.

Words in a Series

Often a general definition of an unknown word can be detected if the word is located in a series. Examples include:

There were marigolds, pansies, and *chrysanthemums* among the flowers.

She earned honors, glory, and *accolades* for her performance as a singer.

Restatements

To clarify, authors often repeat what they have stated. Examples include:

In some places where fresh and saltwater meet, as at the mouth of a river, the water is *brackish*. *Brackish* water is between fresh and salt water in saltiness.

When one reaches the top of a mountain, a flag is placed at the *precipice*. A *precipice* is the top of the mountain.

Comparison and Contrast

A word like *but* often gives clues to a word's meaning. Examples include:

Jerry smiled at Tim, but looked *disapprovingly* at me.

The lady used to be very *vociferous*; however, she doesn't talk much anymore.

Inference

Surrounding words or sentences provide clues. Examples include:

It was necessary to make sure that the coin was as old as the date said it was. Any *artifact* with writing on it is very important to historians.

Lois was so *parsimonious* that she refused to give the children money for popcorn. It was very painful for her to part with her money.

Appositive or Parenthetical

Authors may use appositives or parentheses to help identify the meaning of an unknown word in context. Examples include:

Sesquipedalian (long) words are fun to use with children and adults.

A *ventriloquist*, one who projects his or her voice into a wooden dummy or puppet, is popular with children.

Synonyms

Unknown words may be identified because synonyms have been placed near the unknown word. Examples include:

The *au courant* tour guide was interesting and informative. In fact, no one could have been more knowledgeable about the area.

Jack's argument is *fallacious*, or misleading.

Quick Self-Check 1

1. What is the difference between a semantic clue and a syntactic clue?
2. What are the major types of context clues presented?

Advantages and Limitations of Using Context Clues

As with all types of word recognition strategies, there are advantages and limitations to using context clues.

Advantages

1. Words can be identified in context that cannot be identified in isolation.
2. Readers who can use context clues become independent decoders more quickly. They learn to be good predictors of what the word will be, confirming or rejecting it, based on whether or not it makes sense in the context of what they are reading, and then they quickly read on.
3. Students who have difficulty with phonics skills that require closer attention to visual features may perceive unknown vocabulary more easily in this way.
4. Words that do not follow consistent sound-symbol relationships may be more easily generalized.

Limitations

1. Beginning readers have difficulty using context, as their reading vocabulary tends to be limited.

2. There are many synonyms in English and these could make sense in a given context; therefore, when context is used solely, apart from other word recognition strategies, it does not result in exact word identification. When the exact word is required, readers must reinforce this clue with other word identification clues.
3. The surrounding context may be insufficient or provide misleading information about the word.

Guidelines for Teaching Context Clues

When teachers are preparing to teach students about context clues, a number of guidelines may be followed.

1. Young readers are not always as successful in using context clues as older, more successful readers are for two reasons. First, older readers have had more experience; they have heard, seen, and read more; they have accumulated larger vocabularies; and they have stored more information to draw upon. Second, because of maturation factors, they have developed greater reasoning skills. These enable them to put certain facts together, and to become more successful at decoding unknown words through context.
2. Unfamiliar words that students are initially unable to decode in a selection are often decoded later as the student meets these words in varied contexts throughout the selection. Information in a selection is often accumulative; there is usually more semantic (meaning) information at the end of a sentence than at the beginning, and more information at the end of a paragraph than at the end of a sentence. Combining the meaning of the passage with the physical appearance of the word may lead the student to both an approximate pronunciation and an approximate meaning of the word.
3. Materials that are too difficult present students with a disproportionate number of unknown words. This precludes the students' use of context because they cannot gather enough semantic information to bring the unknown word into focus.
4. Reading materials must be significant and interesting enough for readers to make use of context clues. They must be involved in what they are reading because, if they are not, they will be unaware of the semantic clues available, concentrating instead on individual words.
5. To begin teaching context clues, one must teach about context clues. Students should be familiar with some basic information about context clues:
   a. Most words are learned from context; therefore, it is important to learn to use context well.
   b. Sometimes context clearly tells a word's meaning. Generally, however, it only hints at the meaning of the word.
   c. Context clues may include words, phrases, and sentences that tell something about the unknown word.
   d. Clues can occur before the unknown word and after it. Many times more than one clue relates to an unknown word. Students should be reminded to look before and after the word.
   e. The most useful clues are generally close to the unknown word and often in the same sentence. Sometimes clues occur in other sentences and other paragraphs. (Graves, Juel, & Graves, 2001)

Students and Sentence Clues

Teachers may need to remind students that context clues will vary in sentences. Note the following three groups of context clues. Some sentences provide all the clues needed, some limited clues, and some no clues whatever.

Group 1. *Context does the work for the student.*

1. "It's cold in here. Shut the w_____."
2. When I take an u_______, it never rains.
3. They have one d__ and two sons.
4. On the day David became 10, his Mom had a b_______ party for him.
5. There is no e_______ so you'll have to climb the stairs.

Group 2. *Context clues are present here too, but they do not provide as much constraint as the former sentences. More reading than just the sentence is needed.*

1. How many p____________ are in the book? (pictures, pages)
2. Her coat was tan and bl____________. (blue, black)
3. They like to play in the b____________. (ballpark, basement, band)

Group 3. *Some sentences provide no context clues.*

1. That is a s____________ statement.
2. The l____________ is here.
3. Have you ever p____________?

Students' Dos and Don'ts

When students are learning and practicing the use of context clues, they should consider several recommendations and avoid several strategies.

Do . . .

1. try reading to the end of the sentence in order to figure out the unknown word.
2. search for clues and make certain the meaning "clicks" with what you have been reading.
3. use context when you need a general sense of what you are reading, such as in a story for pleasure reading or to get a general idea of a topic.
4. search across sentences that follow the sentence with the unknown word to determine whether context clues in those sentences can help with the meaning and pronunciation of the unknown word.

Don't Depend Completely on Context . . .

1. when you need the exact meaning of a word.
2. when clues suggest several meanings and you do not know which one is right.

Strategies for Teaching Context Clues

McKee (1948) expressed concern about teaching students how to use the context to unlock the meaning of an unknown word:

> It is indeed unfortunate that, although teachers admonish pupils to use the context to find the meaning of a strange word or group of words, very few children receive any definite instruction in how to use the context. The result is that many of our pupils and students have little if any skill in using this important tool. (p. 73)

Johnson and Baumann (1984) concluded that research regarding children's use of context clues to identify unknown words supports the notion that children effectively use context in word identification; however, there is little research evaluating the effectiveness of strategies to teach the use of context clues. Baumann, Edwards, Font, Tereshinski, Kame' enui, and Olejnik (2002) also conclude that little research evidence exists that supports the use of teaching context clues as a way of learning word meanings. However, they conclude that support does exist for the practice of teaching middle- to upper-elementary students to employ context clues to infer word meanings.

The lack of efficacy research may, in fact, be due to the lack of strategy instruction as suggested by McKee.

Many strategies and approaches for teaching context clues have been suggested by various educators. Some possibilities include teaching taxonomies of context clues first and then application of their use, or teaching generic strategies for obtaining meaning from the sentence or passage containing the unknown word.

General Strategy

To teach students a general process for identifying an unknown word, the teacher should begin by asking the students to identify the unknown word. The students should then look at the sentence before the one containing the word, the sentence with the word, and the sentence after the one with the word in it. A mental or written list should be prepared of the words or phrases that may have something to do with the meaning of the word. Students should reread the sentence containing the unknown word and, using the clues from the list, see if the meaning of the unknown word can be determined. If it cannot, students should be directed to either read more of the passage surrounding the word to see if that helps, or guess at the meaning and see if it makes sense in the context of the sentence and the passage. If the approximated definition makes sense, students should be instructed to continue reading. If a definition cannot be developed, students should determine whether they should skip the word or look it up in the dictionary.

SCANR

Jenkins, Matlock, and Slocum (1989) developed a general strategy for deriving meaning of unfamiliar words that emphasized the use of context clues. They described this strategy with the acronym SCANR (Substitute a word or expression for the unknown word; Check the context for clues that support your idea; Ask if substitution fits all context clues; Need a new idea?; Revise your idea to fit the context).

Think-Alouds

Think-alouds may be used effectively to teach children to use context in determining the meaning of an unknown word encountered in text. The think-aloud process requires that teachers demonstrate the thinking process used when encountering problems while reading. In the case of context clues, the teacher must model the processes used when students come across an unknown word. Demonstrating the think-aloud process requires teachers to read the sentence orally that contains the unknown word, and then to verbalize the processes used to identify the meaning of the unknown word.

1. Select a sentence to read aloud that contains the unknown word. Read the sentence aloud, and have students follow along silently, listening to try to identify the meaning of the unknown word.
2. Talk through the thinking processes used to determine the meaning of the unknown word, modeling the appropriate thought processes. Verbalize the process you are using to determine the meaning of the unknown word.

3. After modeling the strategy using multiple examples, allow students to practice thinking aloud orally with partners as they read sentences to determine the meaning of the unknown words.
4. Have students apply the think-aloud strategies individually as they read silently their own text.

The think-aloud process can be repeated with each type of context clue so that students are aware of the various types of context clues and the thinking process required to effectively use them.

Modification of QAR

Teachers may also modify Raphael's (1984) question and answer relationship strategy for use with context clues. Using Raphael's notion of three types of question-answer relationships (right there, think and search, on your own), teachers can pair the QARs with types of context clues, bypass the formality of teaching the various types with a more informal approach using QARs, or use a combination of the two strategies for a more powerful teaching strategy.

For example, context clues come in three types: the clues are right there beside the word, the words are in the vicinity of the unknown word so the reader must think and search the area for clues, or the word requires that the reader use his/her prior knowledge with some assistance from the text to generate the meaning of the unknown word. Clues that are "right there" may sometimes be referred to as direct context clues, indicating that a word or phrase directly explains or defines the unknown word. Clues that we are identifying as "think and search" or "on your own" may be referred to as indirect context clues. Sometimes the explanation does not appear in the same sentence as the word, or the word may not be explained at all. In this case, the reader must use personal experience and background knowledge to identify the meaning of the unknown word. Using the previous examples of context clues, we can categorize the clues:

Right There (Clue is Right Next to Unknown Word)

Direct Explanation or Definition

Tagliatelli is a type of pasta.

Words in a Series

She earned honors, glory, and *accolades* for her performance as a singer.

Appositive or Parenthetical

Sesquipedalian (long) words are fun to use with children and adults.

Synonym

Jack's argument is *fallacious* or misleading.

Think and Search (Clue is in the Vicinity)

Direct Explanation or Definition

Lobbyists got their name because they used to stand in a lobby or hall outside the room where the laws were passed. They try to influence the laws that are made.

Restatements

When one reaches the top of a mountain, a flag is placed at the *precipice*. A *precipice* is the top of the mountain.

Contrast and Comparison

The lady used to be very *vociferous;* however, she doesn't talk much anymore.

Inference

Lois was so *parsimonious* that she refused to give the children money for popcorn. It was very difficult for her to part with her money.

Synonym

The *aucourant* tour guide was interesting and informative. In fact, no one could have been more knowledgeable about the area.

On Your Own (Prior Knowledge is Required to Identify Meaning)

Experience

In any team, the members must *cooperate* by working together.

Guided Practice

Once students are familiar with one or more of the strategies, they should practice using them under the guidance and direction of their teacher. This can be accomplished by the following steps:

1. Assign a sentence or passage to read that contains words that are unknown to the students.
2. Instruct students to mark the words they do not understand or for which they have no meaning.
3. Prompt students to reread the sentence or passage looking for clues that may help them identify the meaning of the unknown words.
4. Ask a student to think aloud and explain to the rest of the class how s/he arrived at a meaning for the unknown word. Practice this strategy with the different types of context clues.
5. Move to authentic reading situations and ask students to apply the strategy during the reading. They should be encouraged to keep a running log of the words they do not know in the text and should record what they believe the meaning to be and how they obtained the meaning (without using the dictionary).

Quick Self-Check 2

1. Why are younger readers less successful than older readers in using context clues?
2. Where in a passage can readers find context clues?

Activities for Teaching Context Clues

Although a given sentence may lack context clues, the help needed may be in the sentence that precedes or follows it in a paragraph. Context is always more than just a single phrase or sentence.

To help students become aware of context, the teacher may begin by writing a simple sentence containing one unknown word on the board.

She *ambled* slowly down the path.

Discuss with the students possible meanings that make sense in the sentence. Show them how the context limits the word choices they may have.

Suggest to students that when they come to an unknown word they continue reading the complete phrase, sentence, or paragraph. This may help them infer the meaning of the new word. Then, see if they can supply the meaning of the word and find out if it makes sense to them.

Even when students use structural or phonetic analysis to unlock a new word, the final check for accuracy must be the context in which the word is originally found. This is of great help in correctly placing the proper accent and the vowel sound.

I *objéct* to the rule.

She will *condúct* the orchestra.

The *óbject* could not be seen.

Her *cónduct* in the class has improved.

There are other activities the teacher may use to create awareness of context. It must be noted that the success of context clue activities depends on the students' strength in understanding both spoken and written language.

1. a. Read a sentence aloud and omit an "unknown" word, but tell the students the beginning sound. Ask students what they think the word is and why they came to that conclusion.
   b. Discuss the "why" of the choices. Other students will be aided by the how-to-do-it of their peers.
2. Provide examples showing that context clues may precede or follow the unknown word.
   Preceding the unknown word
   People who write about famous persons, places, and events of the past are called *historians.*
   Following the unknown word
   Among them are *antibodies*. These fight germs.
3. Provide examples showing that a context clue may be a phrase, sentence, or paragraph.
   a phrase
   The day was *sweltering*, too hot for any fun.
   a sentence
   She *announced* loudly to everyone that she was leaving.
   a paragraph
   He held the *questionnaire* in his hand. "I need your help," he stated. "I don't know how to fill out the answers to all these questions. Why are they asking so many?"
4. Have students search through some of their favorite books to see how skillfully authors provide many context clues.
   a. But that quietness had been shattered by the coming of Mrs. Scallop, whose voice now *intruded* . . . every morning.
   b. People put out rat poison in their barns to kill the *vermin*.
   c. The old man's voice, its *exasperated* tone, showed Ned he was tired of the cat.
5. Have students write sentences to exchange with their classmates where the context explains the word and where choices are provided.
   a. Mr. Barrows had a way of making the most difficult things seem easy. His *lucid* explanations lit up every subject and helped us understand it.
      interesting relaxed clear
   b. The *prototype* of the automobile was a clumsy three-wheeled carriage invented in 1770 in France. It was propelled by steam and produced to haul cannons.

Though its speed was three miles an hour, it was the forerunner of the swift cars of today.

original model prospect production

c. The first task of a cub pilot on the Mississippi was to learn the *elusive* shape of the river since the shape of the river was constantly altering forever beyond the grasp of the cub pilot's mind and hand.

complicated basic baffling

The Struggling Reader

Struggling readers, who generally have limited vocabularies, are frequently unmotivated or unable to do the amount of contextual reading required to extend their vocabularies (Blachowicz & Lee, 1991). They lag behind able readers in the use of strategies that allow them to gain new word meaning from context (McKecown, 1985). With struggling readers, especially, guided instruction in the use of context is necessary (Jenkins, et al., 1989).

The story below might be used in the following activity in teaching context. The strategy was formulated and used by middle grade teachers and is called C^2QU (Blachowicz, 1993). The acronym stands for the procedures following the excerpts.

> Jimmy felt slighted when the new baby arrived home with his mother and father. The baby was getting all the attention that he used to get from his parents. First, he tried stomping through the house. He was not successful. Mother and Father were still busy getting the new baby settled into the crib. Next, he went to the rocking chair. After rocking the chair *vigorously* for over one hour without success, he decided the best way to get attention was to actually help his parents with the new baby.

C^1: The teacher gives the target word in a broad but meaningful *context.* Students form hypotheses about it and share why they believe the meaning to be as they state.

C^2: The teacher provides *more explicit context* with the word, asking students to reflect on their original choices and refine them.

Q: The teacher asks a *question* that involves semantic interpretation of the word and asks students to try to approximate the definition.

U: The students *use* the word in a sentence, often in summation or in writing about some part of the book or a lesson.

Instruction involves using a transparency on which components of the lesson are revealed one at a time, engaging students in a dialogue similar to the following:

Teacher: (C^1) Will you read this sentence with this italicized word for me?

Student: "Then he rocked the chair *vigorously* . . ."

Teacher: What could *vigorously* mean? (Students discuss.)

Student 1: May be a whole lot.

Student 2: Rocked it very hard.

Teacher: (C^2) "She shook the little bank so *vigorously* that all the coins fell out." Does this match up with what we thought at first?

Student 3: Well, yes, she had to use lots of energy.

Student 4: She had to use lots of force.

Teacher: (Q) Well, how about this. Can people speak *vigorously?* Can they walk *vigorously?* What might be some other things they could do *vigorously?* (This is a good time to show that words only permit themselves to be used in certain contexts.) Let's see if we can agree on a definition and check it with our dictionary. (End of the lesson should result in a working definition.)

Teacher: (U) (Suggests ways students should *use* the new word in their writing.)

SUMMARY

It is generally agreed that using context clues does, in fact, provide students with another option for identifying unknown words they encounter while reading. Context clues are useful because they allow readers to obtain meaning without using the dictionary. Context clues may be of two types: syntactic (grammatical information) or semantic (meaning information). There are various types of context clues. Different taxonomies exist; however, the goal is to *use context clues while reading, rather than to identify and label the various types.*

When instruction with context occurs, teachers must also consider the type of instruction to which students have been exposed. Students taught through a strong decoding approach (relying heavily on phonics) may tend to discount or not use context as a tool. Students who are taught using a strong meaning approach may tend to overuse context clues to arrive at the meaning of an unknown word. Regardless of orientation, one thing is clear: If students are to use context clues successfully, they must be provided with specific instruction in how to use context to derive meaning from text.

Review Questions

1. Can you provide sample sentences for each of the types of context clues described in this chapter?

2. Why is it more important for teachers to teach students how to use context clues than to teach them to identify the types of context clues?

3. How familiar are you with the strategies explained in the chapter? Can you write a lesson plan using one of the strategies outlined in the chapter?

4. What Internet resources are available? Conduct an Internet search for sites that focus on teaching context clues. Are there similarities and/or differences in their approaches to teaching context clues?

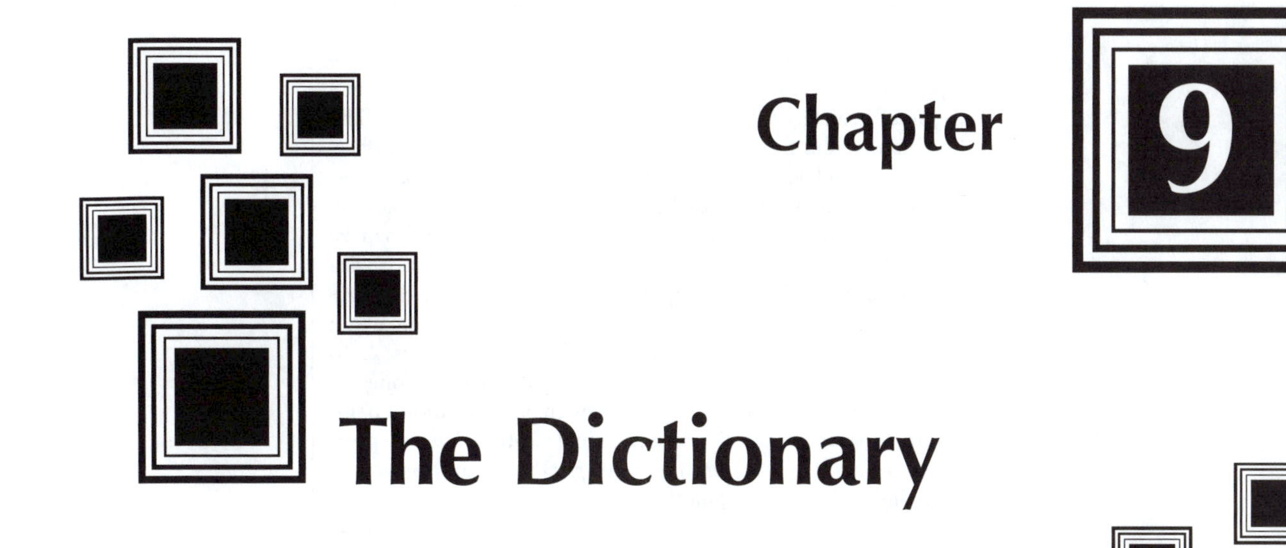

Chapter 9

The Dictionary

As the student moves toward becoming an independent reader, s/he often meets words that cannot be decoded and understood by applying the word recognition skills s/he has learned, including sight words, phonics, structural analysis, and context clues. At these times, the dictionary may be an aid, but only if the student is skilled in its use.

Understanding a Dictionary Entry

While most adult dictionaries are similar in terms of what is contained in an entry, there are some nuances among them. The most effective way to understand a dictionary entry is to find the explanatory section located in the front of the dictionary. Generally, the word will be the first part of the entry and it will be separated by syllables. If the word is a foreign word or phrase, the language of origin is included. Following the word, the pronunciation is enclosed in parentheses. The first pronunciation shown is generally the most frequently used. Next, an italicized abbreviation of the part of speech is included. If the word can be used as more than one part of speech, the italicized part of speech will precede the definition related to it. If an entry has an irregularly inflected form, that form appears next in the dictionary entry. Depending on the dictionary, restrictive labels may also be included. These labels indicate if the word is limited in usage to a particular area, region, or content area. The definitions of the word, usually numbered, come next. Generally, the most-used definition appears first for each part of speech. Variant spellings are included after the definitions and then the etymology of the word. Derivatives of the main entry (called run-on entries) appear next, followed by synonyms and then antonyms. Generally, dictionary entries follow this format; however, changes may be made. Students should be encouraged to examine the explanatory section of the dictionary to determine what is contained in each entry and the order in which it appears.

Using the dictionary sample provided, we can examine the various parts of the entry including the word, the pronunciation, and the part of speech for the definitions that follow. Following the definitions of paint when it is used as a noun, the entry provides definitions of the inflected forms of the word when it is used as a verb. Additional information provided includes idioms, slang, and the origin of the word. Additional forms of the word conclude the entry.

paint (pānt) *n.* **1a.** A liquid mixture, usu. of a solid pigment in a liquid vehicle, used as a decorative or protective coating. **b.** The thin dry film formed by such a mixture applied to a surface. **c.** The solid pigment before it is mixed with a vehicle. **2.** A cosmetic, such as rouge, used to give color to the face; makeup. **3.** See **pinto.** ❖ *v.* **paint•ed, paint•ing, paints** —*tr.* **1.** To make (a picture) with paints. **2a.** To represent in a picture with paints. **b.** To depict vividly in words. **3.** To coat or decorate with paint. **4.** To apply cosmetics to. **5.** To apply medicine to; swab. —*intr.* **1.** To practice the art of painting pictures. **2.** To cover something with paint. **3.** To apply cosmetics to oneself. **4.** To serve as a surface to be coated with paint. —**idiom: paint the town red** *Slang* To go on a spree. [< ME *painten*, to paint < OFr. *peintier* < *peint*, p. part. of *peindre* < Lat. *pingere*.] —**paint'a•bil'i•ty** *n.* —**paint'a•ble** *adj.*

Skills Needed to Use the Dictionary

Students must be proficient in three sets of skills if they are to use a dictionary effectively and efficiently. These include location skills, pronunciation skills, and meaning skills.

Location Skills

A number of skills associated with the dictionary can be identified as location skills. These include the following:

1. *Arranging words in alphabetical order.* Students should begin by arranging words first by initial letter, then by the second letter, followed by the third and fourth letters, and so on. Decisions about the level of difficulty should be based on the developmental level of the student.
2. *Finding words quickly in an alphabetical list.* Students should have command of the letters of the alphabet and alphabetical order to enable them to quickly identify words in a list.
3. *Opening the dictionary to the proper section where the word is to be found.* This includes moving quickly to the section of the dictionary (first half, first third, last third) where the word is to be found.
4. *Using the guide words at the top of the page.* Effective and efficient use of the guide words will enable students to get in and out of the dictionary quickly. If they are able to open quickly to the appropriate section of the dictionary, then they can apply their knowledge of guide words to determine the exact page on which the unknown word is located. Knowing that the word at the top of the left column is the first word on the page and the word at the top of the right column is the last word on the page should help students quickly locate an unknown word.
5. *Recalling the names of letters immediately preceding and immediately following the letter being located.* Automaticity in knowing the alphabet will increase the efficiency with which a student is able to use the dictionary. Opening the dictionary, using the guide words, and finally finding the word depends on knowing the alphabet. The more proficient the reader is in using alphabetical skills, the more proficient s/he will be in locating words in the dictionary.

6. *Using special sections of the dictionary.* Each dictionary is different in terms of its contents. Some dictionaries have a variety of different appendices or sections, such as the pronunciation key at the front, lists of special types of vocabulary (medical terms, slang expressions, musical terms, foreign words and phrases), and additional references (maps, list of U.S. Presidents, Periodic Table).

Words used to teach location skills should be modified according to the age group and ability of the students. More mature readers should be challenged beyond the basics of location skills. Additionally, activities should be developed to provide practice in using the various parts of the dictionary. Teachers will need to determine what the special features of the classroom dictionaries are and then develop activities to facilitate understanding and effective use of the sections.

Alphabetizing Skills

1. Write the word sets in alphabetical order.
   a. demon, monster, robot, giant.
   b. mob, magnet, mermaid, million.
   c. money, moppet, morning, motor.
2. Which word is first? Which is last?
   lightning, light, lighthouse, light-year.
3. Which of these three entry words would be found last?
   birth, birthstone, birthday
4. Which of these entry words would be found last?
   six, sixth, sixteen
5. Arrange the following words according to the way they would appear on a dictionary page.
   termite, test, terrific, tent, tension, testimony, terror, term

Guide Words

1. A dictionary should be thought of as having four sections.
   Section 1 A-E
   Section 2 F-M
   Section 3 N-R
   Section 4 S-Z
   In what section (part) would you find these words?
   a. pepper
   b. black
   c. heroic
   d. scream
   e. kickoff
   f. window
2. Look at the dictionary page. Write the first guide word. Write the second guide word.
   can canteen
   candy canvas
   candle canyon
3. The words *grown* and *gulf* are guide words at the top of one page in the dictionary. Select the words that would appear on that page.
   gull, guide, grumpy, guard, gulf, guess

4. If you were looking for the entry word *honorable*, within what set of guide words would you find it?
   a. hobo hog
   b. hole home
   c. honor hostess

Pronunciation Skills

In addition to finding the word, students must have the skills to pronounce the word, using the guidelines provided by the publisher of the dictionary. These skills include the following:

1. *Using the pronunciation key in the front of the dictionary and those at the bottom of each page.* Each dictionary contains a guide to the diacritical marks used to assist in the pronunciation of a word. These key words are found in the front of the dictionary and on the bottom of each page, or every other page for more advanced dictionaries. Students should learn how to use the key words in the front of the dictionary to help pronounce unknown words. The key words and diacritical marks will help them determine which words have silent letters, long vowel sounds, short vowel sounds, r-controlled vowels, digraphs, diphthongs, schwa sounds, and so forth. They should also practice using the key words at the bottom of the page.

ă	pat	oi	boy
ā	pay	ou	out
âr	care	o͝o	took
ä	father	o͞o	boot
ĕ	pet	ŭ	cut
ē	be	ûr	urge
ĭ	pit	th	thin
ī	pie	*th*	this
îr	pier	hw	which
ŏ	pot	zh	vision
ō	toe	ə	about,
ô	paw		item

Stress marks:
ʹ (primary);
ʹ (secondary), as in
lexicon (lĕkʹsĭ-kŏnʹ)

Partial pronunciation key. Copyright © 2004 by Houghton Mifflin Company. Reproduced by permission from The American Heritage College Dictionary, Fourth Edition.

2. *Identifying stressed and unstressed syllables in words by using and interpreting accent marks.* Students must initially learn that words are divided into syllables in the dictionary using a dot to separate the syllables (a · bol · ish, am · bi · dex · trous). Students must then learn to apply their knowledge of the use of accent marks to determine the pronunciation of unknown words. Failure to do so could cause difficulty in determining whether the unknown word is *con tent'* or *con' tent*. Short words generally have only one syllable that is accented, and this is called a primary accent. However, longer words may have more than one accented syllable. When this happens, we refer to the second accented syllable as the syllable with the secondary accent. It has less stress than the primary

accent, but more stress than the syllables without accent marks. Thus, words can have a primary and a secondary accent. In most dictionaries, the primary accent mark is much darker than the secondary accent mark.

3. *Recognizing differences between spelling, phonetic spelling, and pronunciation* (**phoneme-grapheme relationship**). Words in the dictionary are followed by a phonetic spelling that shows how to pronounce an unknown word. Using the phonetic spelling, the diacritical markings, and the key words located in the front of the dictionary or at the bottom of the pages, students should be able to pronounce or at least approximate the pronunciation of an unknown word. Students will need practice to become proficient at using the dictionary to pronounce unknown words.

As with location skills, the words used in teaching pronunciation skills to students should vary according to the skills and abilities of the students. Words that are more difficult can be used with more advanced readers. However, the skills should be taught and reinforced using less difficult words to start. The level of difficulty may be modified once students demonstrate their comfort and competence in using the resources available in the dictionary.

Pronunciation Key and Stress Marks

1. When you find the entry *impatiently*, you want to know how the word is pronounced. Use the key at the bottom of the page or in the front of the dictionary. The important marks to consider are long and short vowels; the schwa; *r*-controlled vowels; o͝o as in *book*, and o͞o as in *moon*. Also note that the sounds of *ci*, *si*, and *ti* are often /sh/. Most importantly, pay attention to the syllable receiving the stress. With the word *impatiently*, you will note the following syllables and diacritical marks:

   im short *i* (No mark over the vowel in dictionaries also means the vowel has a short sound.)

   pā′ long *a* and the stress mark (Long vowels are indicated by a *macron*, a straight line over the vowel.)

   shənt schwa (looks like an upside-down *e*) receives an uh sound (the schwa can be likened to the sound you make if you get hit in the tummy).

   lē long *e* indicated by the *macron*

   When there is difficulty in pronouncing words of many syllables, say the first syllable, then the first and second syllable together, then the first, second, and third syllable, and finally the last syllable. Repeat the word several times to hear the "tune" of the word. Now try to say the word to yourself.

Phonetic Spelling and Pronunciation

1. Write the correct word for the following phonetic spellings.

   ĕn sī klə pē′ dē ə (encyclopedia)
   ĕg zo͞o′ bər ənt (exuberant)
   rĭ bĕl′ yən (rebellion)

Meaning Skills

The third area in which readers must demonstrate proficiency to effectively use the dictionary is in determining meaning of the unknown word. Knowing the order of the definitions will help students spend less time searching for meanings and more time applying the correct meaning to the text in which the unknown word occurs. In dictionaries, the most commonly used definition of a word appears first followed by various other definitions including figurative meaning, specialized meanings, and then general meanings. Obsolete, archaic, or rare meanings follow. Knowing the definitions is not enough. The reader must be able to apply the appropriate definition to the text to obtain meaning. A number of skills must be learned if the dictionary is to be an effective tool in determining the meaning of an unknown word. These skills include the following:

1. *Using pictures as well as definitions to arrive at meanings of new words.* Readers of all ages must be able to use pictures and written definitions to learn the meanings of unknown words. Understanding the order of definitions that appear in a dictionary entry will expedite the use of the dictionary to obtain meaning.
2. *Selecting the specific meaning for a given context.* Perhaps the most important skill to be learned is applying the appropriate definition to the context in which the unknown word is found. Readers must be able to select the appropriate definition by identifying which one seems to make sense within the context of the passage. Readers may also use the word's part of speech to provide a clue as to the correct definition.

Word Meaning Skills

Activities for teaching word meaning will vary by grade level. Dictionaries for younger children are not as complex and may not contain words with multiple meanings. As students progress through the grades, the sophistication of the dictionaries they use will also increase and the practice activities will become more difficult. The key to word meaning activities is selecting the appropriate definition and transfering it back to the context of the passage in the least amount of time possible. Students must become proficient in determining meaning as quickly as possible to avoid interfering with comprehension.

Word Meaning Practice

1. Look up these unusual words and write the dictionary definition.
   cantankerous
   lionize
   greenback
   expatriate
2. Sometimes dictionary words have more than one meaning and you must decide from the context of the sentence the meaning that is appropriate. Read the dictionary entry for the word *paint* at the beginning of the chapter. Examine the sentences below. What meaning is intended in each?
   a. Mary painted her face before going to the party.
   b. Samuel put too much green paint in the mixture.
   c. Joseph will paint the house tomorrow.

Quick Self-Check 1

1. What are the three skills that readers must use to be proficient in using the dictionary?
2. Alphabetizing is critical to which of the three skill areas?
3. Pronunciation keys are generally found in what two locations in the dictionary?

Motivating Students to Use the Dictionary

A number of activities can be used to motivate students to want to work with the dictionary and to learn how to use it effectively. Examples of some of these activities follow.

1. Dictionary background and development
   a. A good refresher on the history of the dictionary is *The Story of the Dictionary* (Kraske, 1975). Older students may read it independently, or teachers may share it with younger students in class. Students learn, for example, that English dictionaries are really quite "young," dating back only about 400 years, and that listing words in alphabetical order was considered a novel idea at that time. Students also learn that commonly used words had to wait many years to win a place with uncommon words in the dictionary list. All the dictionary aids that we take for granted such as word histories, illustrative sentences, pronunciation symbols, syllabication, accents, parts of speech, and usage notes developed gradually as parts of a typical dictionary entry. Sharing these insights and relating short stories about Noah Webster and Samuel Johnson build an appreciation for the dictionary's use.
   b. Teachers who have access to the compact two-volume edition of the Oxford English Dictionary can build a lot of interest in this study by bringing these volumes into the classroom. The micrography, with 13 volumes compressed to one, and the accompanying magnifying glass will not be easily forgotten by students.
2. Creating original dictionary entries
   a. Students create the sounds, syllables, and definitions for made-up words that reflect various dictionary entries. This increases their familiarity with the different entry parts and their awareness that dictionaries differ in what they include. These words and their entries can be compiled and bound to constitute the class's "Creative Dictionary".

      Example: stratmous. (strat/moos) Eskimo stew made from venison, water, lichens, and moss. "This is the best stratmous I have ever tasted." Noun. (Stratmous has different ingredients depending on the area.)
   b. Proceed as in the previous instance except this time students use their own names and write the appropriate entry. This also helps familiarize students with entries and pronunciation guides.

      Example: Jane Callaway. (Jān Căll å wāy) 1. Third grade student at Hilltop School. 2. Also actress and musician. 3. Blue eyes, black hair, small and thin. Noun.
3. Dictionary scavenger hunts. Students engage in word quizzes. These are appropriate for middle-graders.

   Examples:
   a. Can a centaur be found in a zoo?
   b. Is a poetess a man who writes poetry?
   c. Is a cherubim a delicious fruit?
   d. Is a grackle a kind of noise?
   e. Was Ceres the same as the god Demeter?
   f. Can you wear a waste?
   g. Is a limerick a kind of soft drink?
   h. Would you rather be a spelunker of a philatelist?
   i. Is a statue a law?
   j. Is a puffin a small pillow?
   k. Is an artichoke a disease of the lung?
   l. Is a goatee a baby goat?

4. Integrate dictionary activities into other assignments and make them enjoyable. Students should learn to use the dictionary as part of their everyday routine rather than just during reading class or language arts class.
5. Model the use of the dictionary so students see the dictionary being used in authentic situations.
6. Continuously seek opportunities to incorporate the dictionary into daily activities. The more practice students have, the better they will become at using the dictionary.
7. Allow students frequent opportunities to use the dictionary when they are reading and/or writing in any content area. Viewing the dictionary as a necessary part of learning will benefit the students in the long run.

The Problem with Dictionaries

Rhoder and Huerster (2002) voiced concern over using the dictionary to identify the meaning of an unknown word while actively engaged in reading. They believe that looking up an unknown word while actively engaged in reading could be cognitively disruptive. They explain that the reader must know how to spell the word; stop reading to look for the word; search alphabetically through the dictionary; read through all the definitions, which may contain additional unknown words; select the appropriate connotation; and then apply the meaning back to the passage before continuing on with the reading. They believe that dictionary work alone may be the least effective means of acquiring new vocabulary.

According to Beech (2004), there has been little research on the potential role of the dictionary in furthering the development of reading. He adds that little is known about how the developing reader uses a dictionary. Beech claims that one disadvantage of using the dictionary may be that it disrupts the reading process to a degree that obtaining meaning from the text is inhibited. Beech even questioned whether students had the cognitive skills to use the dictionary. Beech conducted an investigation of students' reported use of the dictionary. He concluded that older readers accessed items faster and with more accuracy than younger readers, and children with reading problems were less efficient than those without reading problems. In his investigation, only 21% of the younger readers and 25.7% of the older readers referred to a dictionary on a daily basis. Beech's investigation supported the notion that as with any skill, the more one practices, the better one should become at its performance. Therefore, to become proficient at using the dictionary, students should have continued practice.

When to Use the Dictionary

If a student is reading a passage and comes to a word s/he does not know and cannot figure out, even after trying all the other word recognition strategies, should the student interrupt his/her reading to use the dictionary? The answer may depend, in part, on the teacher's philosophy of teaching reading; however, the student must learn to determine the relevant importance of the word so that s/he can decide independently what to do. The student must decide whether the unknown word is important enough to stop reading. There are several questions the reader should ask himself/herself to determine the relative importance of the word. First, is the word the focal point of the passage? If the reader cannot determine the main idea of the passage because s/he does not know the word, then s/he should stop and look up the word. Is the word in the title or subtitle? If the word appears in the title or subtitle, it is probably an important word and should be studied prior to reading. Is the word repeated frequently in the text? If it is, then the reader should stop to determine the word's meaning. Finally, does the reader think that not knowing the word will hinder his/her learning?

If so, then s/he should stop and look up the word. If the reader has practiced dictionary skills sufficiently, the short break should not significantly impact comprehension. However, if it takes a while to locate a dictionary, the page, and the correct definition, the reader may consider rereading a portion of the text to ensure comprehension has not been compromised.

Quick Self-Check 2

1. How does a student determine whether s/he should skip an unknown word or look the word up in a dictionary?
2. What is the best way to learn to use a dictionary?

Selecting Dictionaries

Noah Webster is often considered the father of the American dictionary. While teaching school, he compiled an elementary spelling book titled *A Grammatical Institute of the English Language: Part I*, which was published in 1783. Later the title was changed to *The American Spelling Book*. Blue paper covered the binding of the book leading to the nickname "blue-backed" speller. With the sale of well over 20 million copies of the blue-backed speller, Webster helped standardize spelling and pronunciation in the United States. In the 1820s, Webster completed the two-volume *American Dictionary of the English Language*.

Since Webster's time, hundreds of dictionaries have been published. Some are traditional and others are specialized, including a poker player's online dictionary (http://www.gamesandcasino.com/poker-dictionary.htm), the Smiley Dictionary (http://www.smileyworld.com/), and the multilingual Internet Picture Dictionary (http://www.pdictionary.com/).

Many types of dictionaries are available for English language speakers as well as English Language Learners. In addition to the traditional dictionaries with which we are all familiar, there are also bilingual dictionaries, monolingual dictionaries, learner dictionaries, picture dictionaries, and multimedia dictionaries. Bilingual dictionaries use two different languages such as English and French, English and Spanish, or English and Japanese. Monolingual (English-English) dictionaries are for native speakers. Learner dictionaries, such as the Oxford Learner Dictionaries, are leveled English-English dictionaries that have been written by language specialists for students who are in the process of learning the language. Picture dictionaries illustrate the meanings of words. Multimedia dictionaries are computer-based and may be included with the purchase of a computer or may be purchased separately. Some newer dictionaries include words from major subject areas such as computer science. They might also include a mini-thesaurus and vocabulary builders (showing students how to make new words out of prefixes and suffixes), and expand understanding by showing regional differences in pronunciation.

Picture Dictionaries (Pre-School)

Picture dictionaries do not provide written definitions or information about pronunciation, grammar, or use of words. They rely on illustrations to convey the meanings of words. Most of these dictionaries only illustrate concrete nouns. Some examples of picture dictionaries include the following:

- *The New Oxford Picture Dictionary: English/Spanish* teaches English as a second language to Spanish speakers using pictures that deal with everyday topics such as the body, post office, law, travel, and family.

- *The American Heritage Picture Dictionary* contains 900 age-appropriate words with multicultural characters appearing throughout the dictionary. Each word is defined by a sentence using the word to describe what is portrayed in the illustration.
- *Me and My World: Multimedia Picture Dictionary* was created especially for preschool through second or third grade (depending on the developmental maturity of the student). It includes 900 age-appropriate words arranged alphabetically and illustrations using multicultural characters.

First Dictionaries (Kindergarten to Grade Three)

The American Library Association (ALA, 2005) characterizes first dictionaries as those that contain commonly used vocabulary. The entries are short and include simple definitions written as complete sentences that, along with pictures, convey meaning. A representative sample of first dictionaries recommended by the ALA (http://www.ala.org/ala/booklist/speciallists/speciallistsandfeatures3/ChDictionaryRU.htm) include the following:

- *The American Heritage First Dictionary* (2003) contains 1,800 entries of mainly one-and two-syllable words and 650 illustrations. Definitions generally provide plurals, verb forms, and sample sentences. Irregular verb forms (fallen, fell) have their own entries.
- *My First Dictionary* (2000), published by Scott Foresman-Addison Wesley, includes approximately 4,000 entries and 800 illustrations. Cartoon-like drawings, illustrations, and photographs help define words. The definitions are among the most detailed for this age group providing parts of speech, italicized example sentences, inflected forms, and pronunciations (including some variants) for every word defined.
- *Scholastic First Dictionary* (1998) consists of approximately 1,500 headwords and 600 illustrations. It includes an easy-to-understand pronunciation guide. Definitions include sample sentences and inflected forms.

Grade Three to Six Dictionaries

The ALA (2005) explains that dictionaries for the intermediate grades generally include parts of speech, inflected forms, and pronunciation. They also include more advanced features such as syllabification, end-of-line divisions, cross-references, run-on forms, forms using prefixes and suffixes, idioms, word histories, usage notes, and synonym lists. Symbols for pronunciation, and abbreviations for forms and parts of speech may be introduced; pronunciation keys are repeated every few pages. There are fewer pictures in relation to the number of words defined. More scientific and technical terms and proper nouns are defined and in some cases, entries for people and places are included in the A–Z sequence (http://www.ala.org/ala/booklist/speciallists/speciallistsandfeatures3/chDictionaryRU.htm). Recently published examples include the following:

- *The American Heritage Children's Dictionary* (2003), published by Houghton Mifflin, contains approximately 34,000 entries and 800 illustrations. In addition to standard elements, this dictionary includes cross-references, homophones, variants, idioms, italicized examples, either sentences or phrases, synonyms, spelling notes, prefixes and suffixes, and word histories in color-coded boxes.
- The *McGraw-Hill Children's Dictionary* (2003) includes approximately 30,000 entries and 1,000 illustrations. Entries are easy to read, with definitions arranged in three columns. The part of speech immediately follows the word, and the pronunciation is at the end of the entry. There are no usage labels. Boxes identifying word histories, homophone notes, and synonyms provide additional information.

- *Scholastic Children's Dictionary* (2002) consists of approximately 30,000 entries and 1,000 illustrations. The pronunciation guide uses letter sounds instead of symbols, which may be easier for younger readers to decode. Definitions include homophones and sample sentences; highlighted boxes provide information about prefixes, suffixes, synonyms, and word histories.

Grade Six to Nine Dictionaries

Except for larger type, these dictionaries are similar to those used by adults. The ALA (2005) reports that they contain more complex definitions, and fewer illustrations and boxed features. Dictionaries for this age student routinely use abbreviations and pronunciation symbols, and there are generally more usage labels. Some foreign, dialect, archaic, slang, and nonstandard terms and usages are introduced. Fewer titles are available, probably because many children have moved to adult dictionaries (http://www.ala.org/ala/booklist/speciallists/speciallistsandfeatures3/ChDictionaryRU.htm). Following are three representative samples of these dictionaries:

- *The American Heritage Student Dictionary* (Houghton Mifflin, 2003) contains approximately 68,000 entries and 2,000 illustrations. Definitions may include example sentences, synonym paragraphs, and etymologies. Margins contain a "word building" feature (prefixes, suffixes, roots), usage notes, regional notes, word histories, black-and-white photos, and line drawings. Some foreign expressions, British and Scottish forms, and archaisms are included, and labels identify nonstandard, slang, informal, and some offensive terms.
- *Merriam-Webster's Intermediate Dictionary: Revised Edition* (1998) includes approximately 65,000 entries and 1,000 illustrations. This dictionary has an "adult" look and feel to it. Definitions are direct, but the vocabulary is more mature. Some foreign terms are defined. Usage labels include archaic, slang, substandard, nonstandard, British, Scottish, and dialect. Meanings are listed in historical order, and many definitions go into some detail about word histories and origins. They may also include usage notes and illustrations, etymologies, and synonym paragraphs.
- The *Thorndike-Barnhart Junior Dictionary* (Scott Foresman-Addison Wesley, 1997) includes approximately 68,000 entries and 1,200 full-color illustrations. Proper nouns are part of the vocabulary list. Color-coded boxes are used for etymologies and other elements. These features provide some interesting details, such as information on word families and subtle shades of meaning.

High School Dictionaries

The dictionaries in this group have fewer text aids (illustrations, boxed features, and sample sentences). They include more dialect, foreign, obsolete, slang, and archaic terms or usages, as well as more etymologies. While many high school students will have standard adult dictionaries, others may find those designed especially for high school to be more usable (http://www.ala.org/ala/booklist/speciallists/speciallistsandfeatures3/ChDictionaryRU.htm).

Following are some examples of dictionaries designed for high school students:

- The *American Heritage High School Dictionary*, 4th ed. (Houghton Mifflin, 2002) includes approximately 200,000 entries and 2,500 illustrations. This dictionary is exactly like the *American Heritage College Dictionary* except that it contains no vulgarisms or offensive terms.

- *Merriam-Webster's School Dictionary* (1999) contains approximately 85,000 entries and 950 illustrations. The definitions are more sophisticated than those in the company's intermediate dictionary. There are fewer (and different) word-history and synonym paragraphs.
- The *Thorndike-Barnhart Student Dictionary: Revised Edition* (Scott Foresman-Addison Wesley, 1997) contains approximately 100,000 entries and 1,500 illustrations. Line drawings and small black-and-white photos replace the color illustrations found in the junior books. Definitions include example sentences that are more complex and use more sophisticated vocabulary. There are fewer boxed features, and those that remain tend to be more detailed.

Adult Dictionaries

A wide variety of dictionaries are available for college students and home use.

College or Desk Dictionaries

The American Heritage College Dictionary (2002)
Merriam-Webster's Collegiate Dictionary (2003)
Random House Webster's College Dictionary (2001)
Webster's New Explorer College Dictionary (2003)

Comprehensive Dictionaries

Comprehensive dictionaries are more complete than college dictionaries but not as extensive as unabridged dictionaries. Some examples follow:

The American Heritage Dictionary of the English Language (2000)
New Oxford American Dictionary (2001)
The World Book Dictionary (2002)

Unabridged Dictionaries

An unabridged dictionary has not been shortened by omitting terms or definitions; it is a comprehensive dictionary. Following are examples:

Random House Webster's Unabridged Dictionary (2001)
Webster's Third New International Dictionary: Unabridged (1993)

Online Dictionaries

Online dictionaries in many different formats are becoming more and more popular. They generally feature links to other related terms. Examples include the following:

Microsoft Encarta College Dictionary (2001)
The Oxford English Dictionary on CD-ROM: Version 3.0 (2002)
Webster's Third New International Dictionary: Unabridged Online Version

Specialized Dictionaries

The American Sign Language Dictionary combines text, video examples, and animated illustrations. The combination of formats makes learning American Sign Language enjoyable. There are more than 2,600 signs with video demonstrations and illustrations. After listening and watching the demonstrations, users can listen to audio explanations or read the on-screen descriptions. Entries may be searched in five different languages.

The *Franklin KID-1240 Dictionary* is an interactive speaking dictionary. More than 40,000 easy-to-understand definitions are pronounced. The dictionary includes an automatic phonetic spell corrector and an animated handwriting guide that demonstrates print and cursive styles. This dictionary also includes a rhyme finder, five word-building games, and a vocabulary word list that can be created by the user. Headphones may be purchased to use with the dictionary.

English Language Learner Dictionaries

Koren (1997) explored the views of researchers, teachers, and learners regarding the most effective type of dictionary for English Language Learners. The following seven recommendations were reported by Koren:

- Using a monolingual dictionary in the learner's language to facilitate understanding of the definitions of the vocabulary terms
- Using a two-path bilingual dictionary (e.g. English-Spanish and Spanish-English), which provides two-way access to vocabulary
- Using monolingual and bilingual dictionaries together so that students may take advantage of the benefits of both dictionaries
- Using the glossary since it would be directly connected to the text that was being read and would reduce the chance of inappropriate translations
- Using hyper-reference texts with monolingual and bilingual dictionaries
- Using a "bilingualized" dictionary, which is a combination of monolingual and bilingual dictionaries
- Using electronic dictionaries

It is obvious from this list that dictionaries today can include many activities that motivate students to find out about words in interesting ways. Moreover, as students build their vocabularies and their skills in using the dictionary, they become more confident readers. Few students are aware of the wealth of information their school dictionaries contain. Motivation for using the dictionary as a valuable tool can be provided by using some of the special features they provide. Review for dictionaries may be found at the ALA website. Other sources of information include *www.Amazon.com*, *School Library Journal*, Parents' Choice®, and *Publishers Weekly*.

Summary

Using the dictionary as a way of identifying the meaning of an unknown word may be a very effective strategy, unless a student is in the middle of reading a passage; then, the dictionary can be the least effective tool in learning new words. Ensuring that students can effectively and efficiently use the dictionary requires that they have developed location skills, pronunciation skills, and meanings skills. Without the combination of these three skills, the dictionary remains an ineffective tool in unlocking the meaning of unknown words.

Although the activities suggested introduce students to some of the skills needed and engage students in some creative activities using the dictionary, they do not ensure success in locating, pronouncing, and understanding the meaning of an unknown word. Skill in using the dictionary is acquired through frequent and long-time use and interest. To motivate such use and interest, the teacher can serve as a good model, showing students that s/he finds a need to refer to a dictionary on a regular basis.

Review Questions

1. What are the location skills needed to use the dictionary effectively?
2. Can you identify a way to teach location skills not discussed in the chapter?
3. What are the pronunciation skills needed to use the dictionary effectively?
4. What problems might dialect speakers or non-native speakers encounter when trying to use the pronunciation key?
5. What meaning skills are needed to use the dictionary effectively?
6. Why is it probably not a good practice to give students 10 isolated words (no context) to look up and write definitions?
7. Can you generalize a rule or two about how to select an appropriate dictionary?

Chapter 10

Building Fluency Through Word Recognition

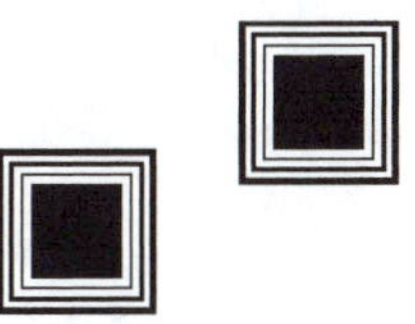

In the sentence "The fire was not extinguished until the house had burned to the ground," the word *burned* may be deduced from the remainder of the sentence, or context. In a second example, "The unhappy lion gave a mighty roar that was heard throughout the darkened jungle," the root of a word or the affixes attached to it may be used as keys to unlock the rest of the word: *unhappy, mighty, darkened.* Third, the arrangement of the letters in a word, or phonics, might suggest that clusters of letters may encode particular sounds such as *igh* /i/ in *mighty;* or *th* /th/ and *ir* /er/ in *thirst.* Last, the glossary or dictionary may help with the division of a word into syllables and give clues to pronunciation; however, the dictionary should only be used as a last resort when previous clues have failed.

Poor readers with poor recognition skills spend too much time trying to recognize words and have very little effort to expend or memory available for comprehension. As word recognition becomes more automatic, space is freed for comprehension. Therefore, one way to improve comprehension is to develop automaticity with word recognition strategies, which should improve fluency and, in turn, increase comprehension.

Word Recognition Strategy Instruction

Cooper, Boschken, McWilliams, and Pistochini (1998) report that below-level readers in the upper grades can generally use word recognition skills in isolation; however, they do not apply them when they are reading text. They suggest that when students come to an unknown word, they stop reading because they cannot use the skills they have to identify the unknown word. Johns, VanLeirsburg, and Davis (1994) postulate that students who have difficulty in reading do not apply all the word-identification strategies they know; whereas, good readers recognize that a variety of strategies must be used depending on the situation.

Pikulski and Templeton (2004) believe that students can be taught strategic behaviors to improve their ability to learn the meaning of words and suggest the following sequence:

1. Look at the word; decide how to pronounce it. Readers should process the letters or chunks of letters and think about the sounds for them.
2. a. Look around the word for context clues; look within the sentence, reread previous sentences, read the next few sentences.
   b. Look for prefixes and suffixes, base words, and root words that might offer clues.
3. Make a guess at the word's meaning; students will probably not get the exact meaning, but a close approximation is fine.
4. a. IF none of the above work and the reader can't guess, AND the word seems important, use a dictionary or glossary. The word is important if the reader is having difficulty with meaning or the word occurs frequently.
   b. If the reader thinks s/he has figured out the meaning of the word or if the word doesn't seem important, keep on reading.

Hendricks and Osborne (2005) recommend the use of the Helping Hand as an aid for word recognition. This mnemonic device, developed by Joseph Nemeth and Jacqueline Stitt in the early 1970s, serves as a reminder to students of what they should be doing regularly when they come to a word they do not know. Although there are some differences between the Helping Hand and the recommendations by Pikulski and Templeton, there is no disputing the notion that strategies for utilizing word recognition skills during reading can and should be taught so that students know what to do when they encounter an unknown word.

The Helping Hand: An Aid for Word Recognition

The Helping Hand is a tool that helps readers remember what to do when they encounter words that are not immediately recognizable. There are five parts to the Helping Hand:

1. Frame It
2. Phonic It
3. Bleep It
4. Part It
5. Consult It

Each of the parts uses a different word recognition strategy. The Helping Hand lists the strategies in an order that allows comprehension to occur. The following directions can be used with students.

Frame It

1. Read the sentence.
2. Place one thumb on each side of the unknown word.
3. Look for letter combinations that are familiar.
4. Look at the shape of the word for distinguishable features (letters above and below line).
5. Does the shape of the word look like any other word you know?
6. Do you know the word? If so, keep reading. If not, go to the next step.

Frame It works if the word is in the student's reading meaning vocabulary but not in the sight word vocabulary. It provides a way to isolate the word for additional recognition.

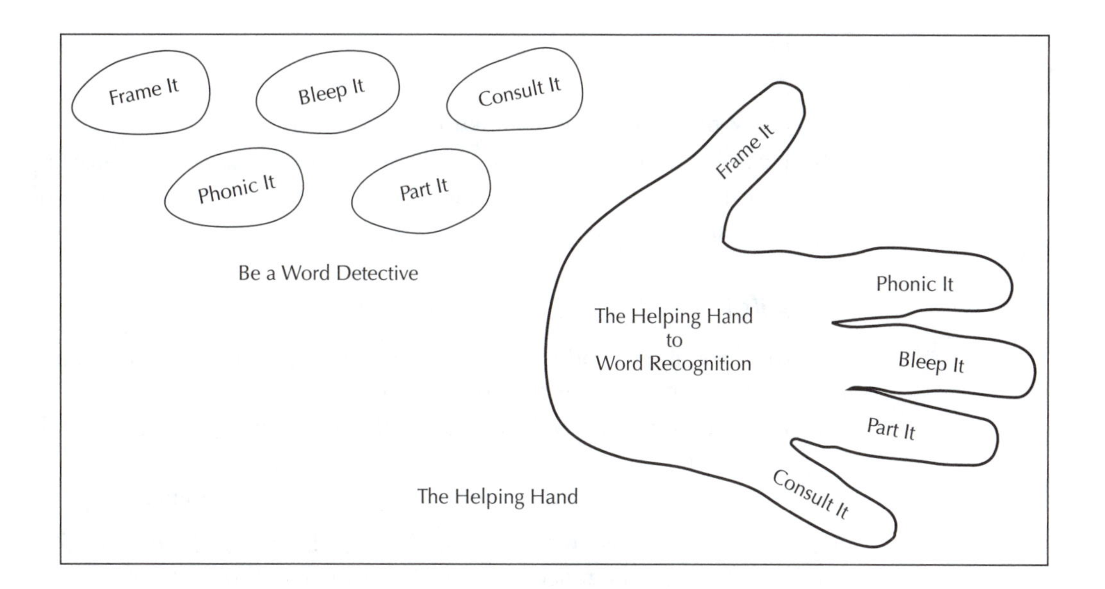

Phonic It

1. Break the unknown word into smaller pieces, called syllables. They are recognized by the vowel sounds.
2. Try to match these sounds with a word you already know.
3. Compare the sounds with language you have heard to find the unknown word.
4. Is the word one you have already heard? If so, continue reading. If not, go to the next step.

   Phonic It works if the word is in the student's listening vocabulary but not in the sight vocabulary or meaning vocabulary.

Bleep It

1. Read the sentence.
2. Determine if the unknown word is necessary for comprehension. Example: The mischievous children devised a clever *jape* to play on their teacher.
3. Reread the sentence, replacing the unknown word with "bleep."
4. Determine the function of the unknown word. What does it do? What part of speech is it?
5. Look for other key words that seem to be related to the unknown word. What is the relationship between or among the key words?
6. Reread the sentence and insert a word for the unknown word. Example: trick, jest, joke
7. If the sentence makes sense, continue with your reading. If not, go to the next step.

   Bleep It will work if the word is not in the meaning or sight vocabulary.

Part It

1. Read the sentence.
2. Identify the largest part of the word (root word).
3. Link that part with words you already know.
4. Look at prefixes (beginning parts) and suffixes (ending parts).
5. Think of words you already know that have these same parts.

6. Example: (bio)graphy
   life written
7. Guess the meaning of the unknown word.
8. Does the meaning make sense in the sentence? If so, read on. If not, go to the next step. Part It will work if the meaning of the word is not in the meaning vocabulary or sight vocabulary.

Consult It

1. After you use the other steps, you may ask a classmate, a teacher, and/or a parent for help in identifying the unknown word.
2. If no one is available to help, use the dictionary or glossary to locate the word, pronunciation, and meaning.
3. Apply the dictionary meaning to the context of the sentence.

Teachers should feel free to modify the Helping Hand for older readers. Changing the Helping Hand to Keys to Unlocking New Words or Be a Word Detective may be more appropriate for older readers. It should also be noted that the specific order of the elements within the strategy may change depending on the student's strengths.

Integrated Processing

Pemberton (2003) developed Integrated Processing, a strategy that can be used to help readers who are hesitant to attempt long words, omit the middle or end of long words, or sound out and blend words without correcting their errors. The objective of the strategy is for the student to read aloud a passage at grade level, correctly processing all the polysyllabic words. For a student to be successful with Integrated Processing, s/he must have an adequate listening vocabulary, a basic sight vocabulary, knowledge about reading consonants, and knowledge of at least one way to produce each vowel.

Implementing the strategy involves reading an expository text orally. When the student encounters an unknown word, s/he draws a line below successive parts of the word, saying each part as it is underlined without lifting the pencil from the paper. The student repeats the parts of the unknown word more quickly. Then, s/he returns to the beginning of the sentence and rereads it. The student then checks the unknown word to determine whether it makes sense in the sentence. When the word has been sounded out and has meaning, the student moves on to the next sentence. Teaching this method involves a number of steps.

1. Present the student with sentences that contain unknown words.
2. Using a pencil, draw a line below successive parts of the word, saying each part as it is underlined. Do not lift the pencil, but pause in the marking while saying each segment of the word. Repeat the procedure, saying the word parts more rapidly.
3. Have the student imitate the procedure. Then ask the student to read the sentence to determine whether the syllables s/he said made a meaningful word that fits into the sentence.
4. Repeat step 2 with new words. Ask the student to imitate the procedure and adjust the approximated pronunciation so that it sounds like a real word. The student should read the sentence to determine whether the adjusted word makes sense in the sentence.
5. Repeat step 2. Students should imitate the procedure, determining if the pronunciation is a real word, and then read the sentence to help determine the pronunciation of the word.
6. Give the pencil to the student. Ask the student to underline and pronounce parts of a new word. Allow the student to divide the word in whatever manner s/he chooses. Wait for the child to complete the process.
7. Repeat with a new word.
8. Continue to repeat.

The student should practice daily so that s/he uses the strategy automatically when encountering an unknown word. Some additional recommendations by Pemberton include keeping a record of the student's performance, withholding praise until the student checks to determine if the word makes sense, pronouncing the word for the student if the student makes more than two unsuccessful attempts, requiring the student to read for 10 to 15 minutes, and beginning the next session by rereading from the previous session.

DISSECT

Lenz and Hughes (1990) developed a word recognition strategy to help struggling readers decode and identify unknown words. According to Lenz and Hughes, there are seven steps to the word recognition strategy, which can be remembered through the mnemonic, DISSECT.

Step 1. Discover the context. Step 1 requires the student to skip the unknown word and read through to the end of the sentence. Then, the student uses the meaning of the sentence to guess what word fits best. If the guess does not match the unknown word, the student moves on to the next step.

Step 2. Isolate the prefix. In Step 2, the student looks for a pronounceable sequence of letters at the beginning of the word (prefix). If a prefix is identified, the student draws a box around it to separate it visually from the rest of the word (for example, in the word *infiltrated*, the *in* would be boxed).

Step 3. Separate the suffix. Similar to Step 2, the student boxes off the suffix if there is one (in the word *infiltrated*, the *ed* would be boxed).

Step 4. Say the stem. In Step 4, the student attempts to pronounce the stem (*filtrat*). If the stem cannot be named, the student moves on to Step 5.

Step 5. Examine the stem. In Step 5, the student divides the stem into small, pronounceable word parts using "the Rules of Twos and Threes" (Lenz & Hughes, 1990, p. 151):

> *Rule 1:* If the stem or part of the stem begins with a vowel, separate the first two letters; if it begins with a consonant, separate the first three letters; continue to apply this rule until the end of the stem is reached (*ac\tiv*, *ac\hie\ve*).
>
> *Rule 2:* If you can't make sense of the stem after using Rule 1, take off the first letter of the stem and use Rule 1 for the remainder of the stem (*a\chi\ev\e*).
>
> *Rule 3:* When two vowels are together, use what you know about pronunciation (for example, pronounce two adjacent vowels as a single sound, and remember that a final *e* following a consonant is usually silent) and try the different possibilities (*a\chiv*, *a\chev*).

Step 6. Check with a teacher, parent, or other student.

Step 7. Try the dictionary. In the final step, the student looks up the word, uses the information to pronounce the word, and reads the definition if the word is unknown.

Lenz and Hughes (1990) do not recommend this strategy for every word; rather, they suggest it should be used only for words that are critical to understanding the text.

Helping Students Develop Flexibility

Once students familiarize themselves with the procedural steps of one of the strategies, they must learn that often a different sequence will be needed to identify a word. For example, context may be used after the word has been partially determined using phonics to make certain the word makes sense in the sentence.

While a series of steps, such as those previously outlined, is useful, the rapid recognition of words, including those met for the first time, is essential so that meaning is not lost. The good reader sifts the options available when meeting an unknown word, selecting one, two, or more in rapid succession. This is what all students must essentially learn to do: *understand the options available and make use of the best one(s) when decoding unrecognizable words.*

Since no single word recognition strategy is adequate, students who rely exclusively on one must be taught to use other strategies. The teacher who wishes to help students become more flexible as they encounter unknown words should do the following:

1. Encourage the student to try, to think, to reason, and to solve word recognition dilemmas.
2. Encourage the expansion of sight vocabulary lists.
3. Obtain insight into the student's sequence of word recognition behaviors by having him/her say precisely what s/he does when s/he meets an unfamiliar word (a student think-aloud).
4. Help the student to develop a procedure for unlocking words and to understand that there are alternative approaches and that sometimes it is a case of trial and error.

Stahl, Duffy-Hester, and Stahl (1998) identified the characteristics of exemplary word recognition instruction:

1. It does not require the teaching of rules, the use of worksheets and/or the use of workbooks.
2. It does not have to be boring or tedious.
3. It depends on direct teacher instruction, followed immediately by student use in authentic reading of connected texts.
4. It provides practice in reading words through (a) reading words in connected text; (b) reading words in isolation through word bank activities, games, and activities; and (c) writing words through dictation and through invented or phonemic spelling.
5. It leads to automatic word recognition.
6. It should be done quickly and with minimal analysis.

Assessing Word Recognition Skill

Samuels (2002) has identified three basic word recognition skill levels that are useful in determining a student's level of expertise with word recognition. The first level is the "nonaccurate stage." The student cannot accurately identify words that are encountered during reading and cannot use word recognition skills during reading.

The second stage is the "accurate but not automatic stage." At this level, the child is able to use his/her word recognition skills when an unknown word is encountered while reading; however, the student is not very quick at it. The child recognizes some words as sight words. Samuels says that at this stage, oral reading is characterized as slow and laborious. Word recognition behaviors are applied accurately; however, they are not automatic.

The final stage is "accurate and automatic," or fluent. Students can read with accuracy and speed. They can also read with expression. They can recognize words and comprehend simultaneously. At this stage, mature reading behaviors are evident.

Quick Self-Check 1

1. What strategies may be used to unlock the pronunciation and meaning of an unknown word?
2. Why is it important that students develop a strategy to use when they come to words they don't know?
3. How can students improve their use of one of the three strategies mentioned in the chapter?
4. What are the three word recognition skill levels identified by Samuels?

Developing Fluency

Some students appear to have word recognition skills when tested on isolated words but seem unable to integrate them with any degree of fluency. In some cases the reading is too slow and labored, lacking the automaticity that must take place if readers are to enjoy and comprehend what they read. Reutzel and Hollingsworth (1993) claim:

> The development of reading fluency has been a neglected part of reading instruction despite the fact that many reading authorities consider it to be an important part of the reading curriculum. In recent years, researchers have turned increasing attention toward unraveling the complexities of how reading fluency is developed and how it can be properly assessed. (p. 325)

Rasinski and Padak (2001) concur: "Fluency is a bridge between word recognition and comprehension. Unfortunately, it is a bridge that is often not sufficiently dealt with in the reading curriculum" (p. 172).

The National Reading Panel (NICHHD, 2000) defines fluent readers as those who ". . . are able to read orally with speed, accuracy, and proper expression" (p. 3–1). The panel explains that fluency depends upon well-developed word recognition skills and develops from reading practice. Bear (2001) adds that fluency takes place at two levels: the phrase level and the word level. At the phrase level, fluency includes reading rate and ease of grouping words. At the word level, fluency includes recognizing words and spelling patterns quickly enough to read for sense and purpose.

The National Reading Panel identified two approaches to reading fluency. The explicit approach provides guidance from the teacher but the implicit approach allows and encourages ". . . students to read extensively on their own or with minimal guidance and feedback" (p. 3–1). Such programs include Sustained Silent Reading (SSR), Drop Everything and Read (DEAR), Accelerated Reader (AR), and various other motivational and incentive-based programs.

Findings from the National Reading Panel Report (NICHHD, 2000) include:

1. Repeated oral reading procedures had a significant positive impact on word recognition, fluency, and comprehension.
2. Research has not yet demonstrated the benefits of encouraging children to read on their own as an effective method for increasing reading fluency.
3. Fluency instruction was appropriate for children in grades two through high school, particularly for struggling readers.
4. Fluency instruction was equally effective for good and poor readers.

Allington (1983) identified six differences between fluent readers and non-fluent readers. These include:

- ❐ Fluent oral readers have models at home and they have learned that fluent reading is the goal of oral reading.
- ❐ Fluent readers are encouraged to focus on elements of expression but poor readers focus on word recognition.
- ❐ Fluent readers have more opportunities for practicing reading.
- ❐ Fluent readers read text at their instructional or independent levels while poor readers are reading texts at their frustration level.
- ❐ Fluent readers have more time to read silently, which means they practice more.
- ❐ Fluent readers realize the goal is accuracy and meaningful expression.

Fluency develops and improves as a result of regular and multiple opportunities to practice reading with a high degree of success. When fluency is the targeted skill, students should be reading text that is at their independent level (95% accuracy, missing only 1 in 20 running words). Otherwise, they will struggle with the words and will not be able to concentrate on working toward becoming a fluent reader. The National Institute for Literacy (1971) recommended that students should be provided with instruction and practice in fluency as they read connected text.

One technique to improve fluency is for students to read passages repeatedly with teacher guidance. Students can read and reread a short passage a certain number of times or until a predetermined level of fluency is reached. Teachers can also use audiotapes, tutors, peers, and other technologies to provide models of fluent reading thereby helping students to achieve a desired level of fluency. In addition, reading aloud daily provides students with models of fluent reading.

Fluency Development Lesson

Rasinski, Padak, Linek, and Sturtevant (1994) developed a 10 to 15 minute lesson plan format for working to develop fluency. The steps to the lesson include the following:

1. Students are given a 50 to 150 word text to read. The teacher introduces the text and invites predictions.
2. The teacher models by reading orally to the whole class while students follow along silently with their own copies of the text.
3. The teacher leads the class in a discussion of the text, in addition to a discussion of the oral reading, which includes the rate, pitch, phrasing, and intonation during reading.
4. The class reads the text chorally several times with the teacher.
5. Children are paired and read the text orally several times to their partners, who provide feedback on the other's reading performance. Then the pairs are switched and the process is repeated.
6. The teacher invites pairs or individuals to read for the class.
7. The students and teacher select words from the text to study.
8. Students take the text home to read to their parents.

The Imitative Method

Teachers engage in creative activities to encourage older readers to develop automaticity. To improve fluency, Cunningham (1979) suggested a procedure called the "imitative method," first suggested by Carol Chomsky (1976), a noted linguist.

Briefly, the teacher locates an interesting short story at the student's independent reading level and records it on cassette in an appealing and dramatic form. While listening to the tape, the student follows along, reading the story from the book until it is mastered. Patience is required of both the teacher and the student because it may be several weeks before true reading mastery of the story occurs. When it does, the student is encouraged to read the story to parents, friends, and classmates. The story has not been memorized, and the student will need the book, but elements of memorization are certainly present. Nevertheless, this approach to reading enables the student to have the experience of successful, effective, fluent reading for perhaps the first time.

Neurological Impress Method

Heckelman (1969) developed the Neurological Impress Method to assist students with fluent reading. A selection at the student's independent level is given to the student to read silently. The teacher sits behind the child, practically reading into the student's ear. The student and teacher read the material together orally; the child follows the teacher's voice with the teacher reading louder and faster than the student to set the pace. The teacher also moves his/her hand along under the lines being read. Upon rereading the story, the teacher reads softer and allows the child to take control of the reading while helping the child run his/her hand under the line of text. The name of the procedure suggests what the teacher is attempting to do—to impress the words on the mind of the student through repeated practice.

A modified method is suggested by Eldredge and Butterfield (1986) whereby slower students can be assigned to read with more skilled students. Students sit side by side, reading aloud from one book. The faster reader reads at her/his normal rate touching each word as s/he reads it. The slower student is instructed to follow and repeat each word as quickly as possible. As the slower reader gains skill, the more rapid reader reads silently, supplying words only when needed.

Repeated Readings

Another procedure, originated by Samuels (1979), involves a method called "repeated readings." Students are given a selection at their independent level or may choose a selection of about 100 words and are then asked to read it multiple times to increase accuracy and speed. Samuels set 85 words per minute as the target speed. Samuels does not require error-free reading because he believes that would inhibit some readers. Each time the child reads, s/he should read at a faster pace and should mispronounce fewer words. The story is repeated until the child is able to read fluently and without errors. The teacher may use this method in a group, listening to one student while others are practicing. Again, the idea is to improve the rate and give the student the feeling of fluency for perhaps the first time.

Two modifications to the procedure are suggested by Lauritzen (1982). These lie in the choice of materials and in the initial method of presentation. Materials chosen should have a singing quality that children love with a definite rhyme, strong rhythm, identifiable sequence, and oral literature patterns. These are all prevalent in folk literature such as Henny Penny, the Gingerbread Boy, and the Old Woman and Her Shoe. First, the teacher reads the entire selection while the children follow the print, either from a book or from a copy on a chart or board. Then the children echo-read a line, a sentence, or a paragraph with length determined by the structure of the poem or story. Eventually the teacher and children read the entire selection in unison. The children may read individually, in pairs, or in small groups as many times as they wish. Because the teacher models fluent reading from the beginning, the children imitate it. Difficult material is mastered, and children can be motivated to improve their reading because of success.

Another modification of repeated readings is suggested by Swaby (1982) in what is called an *instructional* repeated reading program. Here a teacher, aide, or other adult works individually with a child. A short passage written at the student's instructional level is chosen. The passage is divided into three or four paragraphs or short segments. If the student has previously read the materials (which is preferred), s/he should be reminded of the major concepts. If the material is new, the major concepts are discussed briefly. A segment of a passage is read at a time, and word errors made by the student are recorded. The segment is read back to the student to see if errors are recognized. Errors are analyzed to determine whether they were errors of phonics, structure, or context. Often the word choice is poor; for example, a student might read *chain* for *chair*. The semantic clues that make *chain* a poor choice are highlighted so that the student learns to recognize the type of errors made—phonetic, structural, or contextual—to avoid them in the future.

A final modification from the original work by Samuels involves the number of times a student reads the material. One suggestion is that the passage be read repeatedly a total of four times (Rashotte & Torgesen, 1985). Another recommendation is that the student purposefully rereads the passage until a rate of at least 85 to 100 words per minute is achieved (Dowhower, 1987; Herman, 1985).

Student Sharing

Many teachers advocate co-authoring and reading as a method of improving fluency. This method has many variations. Davis (1989) pairs her first grade class with fifth graders who act as teachers as the two create books together. Kemp (1990), a second grade teacher, works with a fourth grade teacher. The two have their students meet one day a week for 30 minutes to read and enjoy books. A guideline for older students is to allow wait time before they help with a difficult word. Visser (1991), appreciating the importance of sports, persuaded a high school football team to come to her class to read to her students. Juel (1991b) asked university athletes to wear their football jerseys, come to class, and read aloud to elementary school classes. The program benefited the students, who saw reading as a positive experience for some of their idols, and it also benefited the athletes, who became enthusiastic about reading.

Choral Reading

Sometimes called unison reading, this strategy has the teacher and students reading the text together. Choral reading involves repeated readings of a passage, which provides practice in oral reading. Rhymes, poetry, lyrics, and short stories are ideal for choral reading. The teacher's role is to set the pace and model proper pronunciation. The less fluent students learn expression as they read along with skilled readers. Basic guidelines include keeping the passage short, choosing material on grade level, and selecting a passage that is fun and can come alive during reading. Before reading the passage orally as a class, new vocabulary words should be taught and children should have an opportunity to read the passage silently. This strategy may be altered by dividing the class into halves, thirds, or quarters with each section reading a different part. Readers may vary the tone and the volume and speed at which they are reading. Teachers should feel free to experiment with variations appropriate to the classroom setting.

Echo Reading

Fluency is modeled when students immediately echo a phrase read by a skilled reader, who may or may not be the teacher. Short phrases are replaced with full sentences as the students' skills increase. Predictable text, plays, poems, and small portions of a selection are appropriate. Students are told that they should echo the way the reader reads the passage, including reading with similar expression.

Paired or Partner Reading

A capable reader and a student who is having difficulty reading are paired or partnered together. One of the partners reads the first page or paragraph, and then the other partner reads the next page or paragraph. Learners decide for themselves when to read without help, which gives them confidence to try reading without fear of failure.

Assisted Reading

Richek and McTague (1988) have developed another type of reading to facilitate fluency called assisted reading. Richek and McTague developed this strategy for use with struggling second- and third-grade readers. In addition to introducing the book in an appropriate fashion, the goal is to read the story repeatedly. During the first reading, children listen to the story. During subsequent readings, it is recommended that the teacher stop reading when s/he comes to predictable words and let the children read them. Next, the children read the story by themselves, followed by the children dictating their own version of the story. The next day the procedure is repeated, and it continues until the story ends. Depending on the text selection, the children, and the goal of the lesson, the readings could take one day or multiple days.

Readers' Theater

Readers' Theater allows students to turn any piece of literature into a script. Students practice reading script parts and then present the script to an audience. The keys to implementation include no full memorization, no full costume (partial may be used), and no full stage sets (minimal or simple may be used). Teachers should choose texts that are interesting and that have several characters. Students should be given time to rehearse, read, and perform in class.

Technology-Assisted Reading

One way that students can listen to and practice fluent reading is to read along in their books as they listen to an audiotape recording of the book by a fluent reader (Chomsky, 1978). CD-ROM interactive stories, which can also be used to increase fluency are useful for intermediate grade struggling readers. In one-computer classrooms, interactive stories can be read with partners. While reading interactive stories, students can mouse click on a word in the story and the word will be pronounced.

Shared Reading

With shared reading (Holdaway, 1979), the teacher generally uses a predictable big book to practice fluency and expression. The big book with text and pictures allows children to focus their attention on the text, pictures, and other visuals that may be included in the selection. To begin, the teacher introduces the book to the children by reading the title as well as the names of the author(s) and illustrator(s) while pointing to the print. The pictures are discussed with the children. Then the teacher reads the story to the children while pointing to the words so the children can see. This draws children's attention to the print and models early reading behaviors such as moving from left to right and matching words and sounds. After several readings, the teacher invites the children to read the story as a whole group from the big book and then with partners working with little books. The children's memory of the story and the pictures guide their reading of the text.

Evaluating Fluency

In 1995, the National Assessment of Educational Progress (Allen, McClellan, & Stoeckel, 2005) set out to assess the oral reading fluency of fourth-grade students. The NAEP definition of fluency included three elements: (a) grouping or phrasing of words revealed through intonation, stress, and pauses; (b) adherence to author's syntax; and (c) expressiveness of the oral reading—interjecting a sense of feeling, anticipation, or characterization. Accuracy (students' misread words), and rate (words per minute) were also assessed.

Of the fourth-grade students tested, 55% read at levels 3 and 4. Only 13% of the students were at level 4 even though they had read the passage silently twice. Students who read more fluently read the passage considerably faster than those who read less fluently. The more fluent readers were, on average, somewhat more accurate than the less fluent readers. The criteria were as follows:

Level 1 Reads primarily word-by-word. Occasional two-word or three-word phrases may occur, but these are infrequent and/or they do not preserve meaningful syntax.

Level 2 Reads primarily in two-word phrases with some three- or four-word groupings. Some word-by-word reading may be present. Word groupings may seem awkward and unrelated to larger context of sentence or passage.

Level 3 Reads primarily in three- or four-word phrase groups. Some smaller groupings may be present. However, the majority of phrasing seems appropriate and preserves the syntax of the author. Little or no expressive interpretation is present.

Level 4 Reads primarily in larger, meaningful phrase groups. Although some regressions, repetitions, and deviations from text may be present, these do not appear to detract from the overall structure of the story. Preservation of the author's syntax is consistent. Some or most of the story is read with expressive interpretation.

Rasinski and Padak (2004, p. 111) provide some approximate benchmarks from which to judge students' reading rates.

Grade	Fall	Winter	Spring
1			60
2	53	78	94
3	79	93	114
4	99	112	118
5	105	118	128
6	115	132	145
7	147	158	167
8	156	167	171

Additional informal measures can be used to assess fluency such as informal reading inventories, miscue analysis, running records, and reading rate measures.

Although there are many ways of measuring reading rate (instructional rate, independent rate, silent rate, oral rate, etc.), the calculations are basically the same; it is the interpretation of the information that changes and the accuracy with which one can compare a student's progress to existing levels of performance. One such example includes recording the number of words in the passage and dividing that by the number of seconds it took to read the passage. This quotient is multiplied by 60 to determine the reading rate in words per minute. Let's say that the teacher has selected a passage of 150 words. It took LeeAnn 40 seconds to read the passage.

$$150 \text{ words}/40 \text{ seconds} = 3.75 \text{ words/second} \times 60 \text{ seconds}/1 \text{ minute}$$

$$\text{LeeAnn's reading rate} = 225 \text{ words per minute.}$$

Now, let's calculate the words correct per minute. Using the information from the same problem, we can calculate LeeAnn's accuracy rate. If she made 10 errors/40 seconds = .25 errors/second × 60 seconds/minute

$$.25 \times 60 = 15 \text{ errors per minute}$$

Then subtract the number of errors from the words read:

$$225 \text{ words per minute} - 15 \text{ errors per minute} = 210 \text{ words correct per minute}$$

Another way to calculate this is to find the number of CORRECT words read (150 − 10 = 140). Then divide by the number of seconds (140/40) to get the correct words per second (3.5). Multiply 3.5 by 60 seconds to get 210 words correct per minute. The results obtained could be compared with standards like those shown in this chapter. Progress charts could be made to keep a running record of the student's performance with oral reading accuracy.

Quick Self-Check 2

1. What is the basic difference between explicit fluency instruction and implicit fluency instruction?
2. When students are practicing fluency, reading materials should be at their independent, instructional, or frustration level?
3. We might generalize that a reader becomes more fluent by being provided a variety of different opportunities to ____________.

Guidelines for Word Recognition Materials and Activities

The commercial market is inundated with materials to teach basic sight words, structural analysis, use of context, and dictionary skills (see Appendix F for an evaluation form). A few questions teachers should ask about these materials (Cunningham, 1981; Spiegel, 1990) follow:

1. Will the materials assist in meeting your reading goals? They should be an integral part of your reading program.
2. Are the materials flexible? Good materials should meet a variety of instructional goals.
3. Do they teach what they say they do? Close perusal often shows that the skill is not what it is purported to be.
4. Are the skills taught important to reading? Knowing that a word is a noun and not a verb may be important to language instruction, but that knowledge does not help readers identify words or get meaning from them.
5. Are the skills taught appropriate for the level of the readers with whom you intend to use the material? Not all skills are important at all levels. Skill emphasis shifts from word identification, to vocabulary and comprehension. If the skills are important, are they important to your particular level of readers?
6. Are skills taught at the application level? Do students actually apply the skills or is it expected they will automatically transfer the knowledge to real reading? You may still purchase the materials but recognize you need to provide the application practice and assessment.
7. Are the materials intrinsically motivating? Avoid boredom. You may still have to use some extrinsic motivation to get students to start working on a piece of material, but if it is interesting, worthwhile, and varied, students' intrinsic motivation system takes over.
8. What is the ratio of time spent actually reading? Materials that have students spend twice as much time doing things other than actual reading should get a very low rating.
9. Is there bias or stereotyping? Note the questions and illustrations.
10. Is the material worth the cost? How durable and sturdy is the material? How many children's needs will it help meet? Are there less expensive materials that meet the same instructional criteria?

Do-it-Yourself Materials and Activities

Using Cereal Boxes

Cereal boxes may be one of the most overlooked and underused materials. Almost everyone reads cereal boxes at the breakfast table—children are also eager to find the free offerings. These boxes are easy to obtain, and the variety can be interesting. Students can use different boxes for the same lesson, a change from the usual way. Adapt the following ideas to any grade level.

Objective: Word Recognition

1. *Word recognition.* How many words do you see on the box that you recognize? Write these words.
2. *Suffixes.* Find words that have these endings: *s, es, ing, ed.* Find other suffixed words.

Sports Names

Objective: Word Recognition

Read and discuss with students the following examples of sports team tongue twisters:

The Pittsburgh Penguins pretended to have a particular pathway to the park.

The Chicago Cubs constantly came close to confessing the crisis.

Then direct the students to use the following list of team nicknames to write sentences containing their own creative tongue twisters:

List of Team Nicknames

Hockey	Baseball	Basketball
Philadelphia Flyers	Philadelphia Phillies	New York Knicks
Pittsburgh Penguins	Pittsburgh Pirates	New Jersey Nets
Boston Bruins	New York Yankees	Los Angeles Lakers

Football

Buffalo Bills

Kansas City Chiefs

San Francisco 49ers

Wordsplash

Write words that tell about you on the lines. Add other words or pictures in any spaces. Trade wordsplashes with a classmate. Take turns using your wordsplash to get to know one another.

Favorite Movies	Greatest Moments	Favorite TV shows
____________	____________	____________
____________	____________	____________
____________	____________	____________
Best Books I've Read	**Best Vacation**	**Special Talents**
____________	____________	____________
____________	____________	____________
____________	____________	____________

Adapted from the September issue of Learning 1991, Copyright The Education Center®, 1607 Battleground Ave., Greensboro, NC 27408.

TABLE 10.1 Pros and Cons of Teacher-Produced and Commercially Produced Materials

TEACHER-PRODUCED		COMMERCIAL	
Pros	**Cons**	**Pros**	**Cons**
1) Can be designed to meet specific needs and interests of target group.	1) Durability of the constructed material is sometimes questionable.	1) Material can be geared to specific needs of children.	1) May use a too difficult vocabulary or a different approach to skill development.
2) Use an appropriate vocabulary and level of difficulty.	2) Constant remaking or mending may be required.	2) Material is durable, legible, and colorful. Looks professional and may be long-lasting.	2) May be limited in usefulness.
3) Children can be actively involved in game production.	3) Construction must reflect high standards of neatness and legibility.	3) A wide variety is already available in the marketplace.	3) Require much time to locate, evaluate, purchase.
4) Kits and activity game files can be expanded as needed.	4) Directions must be carefully thought out.	4) If teacher time is a factor, may be less expensive than "homemade."	4) Lost items are expensive to replace.
5) Favorite "old" games can be easily adapted.	5) Construction sometimes requires more time than is warranted.		5) Frequently considered too expensive.
6) Materials are sometimes more economical.	6) Easily available commercial materials are sometimes more economical.		

A group of pre-service teachers (Snyder, 1981) experimented with producing reading games for fourth to sixth grade children, evaluating whether or not the activities were worthwhile. Their final consensus was that, while purposeful activities and games have a place in the school environment, the "greatest game in town" is still book reading.

There are many advantages and disadvantages to both teacher-produced and commercially produced materials. Table 10.1 illustrates both the advantages and the disadvantages.

Technology

Technology has the potential to provide students with significant assistance in learning word recognition skills. From software to the Internet, technology provides learning opportunities beyond what we can imagine. There are multiple benefits from all the advancements brought about by the computer age; however, there are also some pitfalls. Using the technologies requires a careful and critical evaluation of materials. Understanding some basics about the materials that are available can help teachers make informed decisions about the resources at their disposal.

Type I Software

Software today can be identified as one of two types. Type I software tends to support more traditional teaching:

- ❒ Skills have been predetermined by the software developers.
- ❒ There is limited potential interaction between learner and machine.
- ❒ It involves a format with few variations.

Examples would include most drill and practice, tutorial, and assessment uses. Most computer programs involving word recognition skills are Type I. Some of these are designed to move in short, repetitive steps in case the student is having difficulty. Other programs switch to longer, faster steps as students easily grasp the materials. The majority of programs require that materials at each level be mastered before proceeding. The student is often rewarded with stars, pluses, or printed or audio recognition after each response.

Most available software programs in word recognition are found in these areas: the alphabet, consonants, blends, and vowels. Programs that teach the consonant and vowel digraphs and the diphthongs are more limited. Programs to teach the basic sight words, context clues, and syllabication rules are also available but, like digraphs and diphthongs, are more limited in number. In the area of structural analysis, many programs are available to teach the inflectional endings and contractions. Most prominent are programs with affixes. Programs that teach dictionary skills are also available.

Type II Software

Type II software tends to emphasize a more cognitive approach:

- ❐ It is controlled by the user, rather than the software developer.
- ❐ It involves a highly varied (sometimes unlimited) repertoire of acceptable responses between learner and machine.
- ❐ It often requires days or weeks of use before all the software's capabilities have been observed.

Type II examples include simulations, problem-solving, graphics, writing aids, and word processing.

After some educators criticized software for lacking follow-up reading application, newer software was developed to provide for greater student involvement. Newer programs allow students to actively take part as they interact with stories, adding their own text to them. Programs also exist that enable students to create their own "big books."

Story Software

Books and reading passages are available as software and on the Internet for students to use to improve their reading. Popular children's books are now available as electronic books. Graphics, animation, and voice make electronic books a favorite among children. Some books allow readers to choose with or without voice; others provide the opportunity to click on a word and learn the meaning while hearing the word pronounced.

Websites

The Internet has provided teachers and students with a whole new world of resources for reading instruction. Websites provide opportunities for getting assistance, enriching instruction, sharing ideas, explaining processes, providing resources, and communicating with others around the country and around the world (see Appendix F for sample evaluation tools).

While the merits of computer-assisted instruction are still debated, the use of computers in the classroom continues to grow. This is commendable; however a great investment of time and money is needed in many areas of the country that lack computers for students and adequate computer training for teachers. The result is that many American children are not acquiring the necessary computer and technological skills they will need in the coming century.

Quick Self-Check 3

1. What are some major considerations in selecting materials for teaching word recognition skills?
2. What is the difference between Type I and Type II software?

Summary

The two major components of the reading process are word recognition and comprehension. According to the National Reading Panel (NICHHD, 2000)

> . . . one process involves learning to convert the letters into recognizable words. The other involves comprehending the meaning of the print. When children attain reading skill, they learn to perform both of these processes so that their attention and thought are focused on the meaning of the text. . . . (p. 2–106)

This chapter focused specifically on using the word recognition tools (sight words, phonics, context, structural analysis, and dictionary) collaboratively to help with the pronunciation and meaning of unknown words. Using a combined approach enhances the probability that the student will be able to determine the meaning of an unknown word. Because word recognition involves both meaning and pronunciation (Rubin, 2002), children must be instructed to use strategies collaboratively if they are to obtain an approximate pronunciation and an approximate meaning for unknown words. A heavy emphasis on one strategy over another (phonics over context, for example) will be detrimental to students' success in word recognition and, more importantly, to their success in comprehension.

The chapter also focused on fluency, which is one of the most important considerations while reading, but one of the least taught. Obviously, the more fluent the child is in reading a passage, the more likely the child is to gain meaning from the text. Fluency instruction must be planned, not accidental or incidental, if students are to become proficient readers!

Many strategies, techniques, and materials are available to help teach word recognition skills that, when combined with appropriate instruction, will yield fluent readers who focus their energies on comprehending what they read.

Review Questions

1. In this chapter, we refer to a five-step word recognition strategy known as The Helping Hand. We also suggested this strategy could be Keys to Unlocking New Words or Be a Word Detective. Can you think of another thematic approach to this strategy?
2. With which of the three strategies (Helping Hand, Integrated Processing, DISSECT) do you feel most comfortable? Why?
3. Fluency may be approached explicitly or implicitly. Can you distinguish between the two? Can you provide examples of each?
4. Using the methods for teaching fluency, which do you believe are more applicable in one-on-one settings, in small groups, and for the whole class?
5. What do you believe are the most important considerations when selecting materials for teaching word recognition?
6. What materials are available via the Internet? You should do a search to find out what type of activities and programs are available for teaching word recognition and fluency.

Appendix A

Answers to Quick Self-Checks

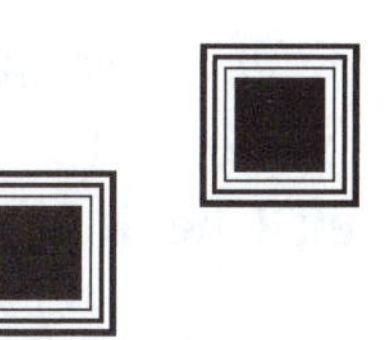

Chapter 1

Self-Check 1

1. They allowed teachers to focus on the phonic method, the word method, the alphabet method, or a combination.
2. Initial Teaching Alphabet, Linguistic Approach, Words in Color, Utility of Phonics Generalizations, First Grade Studies, The Great Debate.
3. *Preventing Reading Difficulties in Young Children, Report of the National Reading Panel*

Self-Check 2

1. Not all children learn at the same rate; provides benchmarks from which to evaluate student performance and growth
2. Scientifically based uses rigorous, systematic, and objective procedures to obtain knowledge relevant to reading development, reading instruction, and reading difficulties; evidence-based reading instruction means that a program, strategy, or technique has a record of success.

Chapter 2

Self-Check 1

1. Generally they decode as the soft sound when they follow the vowels *e*, *i*, *y*.
2. Generally they decode as the hard sound when they follow the vowels *a*, *o*, *u*.
3. Answers will vary.
4. /s/ as in sat, /z/ as in his, and /sh/ as in sugar.
5. /ks/, /gz/, /z/, or no sound.

Self-Check 2

1. a. *ch*, /ch/, /k/, /sh/
   b. *gh*, /g/, /f/
   th, /th/, /th/
   wh, /w or hw/, /h/
   c. *ph*, /f/
   sh, /sh/

Self-Check 3

1. The first letter of each digraph is silent.
2. They encode one sound.
3. All follow a short vowel and usually come at the end of a word.

Self-Check 4

1. *r, l, s,* and *w*
2. *r, l, w*
3. *s*
4. *str, scr, spr, spl, shr, squ, thr*

Self-Check 5

1. *ct, ft, ld, lf, lk, lm, lp, lt, mp, nt, nd, nk, ng, pt, st, sk, sp, sm, st*
2. *nge, nce, nse, nch, tch*

Chapter 3

Self-Check 1

1. a. *u*, /oo/
   b. *a, o, u*. They are sometimes taught as sight words.
   c. It is similar to the sound of /uh/, and is usually heard in unaccented syllables.

Self-Check 2

1. English words do not end in the letter *v*.
2. A final vowel is needed to complete the final syllable; therefore, the first vowel remains long.
3. Final *e* gives *c* a soft sound.
4. Final *e* indicates the preceding vowel has a long sound.
5. Final *e* is present for historical reasons.

Self-Check 3

1. English words do not end with *i*. *Ai* and *ay* encode a long /a/ sound.
2. English words do not end with *u*. Au and aw encode the /a/ sound.
3. The sounds encoded by these graphemes do not vary.

Self-Check 4

1. *ee*
2. *ei*
3. *ea*
4. *ey*
5. *ie*
6. The e digraphs decode mainly as long *e* and sometimes as long *a*.

Self-Check 5

1. *ou*, /ow/ as in proud, /u/ as in touch, /o/ as in soul, /oo/ as in group, /ow/ and /u/
2. English words do not end with *i*.
3. *oa*, /o/
4. /ow/ as in cow, /o/ as in know
5. /oo/ as in moon, /oo/ as in book

Self-Check 6

1. At the beginning of words.
2. Yes, as a consonant; cry, as a vowel; play, as part of a digraph; royal, as part of a diphthong.
3. When it occurs after a vowel.
4. Vowel: cow, draw, now; consonant: water, winter, watch

Self-Check 7

1. All have the same sound
2. When the letter *w* precedes or, the *or* encodes the /er/ sound.
3. It has a variety of sounds.
4. *Ai* and *ee*. /Ar/ as in pair and /er/ as in peer.

Self-Check 8

1. No. George Bernard Shaw, who disliked the English writing system and offered money to anyone who would improve upon it, once suggested that *ghoti* should be read as fish. This is not so because the consonant digraph *gh* only decodes as /f/ at the end of some words, never at the beginning. The *o* in *ghoti*, he claimed, could decode as short /i/ as in *women*. The word *women* is the only instance in which *o* has this sound because the word has undergone spelling changes. Also, the *ti*, which he claimed would decode as /sh/ as in *nation*, is equally incorrect. The combination *ti* is rarely found at the end of words.

A foreign adopted word such as *spaghetti* is pronounced differently.

2. The combination *ti* is only pronounced as /sh/ when it appears in the middle of the word.

Chapter 4

Self-Check 1

1. Different font types yield different forms of letters, particularly with letter *a*, *g*, *q*.
2. Personalizes learning the alphabet, allows students to select their own key words to match the letters, makes the alphabet meaningful.

Self-Check 2

1. Phonological awareness is the overarching concept of which phonemic awareness is a part. Phonemic awareness is a phonological awareness task.
2. Phoneme isolation, phoneme identity, phoneme categorization, phoneme blending, phoneme segmentation, phoneme deletion.
3. Ch is the onset; *at* is the rime.
4. Blending requires putting sounds together into words; segmenting is taking words, sentences, or syllables apart; adding is putting sounds at the beginning of a word; deleting (elision) is taking letters from a word; and substituting is replacing part of a word with another letter/sound.

Chapter 5

Self-Check 1

1. Basic appear frequently in print; content specific are words that frequently appear within a content area; signal words cue readers to what is coming next.
2. Larger sight vocabularies mean more time on comprehension; some words cannot be decoded; may be able to use knowledge of sight words to decode other words.
3. High frequency, words in reader's oral vocabulary for which reader has meaning, words that can be identified through picture clues.

Self-Check 2

1. Reading interesting stories and articles; learn in context.
2. Repetition.
3. Timing—sight words are recognized automatically, no decoding is necessary.

Chapter 6

Self-Check 1

1. Some programs focus on rules, and others do not. Some programs focus on all letter combinations; others focus only on the most frequently occurring ones.
2. Single consonant letters with one sound, single consonant letters with more than one sound, digraphs, blends, special combinations.
3. Vowel divisions typically are single vowels (long, short, and special sounds), schwa, digraphs, and diphthongs.

Self-Check 2

1. a. Explicit: teacher gives the rules and gives examples.
   b. Implicit: teacher gives examples and students generate generalization.
   c. Analogy: teaching is conducted using word families such as *at* (at, bat, cat, fat, hat, mat, pat, rat, sat)
   d. Embedded phonics: phonics instruction evolves from the readings assigned.
2. Demonstration and immersion, attention to detail, guided practice, application and extension.

Chapter 7

Self-Check 1

1. Sometimes a compound word has the combined meaning of the two root words, but sometimes it does not.
2. Cyberspace, download, cranapple.

Self-Check 2

1. Prefixes are usually found before a base word or root; suffixes are placed after the base word or root. Prefixes usually change the word meaning but not the part of speech. Derivational suffixes may alter both.
2. Affix is the general term that includes both prefixes and suffixes.

3. Absorbed: recent, insist.
   Active: prepay, uncertain, dislike, impersonal.
4. Inflectional: singing, jumps, called.
   Derivational: foolish, cleverness, safely.
5. a. Drop the final e when adding an ending that begins with a vowel
   b. Double the final consonant when adding a suffix that begins with a vowel if the word
      i. ends in a single consonant
      ii. is preceded by a short vowel
      iii. is a one-syllable word
   c. Do not drop the letter *y* when adding *ing*.
6. Through wide and varied reading and through classroom discussion that clarifies affixed words.
7. As students move through the grades, they encounter more and more affixed words.

Self-Check 3

1. Closed syllable, open syllable, consonant-*le*, double vowel, vowel-consonant-*e*, *r*-controlled.
2. The syllable is the basic unit of pronunciation. Each syllable contains one and only one vowel sound.

Chapter 8

Self-Check 1

1. A semantic clue focuses on meaning, while a syntactic (syntax) clue focuses on grammatical aspects of a word, such as the part of speech.
2. Direct explanation or definition, experience, words in a series, restatements, contrast and comparison, inference, appositive or parenthetical, and synonym.

Self-Check 2

1. Older readers have more experience and more developed reasoning skills.
2. Context clues may be found before the word, after the word, or in the sentence before or after the unknown word.

Chapter 9

Self-Check 1

1. Location, pronunciation, and meaning.
2. Location.
3. In the front of the dictionary and at the bottom of each page.

Self-Check 2

1. Determine the importance of the word with respect to the passage.
2. Practice.

Chapter 10

Self-Check 1

1. Phonics, structural analysis, context clues, dictionary.
2. Because the more time spent decoding means less time spent comprehending.
3. Practice.
4. Non-accurate, accurate but not automatic, accurate and automatic.

Self-Check 2

1. Explicit involves teachers providing guidance. Implicit involves students reading on their own.
2. Independent level.
3. Read.

Self-Check 3

1. Are they age appropriate? Are they developmentally appropriate? Do they focus on the intended skills? Do they provide practice in the targeted areas?
2. Type I generally consists of drill and practice, tutorials, and assessment. Type II involves simulations, problem-solving, graphics, writing aids, and word processing.

Appendix B

Example Word Lists

Structural Elements Taught At Particular Levels

Initial Consonants

b	c	d	f	g	h	j	k	l	m
baby	cab	dark	face	gag	hail	jab	kangaroo	lace	mad
bag	cage	date	fact	gale	hall	jack	keep	lad	magic
ball	cake	day	fade	game	ham	jade	keg	ladder	magnet
band	call	den	fail	gang	hand	jam	kennel	lady	make
bang	can	dent	fan	garden	happy	jar	kettle	lake	man
bank	cane	desk	farm	gas	hat	jaw	key	lamb	map
bat	cap	dig	fat	gate	have	jeep	kick	lamp	mask
bed	car	dike	feed	gaze	hay	Jell-O	kid	land	match
bee	cat	dill	feet	goat	head	jet	kill	lap	mice
belt	cave	dim	fig	gob	heat	jig	kind	last	milk
big	coat	disk	file	gold	help	joke	king	lawn	mirror
bike	cob	doe	fin	golf	hen	jolly	kiss	leaf	mitt
bill	Coke	dog	find	gone	hike	job	kit	leg	mix
bird	cold	doll	fish	good	hill	judge	kitchen	lemon	money
box	cone	door	five	gorilla	hip	jug	kite	lend	mop
boy	cub	dot	fix	got	home	juice	kitty	letter	mother
bud	cube	down	fond	gull	honey	jumbo		like	mud
bug	cuff	duck	fox	gum	hop	jump		line	muff
bus	cup	dull	funny	gun	hot	jungle		lion	mug
buzz	cut	dust	fuzz	gust	hug			listen	must

Initial Consonants (con't)

n	p	q	r	s	t	v	w	x	z
nag	page	quack	rabbit	sack	table	vacation	wade	Xmas	zeal
nail	pail	quail	radio	sad	tack	valentine	wag	X ray	zebra
name	pan	quake	rag	said	taffy	valley	walk		zero
nap	paper	quarrel	rain	sailboat	tail	van	wall	**y**	zest
near	paw	quart	rake	salt	tall	vane	war	yacht	zigzag
neck	peanut	quarter	rat	sat	teacher	vase	warm	yank	zinc
need	pear	queen	rattle	save	team	vast	was	yap	zing
needle	pen	queer	read	saw	teeth	veil	watch	yard	zinnia
net	penny	quick	red	seal	ten	vein	water	yarn	zip
never	pet	quiet	ride	see	tiger	velvet	web	yawn	zipper
nice	pickle	quirk	ring	sell	time	vent	wedding	year	zone
nickel	picture	quit	road	seven	tire	verb	well	yeast	zoo
night	pie	quite	roar	sew	today	verse	west	yell	
nine	pig	quiver	rob	sick	toe	vest	wet	yellow	
nod	pill	quiz	robin	sing	top	vet	wind	yelp	
nose	pizza		rock	sink	toy	vim	window	yes	
note	pop		rocket	sister	tug	vine	wing	yield	
now	puff		rope	six	tummy	violet	wink	yogurt	
number	puzzle		rose	sock	turkey	violin	wolf	yolk	
nurse			run	sun	turtle	visit	wood	you	
								young	
								yoyo	
								yule	

Consonant Blends

bl	cl	fl	gl	pl	br	cr
black	clam	flag	glacier	place	brace	crab
blade	clap	flake	glad	plan	braid	crack
blank	class	flap	glass	plant	brain	cradle
blast	claw	flash	gleam	planet	brash	cream
blaze	clay	flat	glee	plaster	brave	crayons
block	clean	float	glide	play	bread	crib
blond	clock	flock	glitter	please	break	crisp
blood	close	floor	glory	plenty	brick	cross
bloom	clothes	flower	glove	plot	bride	crow
blow	cloud	fluid	glow	plug	bring	crown
blouse	clover	flush	glue	plus	brittle	crust
blue	clown				brown	cry
bluff					bruise	
dr	**fr**	**gr**	**pr**	**sc**	**sk**	**sl**
dragon	fraction	grab	prance	scab	skate	slam
drain	frame	grand	pray	scale	skeleton	slap
drape	freckle	grape	press	scald	ski	sled

Consonant Blends (con't)

dr	fr	gr	pr	sc	sk	sl
drawer	free	graph	pretzel	scalp	skillet	sleep
dream	freeze	grass	pride	scan	skin	sleeve
dress	fresh	gravy	prince	scar	skinny	slice
drink	friend	graze	princess	scare	skip	slime
drip	frizz	green	print	scarf	skirt	sling
drive	frog	grin	prize	scatter	skull	slip
drop	frost	grip	proud	scooter	sky	sliver
drown	frozen	grocery	prune	scout		slot
drum		grow				

sm	sn	sp	st	sw	tr	tw
smack	snail	space	stain	swam	tractor	tweed
small	snake	spat	stamp	swarm	trade	tweet
smart	snap	speak	stand	swat	traffic	tweezers
smash	snatch	spear	staple	sway	train	twelve
smear	sneak	speed	star	sweat	trap	twenty
smell	sneeze	spell	stay	sweep	treat	twice
smile	sniff	spend	stem	sweet	tree	twig
smock	snooze	spill	still	swerve	tribe	twin
smoke	snore	spin	sting	swift	trick	twirl
smoky	snow	spoon	stitch	swing	trip	twist
smooth	snug	spot	stop		trot	
smuggle	snuggle				truck	

Variant Consonant Sounds

c/k/	c/s/	g/g/	g/j/	s/s/	s/z/
cabin	cedar	galaxy	gelatin	sack	babies
cage	ceiling	gallant	gem	saddle	boys
cake	cell	gallon	general	safe	chairs
camel	cement	gallop	gentle	sail	cookies
camp	census	garage	geography	salt	enemies
card	center	garbage	geometry	sample	families
cat	century	goat	germ	sand	frogs
coconut	cider	golf	giant	satin	girls
coffee	cigar	goose	ginger	second	please
collar	cinnamon	gorilla	giraffe	seed	rose
collie	circus	gown	gym	send	sees
cube	city	guard	gyp	settle	shelves
cucumber	cycle	guess	gypsy	single	stories
cute	cyclone	guide	gyrate	soft	surprise
	cypress	guitar	gyro	some	wives
				soup	

Consonant Digraphs

***ch*/ch/**	***ch*/k/**	***ch*/sh/**	***gh*/g/**	***ph*/f/**	***sh*/sh/**
chain	character	chalet	ghastly	phantasy	shade
chalk	chasm	champagne	ghetto	phantom	shake
champ	chemical	chandelier	ghost	phase	shame
change	choral	charade	ghoul	pharmacy	shape
chart	chorus	chef		pheasant	shark
chase	chlorine	chenille	***gh*/f/**	phone	sharp
check	christen	chivalry	cough	phoneme	shave
cheese	chrome		enough	phonics	shawl
chest	chrysalis		laugh	phonograph	shed
chick	scheme		rough	phony	sheep
chief	school		tough	phosphate	shelf
child				photograph	shell
chill				phrase	shine
chin				physical	ship
choose					shirt
church					

***th*/th/ (voiced)**	***th*/th/ (voiceless)**	***thr*/thr/ (digraph-blend)**	***wh*/wh/**
than	thaw	thrash	whack
that	theater	thread	whale
the	theft	threat	wharf
their	theme	three	wheat
them	thick	thresh	wheel
themselves	thief	thrift	where
then	thimble	thrill	whiff
there	thin	throne	whimper
these	thing	through	whine
they	think	throw	whip
this	third	thrust	whirl
those	thirsty		whisk
though	thirty		whisper
	thorn		whiz
	thought		whopper
	thousand		
	thumb		
	thunder		
	Thursday		

Consonant Digraphs with First Silent Letters (Also *tch, dge,* and *ng*)

***gn*/n/**	***kn*/n/**	***wr*/r/**	***ck*/k/**	***tch*/ch/**	***dge*/j/**	***ng*/ng/**
align	knack	wrack	back	batch	badge	bang
campaign	knapsack	wrangler	brick	catch	bridge	flung
design	knead	wrap	crack	crutch	dodge	gang

Consonant Digraphs (con't)

gn/n/	*kn*/n/	*wr*/r/	*ck*/k/	*tch*/ch/	*dge*/j/	*ng*/ng/
foreign	knee	wrapper	chick	hitch	edge	gong
gnarl	kneel	wreath	clock	itch	fudge	hung
gnash	knelt	wreck	dock	latch	grudge	long
gnat	knew	wrestle	duck	match	ledge	lung
gnaw	knife	wring	flick	patch	ridge	prong
reign	knight	wrinkle	kick	pitch	sludge	song
resign	knit	wrist	lick	splotch		sing
sign	knob	write	lock	stretch		strung
	knock	wrong	luck	stitch		thing
	knot	wrote	peck	watch		wing
	know	wrung	pick	witch		
	knuckle	wry	quack			
			quick			
			shock			
			slick			
			stack			
			stick			
			tack			
			tick			
			thick			
			trick			
			track			
			truck			

Short Vowels

ă	ĕ	ĭ	ŏ	ŭ
act	bed	bib	block	bud
add	best	big	box	bus
as	den	bit	clock	cub
ask	end	dig	cop	cup
ax	ever	fig	dot	fun
bad	hem	fish	fox	gum
bag	jet	hid	got	gun
cab	led	hit	hop	jug
cat	men	if	lot	jump
dad	nest	ill	mop	lunch
fast	net	in	odd	mud
gap	next	inch	ox	nut
hat	pep	its	pot	pup
map	pet	kick	rob	rug
nap	red	milk	rot	sun
pat	sent	nip	shock	truck
sand	ten	pin	sock	tug
sat	web	sit	spot	under
tan	wet	wig	stop	up
tap	yes		top	us

Long Vowels and Silent *e*

ā	ē	ī	ō	ū	u as o͞o
bake	extreme	bite	bone	abuse	brute
base	impede	dime	cone	cube	bugle
cave	obese	file	drove	cure	flute
date	scene	five	hole	cute	parachute
game	scheme	hide	home	fuel	prune
gate	serene	hike	hope	fuse	rule
gave	stampede	life	joke	huge	salute
lake	supreme	like	poke	mule	sue
made		mile	nose	music	tube
race		pine	note	mute	tune
sale		pipe	robe	refuge	
take		ripe	rope	use	
tame		rise	smoke		
tape		time	tone		
wave					

y as a Vowel

y/ī/		*y*/ē/*	
by	sly	busy	penny
cry	sty	dirty	pity
dye	style	foggy	plenty
fly	stylus	foxy	pony
fry	styrofoam	funny	puppy
my	try	heavy	snowy
myself	wry	juicy	spotty
rye			

*In some dialects dialects /ĭ/

Vowel Digraphs

ai/ā/	*ay*/ā/	*ea*/ē/	*ea*/ĕ/	*ee*/ē/	*ie*/ē/
aim	away	beach	ahead	beef	achieve
bail	bay	bean	bread	bleed	believe
braid	clay	cheat	dead	creek	brief
claim	decay	clean	head	creep	chief
drain	gray	creak	read	deep	field
faint	may	cream	spread	flee	hygiene
grain	play	flea	thread	free	piece
hail	pray	heat	tread	geese	priest
mail	ray	peach		green	rabies
paid	relay	reach		jeep	relief
paint	slay	scream		peel	shield
rain	spray	seat		queen	shriek

Vowel Digraphs (con't)

ai/ā/	***ay***/ā/	***ea***/ē/	***ea***/ĕ/	***ee***/ē/	***ie***/ē/
sail	stay	steam		seed	thief
snail	stray	team		sleep	wield
train	tray	treat			
		wheat			

ie/ī/	***ei***/ē/	***ei***/ā/	***ey***/ē/	***igh***/ī/	***oa***/ō/
cried	ceiling	beige	barley	bright	boast
die	conceive	eight	donkey	fight	cloak
dried	deceive	freight	galley	flight	coal
fried	either	neighbor	hockey	fright	coast
lied	leisure	reign	honey	high	coat
pie	neither	rein	jockey	knight	float
pried	protein	skein	journey	might	foam
relied	receive	sleigh	kidney	night	goat
replied	seize	veil	medley	plight	load
spies		vein	money	right	
tie		weigh		sigh	
tied				sight	
tried				slight	
				tight	
				thigh	

Diphthongs

oi/oy/	***oy***/oy/	***au***/ä/	***aw***/ä/	***oo***/o͞o/	***oo***/o͝o/
appoint	ahoy	applause	awning	balloon	book
avoid	alloy	auto	brawl	bloom	hood
boil	boy	because	crawl	broom	hoof
choice	convoy	caught	dawn	cartoon	hook
coil	decoy	cause	draw	cool	look
coin	destroy	fault	fawn	drool	stood
foil	employ	haul	flaw	goose	took
join	joy	launch	hawk	moon	
moist	joyful	laundry	jaw	pool	
noise	loyal	naughty	law	school	
oil	oyster	sauce	lawn	scooter	
soil	royal	saucer	raw	smooth	
spoil	tomboy	taught	saw	spool	
voice	toy	vault	yawn	spoon	
				tooth	

Diphthongs (con't)

ow/ō/*	*ow*/ow/	*ou*/ow/	*ew*/o͞o/	*ue*/yū/	*ui*/o͞o/
below	allow	blouse	blew	cue	fruit
blow	brow	bounce	brew	due	juice
elbow	clown	cloud	chew	hue	nuisance
flow	cow	found	crew	rue	suitor
follow	cowboy	ground	drew	sue	
glow	drown	house	few		
grow	flower	loud	jewel		
know	frown	mouse	mew		
pillow	gown	ouch	new		
rainbow	plow	ounce	newly		
shadow	power	out	screw		
show	shower	pound	slew		
snow	towel	round	stew		
sparrow	tower	shout	strewn		
throw	town	sound	threw		
			view		

*Here, *ow* decodes as a long vowel sound.

r-Controlled Vowels

ar/ar/	*or*/or/	*er*/er/	*ir*/er/	*ur*/er/
alarm	born	clerk	birch	burn
arch	corn	fern	bird	burst
ark	ford	germ	birth	church
arm	horn	herd	chirp	curb
armor	morning	jerk	dirt	curve
artist	north	nerve	firm	hurl
barn	orange	perch	shirk	nurse
cart	order	perk	shirt	purse
chart	short	refer	skirt	surf
dart	sort	serve	squirm	surface
mark	sport	stern	squirt	turf
part	stork	term	stir	turkey
shark	torch	verse	twirl	turtle
	torn	worker	whirl	urge
	sworn	zipper		

The following list of prefixes (active and absorbed) and suffixes have a designated grade level following them. These levels are suggested by Edgar Dale and Joseph O'Rourke in *The Living Word Vocabulary*[1] and are based on considerable research. (Testing was not done at grades three, five, and seven.)

Teachers, however, should use their own discretion in determining whether students in their classroom would profit from learning to decode these words. Note how many words at the fourth, sixth, and eighth grade levels are derived from the use of the following prefixes: *dis*, *in*, *un* and the suffixes *tion*, *less*, *ly*, *ment*, and *ness*.

[1] From *The Living Word Vocabulary* by Edgar Dale and Joseph O'Rourke. © 1976 by Field Enterprises Educational Corporation.

Active Prefixes

dis

discharge (6)
discolor (6)
discomfort (6)
disconnect (4)
discontent (6)
discontinue (6)
discourage (8)
discouragement (8)
discourtesy (6)
disentangle (8)
disfavor (6)
disharmony (8)
dishonor (6)
disinherit (6)
disinterest (6)
dislocate (6)
dislodge (8)
disloyal (4)
disloyalty (6)
dismount (4)
disobedience (6)
disobey (4)
disorder (4)
disorderly (8)
disorganize (6)
displace (8)
displeasure (6)
disqualify (4)
disregard (6)
disrespect (6)
disrespectful (6)
dissatisfaction (6)
dissatisfy (4)
dissimilar (6)
distrustful (6)

en

enclose (4)
encourage (4)
encouragement (4)
endanger (6)
endear (8)
enforce (6)
enjoy (4)
enjoyable (4)
enjoyment (4)
enlarge (4)
enlargement (4)
enlist (4)
enlistment (4)
enrage (6)
enrich (6)
enroll (6)
enrollment (6)
ensure (4)
entangle (6)
entrust (6)

for/fore

forearm (6)
forefathers (6)
foregone (6)
foreground (6)
foreknowledge (6)
foreleg (6)
foreman (4)
forenoon (4)
forepaw (4)
foresaw (6)
foresee (6)
foreseen (6)
foresight (6)
foretell (6)
forethought (6)
foretold (6)
forever (4)
forevermore (4)
forewarn (6)
forgave (6)
forward (8)

im
(means *not*, also *in*)

immature (6)
immeasurable (6)
immigrant (6)
immigration (6)
immodest (8)
immortal (8)
immortality (8)
immovable (6)

in
(means *not*, also *in*)

inability (6)
inaccurate (6)
inactive (8)
inadequate (8)
inappropriate (8)
incapable (6)
inclose (4)
inclosure (6)
indirectly (8)
indisputable (8)
indistinct (8)
indoors (4)
inedible (8)
ineffective (6)
inefficient (8)
inestimable (8)

inter

intermarriage (8)
intermediate (8)
intermixture (8)
international (8)
internationalize (6)
intersection (6)
interview (6)
interweave (8)

Active Prefixes (con't)

im
(means *not,* also *in*)

immunize (8)
impassable (4)
impatience (6)
impatiently (6)
imperfect (6)
imperfection (6)
impersonal (8)
impolite (4)
import (6)
impossible (4)
impress (6)
impressive (6)
imprint (8)
imprison (4)
imprisonment (6)
improbable (8)
improper (6)
impure (6)
impurity (6)

in
(means *not,* also *in*)

income (6)
incoming (8)
incomparable (6)
incompetent (8)
incomplete (4)
inconsiderate (6)
inconvenience (8)
incredible (6)
incurable (6)
indebted (6)
indebtedness (8)
indecent (6)
indecision (6)
indefinite (8)
independence (4)
independent (6)
indestructible (8)
indigestible (6)
indirect (8)
inevitable (8)
inexact (6)
inexpensive (6)
inexpressible (8)
infield (8)
inflammable (6)
inflammation (8)
ingratitude (8)
inhospitable (8)
inhuman (6)
inhumane (8)
inscribe (6)
inscription (8)
insecure (4)
insensitive (8)
inseparable (6)
insoluble (8)
insufficient (8)
intake (4)

mis

misapply (8)
misbehave (4)
misbehavior (8)
misconduct (6)
miscount (4)
misdeal (4)
misfit (6)
misfortune (4)
misjudge (4)
mislay (4)
mislead (6)
misleading (6)
mismanage (6)
misplace (4)
misprint (4)
mispronounce (6)
misquote (8)
misread (4)
misrule (6)
misspell (4)
misspent (6)
mistrust (6)
misunderstand (4)
misuse (6)

non

noncombatant (8)
nonconductor (8)
nonprofit (8)
nonresident (4)
nonsense (4)
nonstop (4)

re (meaning *again*)

rebirth (6)
reborn (8)
rebound (6)
rebroadcast (4)
rebuilt (4)
recall (4)
recapture (6)
recombine (6)
recondition (8)
recycle (6)
rediscover (6)
refill (4)
reforest (6)
refresh (4)
regain (4)
removable (6)
rename (4)
renewal (8)
reopen (4)
reorganize (4)
repaid (4)
repayment (6)
replace (4)
reprint (4)
reproduce (8)
retake (4)

Active Prefixes (con't)

	un	
unable (6)	uncomfortable (6)	unorganized (6)
unacquainted (4)	unconcern (6)	unpopular (4)
unaffected (8)	uncontrollable (6)	unreality (6)
unafraid (4)	undiscovered (6)	unsaddle (4)
unaided (6)	undisturbed (4)	unscramble (6)
unarmed (4)	unearth (8)	unscrew (6)
unattached (4)	uneasily (6)	unselfish (4)
unattainable (8)	unemployed (6)	unsettled (6)
unattended (8)	unequal (4)	unskilled (4)
unattractive (6)	uneven (4)	unsuccessful (6)
unavoidable (8)	unexpectedly (6)	unsuitable (6)
unbalanced (4)	unfold (4)	untangle (6)
unbeaten (8)	unfortunate (6)	untiring (6)
unborn (4)	unfurl (8)	untouchable (4)
unbreakable (4)	unguarded (8)	untried (6)
unbroken (4)	unhappily (6)	untrue (4)
unbuckle (4)	unkindness (4)	untwist (4)
unbutton (4)	unlikely (4)	unwashed (4)
uncertain (4)	unlively (6)	unwelcome (4)
unchanged (4)	unmerciful (8)	unwilling (4)
unchecked (6)	unnatural (4)	unwind (6)
uncivilized (6)	unoccupied (8)	unwisely (4)
unclasp (4)	unopened (4)	unworthy (8)
unclothed (4)		

Absorbed Prefixes

com	con	de	
combine (4)	conceal (6)	debate (6)	defrost (4)
comfort (4)	concern (6)	decay (4)	delay (4)
comment (6)	conclude (6)	decent (8)	deliver (4)
commit (8)	condense (8)	decide (4)	demand (6)
common (6)	conflict (8)	decision (4)	depend (4)
compass (8)	confuse (4)	declare (6)	deposit (4)
compete (8)	connection (6)	decline (8)	detail (8)
compose (6)	consist (6)	defeat (6)	detract (8)
composition (6)	construct (4)	define (6)	
compound (6)	contact (6)		
compromise (8)	contest (4)		
	contract (6)		
	contraption (8)		
	contrast (8)		

Absorbed Prefixes (con't)

ex		pre*	pro
examine (4)	execute (4)	precipitation (6)	procedure (8)
example (4)	exhaust (6)	predict (6)	proceed (4)
excellent (4)	exile (8)	prefer (6)	process (6)
except (4)	exit (4)	premium (6)	produce (6)
excess (8)	explain (4)	preparation (4)	production (6)
excite (4)	explode (4)	prepare (4)	program (4)
exclaim (6)	expose (6)	present (4)	prolong (8)
exclude (8)	express (6)	pretend (4)	promote (4)
excuse (4)	extend (8)	prevent (4)	propose (4)
		previous (6)	protest (6)

*The prefix *pre* is also an active prefix in words as *predetermine*, *prejudge*.

Derivational Suffixes

able		ance	ess
acceptable (8)	movable (4)	acceptance (8)	authoress (8)
accountable (6)	navigable (8)	acquaintance (8)	duchess (8)
admirable (6)	notable (8)	admittance (8)	enchantress (8)
allowable (4)	observable (6)	allowance (6)	huntress (6)
believable (4)	portable (4)	appearance (4)	lioness (6)
charitable (8)	presentable (6)	appliance (4)	poetess (6)
comfortable (4)	punishable (6)	assistance (4)	princess (4)
dependable (4)	reasonable (6)	ordinance (8)	stewardess (6)
desirable (6)	respectable (6)	performance (4)	tigress (6)
fashionable (4)	sizable (8)	remembrance (8)	
favorable (8)	traceable (6)	repentance (8)	
flammable (6)	treasonable (8)	resistance (8)	
honorable (6)	usable (4)	tolerance (8)	
justifiable (6)	valuable (4)		
manageable (6)	washable (4)		

ful	ify	ion	
beautiful (4)	clarify (6)	abbreviation (4)	navigation (8)
blissful (8)	classify (6)	accusation (8)	nomination (6)
careful (4)	crucify (6)	addition (4)	persuasion (8)
cheerful (4)	glorify (6)	admiration (6)	presentation (8)
colorful (8)	horrify (6)	admission (6)	production (6)
cupful (4)	identify (6)	adoption (4)	protection (4)
doubtful (6)	intensify (8)	affection (6)	radiation (4)
faithful (6)	justify (6)	amputation (8)	reflection (4)
forgetful (4)	magnify (6)	application (8)	sensation (6)
graceful (6)	mystify (8)	attention (6)	starvation (4)
handful (4)	notify (6)	attraction (6)	supervision (4)
harmful (4)	pacify (8)	construction (6)	taxation (6)
joyful (4)	terrify (4)	division (4)	temptation (6)
lawful (4)		elevation (6)	tension (6)

Derivational Suffixes (con't)

ful

masterful (6)
meaningful (6)
merciful (6)
mournful (6)
playful (4)
shameful (8)
sinful (6)
sorrowful (4)
spoonful (4)
thankful (6)
thoughtful (4)
trustful (4)
truthful (4)
wonderful (4)

ion

expression (4)
formation (6)
introduction (4)
irritation (6)
vaccination (6)
vegetation (8)
vibration (6)
violation (8)

ish

banish (8)
bookish (8)
boyish (4)
brownish (4)
childish (4)
devilish (6)
foolish (4)
girlish (4)
grayish (6)
reddish (8)

ism

alcoholism (4)
Americanism (4)
barbarism (8)
cannibalism (6)
Catholicism (6)
colonialism (6)
communism (6)
criticism (6)
idealism (8)
liberalism (8)
patriotism (6)
terrorism (8)
vandalism (6)

ist

abolitionist (8)
accompanist (6)
biologist (6)
botanist (8)
chemist (6)
columnist (6)
duelist (8)
finalist (8)
humorist (8)
opportunist (8)
organist (4)
panelist (8)
terrorist (6)
tourist (6)
violinist (4)
vocalist (6)
zoologist (8)

ity

ability (4)
activity (8)
actuality (8)
authority (6)
cavity (6)
community (6)
curiosity (8)
deformity (8)
elasticity (8)
humanity (8)
legality (8)
locality (6)
majority (6)
maturity (8)
minority (8)
nobility (8)
opportunity (6)
personality (4)
possibility (6)
prosperity (8)
rapidity (4)
regularity (6)
scarcity (6)
security (6)
sincerity (8)
stability (8)
stupidity (6)
utility (6)
vitality (8)

Derivational Suffixes (con't)

ive

attractive (4)
defensive (8)
locomotive (4)
possessive (6)
preventive (6)
productive (6)
sensitive (8)

ize

apologize (4)
legalize (6)
materialize (8)
modernize (4)
organize (6)
specialize (6)
sterilize (4)
terrorize (8)
vaporize (4)

less

aimless (6)
bottomless (4)
boundless (8)
brainless (4)
breathless (4)
ceaseless (8)
cheerless (4)
childless (4)
defenseless (6)
doubtless (6)
fatherless (4)
faultless (8)
formless (4)
friendless (4)
guiltless (6)
helpless (4)
hopeless (4)
landless (4)
listless (8)
matchless (8)
meaningless (6)
merciless (6)
motionless (6)
needless (8)
noiseless (4)
painless (4)
pointless (6)
regardless (6)
shameless (8)
shapeless (4)
sleepless (4)
spiritless (8)
spotless (6)
stainless (6)
thoughtless (4)
timeless (6)
treeless (4)
valueless (6)
voiceless (6)

ly

actually (6)
awfully (4)
carefully (4)
certainly (4)
cheaply (4)
correctly (4)
currently (8)
directly (8)
doubly (6)
earthly (6)
easily (4)
especially (6)
feelingly (6)
frequently (4)
friendly (4)
furiously (6)
hourly (6)
knowingly (6)
mannerly (4)
mostly (4)
naturally (6)
nearly (4)
orderly (8)
ordinarily (6)
patiently (4)
personally (4)
positively (6)
probably (6)
saintly (6)
scarcely (4)
seemingly (8)
severely (6)
shapely (4)
sincerely (6)
slightly (6)
sparingly (6)
stubbornly (6)
supposedly (8)
swiftly (4)

ment

achievement (6)
advertisement (4)
agreement (4)
ailment (4)
amendment (6)
amusement (4)
announcement (4)
apartment (4)
appointment (4)
argument (6)
arrangement (4)
assignment (4)
detachment (8)
development (6)
employment (6)
enchantment (6)
engagement (4)
environment (6)
government (6)
judgment (6)
pavement (4)
payment (6)
punishment (4)
refreshment (4)
replacement (4)
resentment (8)
retirement (4)
sentiment (8)
settlement (4)
shipment (4)
statement (4)
temperament (8)
treatment (4)

Derivational Suffixes (con't)

less	**ly**
witless (6)	variously (6)
	vertically (8)
	vocally (6)

ness

alertness (6)	foolishness (4)	shyness (4)
attractiveness (4)	freshness (4)	smoothness (6)
bashfulness (4)	greatness (4)	steadiness (8)
bitterness (4)	greediness (6)	stiffness (4)
blindness (4)	greenness (4)	stillness (4)
briskness (6)	keenness (6)	strangeness (4)
closeness (6)	kindness (6)	suddenness (4)
coarseness (6)	largeness (4)	sweetness (4)
darkness (4)	lawlessness (6)	swiftness (4)
dimness (4)	loneliness (4)	tardiness (4)
drowsiness (6)	nearness (4)	tenderness (4)
drunkenness (4)	nervousness (4)	thankfulness (4)
dullness (6)	nobleness (6)	thickness (4)
duskiness (6)	pleasantness (6)	thoughtfulness (4)
emptiness (6)	prettiness (4)	usefulness (4)
exactness (6)	rashness (4)	watchfulness (6)
fatness (4)	readiness (4)	weakness (4)
feebleness (6)	restlessness (6)	weariness (6)
filthiness (6)	roominess (6)	whiteness (4)
fitness (8)	rottenness (4)	willingness (6)
flabbiness (6)	seriousness (6)	

ogy	**ous**	
archeology (8)	courageous (4)	mysterious (6)
astrology (8)	dangerous (4)	nervous (6)
biology (8)	glorious (6)	numerous (6)
criminology (8)	humorous (4)	odorous (8)
ecology (8)	joyous (6)	poisonous (6)
geology (6)	luminous (8)	prosperous (8)
mineralogy (6)	marvelous (4)	studious (8)
	miraculous (6)	treasonous (8)
	mountainous (6)	

Practice Words for Syllabication

2 syllables	3 syllables	4 syllables
captive	belittle	declaration
carbon	capital	deliberate
carefree	correctly	embarrassment
cortex	corridor	encouragement
extent	exposure	exceedingly
extreme	extension	impersonal

Practice Words for Syllabication (con't)

2 syllables	3 syllables	4 syllables
formal	external	introduction
fungus	fantastic	magnesium
furnace	foundation	majority
junction	important	mathematics
mailman	imposter	mechanical
picket	impression	necessary
picture	janitor	pacifier
proverb	magnetic	predetermined
provoke	mastermind	recognition
return	matador	relationship
royal	mechanic	revolution
rubber	medicine	sensational
twilight	medium	spectacular
upstream	opportune	supervisor
waistline	preamble	totality
waitress	prospector	unsuspected
welfare	resident	violinist
	stimulus	

Appendix C

Phonogram List

ab	each	ice	oar	ub
ack	eal	ick	oat	uck
ad	ean	id	ob	ug
ag	eat	ight	ock	ule
ail	ed	ill	on	ull
ain	eed	im	one	um
ait	eel	in	ong	ump
ake	eep	ind	ook	un
all	eet	ine	ool	ung
am	eg	ing	oom	unk
ame	ell	ink	oon	unt
and	en	int	op	up
ang	end	ip	ore	uss
ank	ent	iss	ort	ut
ap	est	it	oss	ute
at	et	ite	ot	
ate	ew		ote	
ay			ound	
			out	
			ow	

Appendix D

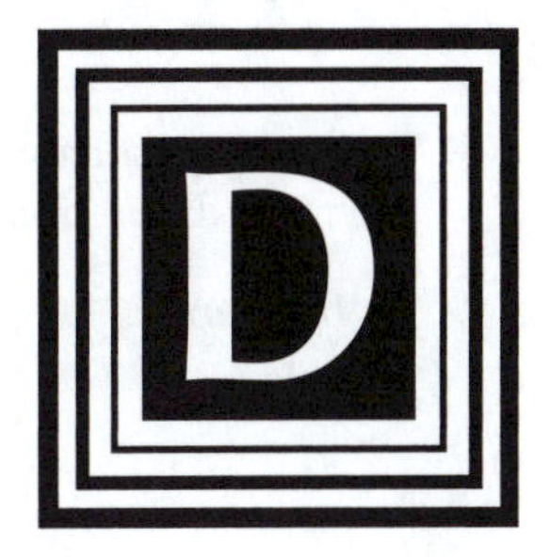

Tests

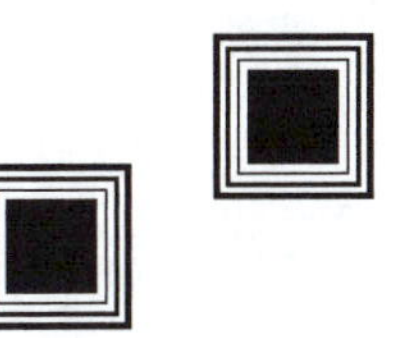

Teacher's Test of Decoding Skills

Part I

1. Define a consonant digraph. (1) List and organize them into (a) digraphs with *h*, (b) digraphs with an initial silent letter, (c) three-letter digraphs. (2) Indicate the sound/sounds each encodes. (3) Give a word/example of each and underline the digraph in the word.

   Definition:

Digraphs	**Sound/Sounds**	**Word Example/Examples**
(a)		
(b)		
(c)		

2. Some single consonant letters in our alphabet encode more than one sound. What are these letters? What sounds do they encode? What vowels condition these sounds? Give word examples of each.

Letter	**Sound/Sounds**	**Vowels That Condition**	**Word Example/Examples**

3. The letter *y* functions as both a consonant and a vowel. Explain and give word examples.

4. Define a consonant blend. Give two examples of each kind of blend, underlining the blend. What is/are the main difference/differences between them?

   Definition:

   Blends **Examples**

5. At the end of some words *ck* is used as the /k/ sound. At the end of other words *ke* is used as the /k/ sound. Explain.

6. Give word examples of the five short sounds of the vowels.

7. Some vowels encode a third in addition to the short and long sounds. What are these vowels? What sounds do they encode? Give word examples.

8. List four "regular" vowel digraphs that follow the rule used by many primary teachers: "When two vowels go a walking, etc." Give word examples.

   Vowel Digraph **Word Examples**

9. The /o͞o/ sound as in the word *spoon* can be encoded in many ways. List the six additional letters or letter combinations that encode this sound. Give word examples.

Sound	Letter Combination	Word Examples
/o͞o/	oo	spoon

10. Give word examples to show the effect of a final *e* on words. You should have five different examples to indicate five reasons why final *e* appears.

11. Long *e* may be encoded many ways. List the letters that combine to encode this sound. Give word examples.

Sound	**Letter Combinations**	**Word Examples**

12. Define a diphthong. What sounds do these diphthongs encode? Give word examples.

Definition:

Diphthongs	**Sounds**	**Word Examples**
oo		
ou		
ow		
oi		
oy		

13. Long *i* may *usually* be encoded three ways in addition to the letter *i*. Give the letter combinations with word examples.

/i/	**Letter Combinations**	**Word Examples**

14. What do *ir*, *er*, *ur*, and *wor* have in common?

15. What is the schwa sound? Where is it found? How is it written? Give example words.

16. What happens to words such as *jog* and *brim* when an ending is added that begins with a vowel? Why is this?

17. Add the endings *ing* and *ed* to the nonsense words below.

blath
gute
pem
shane
colnep
theg
cay

18. What suggestions would you make to students when they come to an unknown word?

Part II

1. Circle the vowel digraphs
2. Underline the blends
3. Place a square bracket around the consonant digraphs
4. Place a checkmark before a word with a diphthong

character	afraid	relative	coarse
shook	flight	back	chaise
receive	known	surprise	athlete
treasure	toil	illustration	whether

Part III

1. (a) Define the term sight words and give some examples.
   (b) What is the importance of these words?

2. What is the difference between an absorbed and a regular prefix?

3. What is the difference between an inflectional and a derivational suffix?

4. What is the difference between a semantic and a syntactic context clue?

5. What syllabication principles would you suggest that students incorporate when they meet an unfamiliar word?

Answers to the Teacher's Test of Decoding Skills

Part I

1. Definition: two consonant letters together encoding one sound

   (a) *ch*/ch/ /k/ /sh/ — *ch*amp *ch*aracter *ch*ef
   gh/g/ /f/ /-/ — *gh*ost thoug*h* boug*h*
   ph/f/ — *ph*armacy
   sh/sh/ — *sh*ape
   th/th/ /th/ — *th*icket *th*em
   wh/w/ /h/ — *wh*en *wh*ole

   (b) *gn*/n/ — *gn*ome
   kn/n/ — *kn*ife
   wr/r/ — *wr*inkle
   ck/k/ — che*ck*

   (c) *dge*/j/ — bri*dge*
   tch/ch/ — ca*tch*

2.

Letter	Sound/Sounds	Vowels That Condition	Word Example/Examples
c	/k/ /s/	When *a*, *o*, *u* follow *c*, *c* encodes /k/. When *i*, *e*, *y* follow *c*, *c* encodes /s/.	camera, cycle

Letter	Sound/Sounds	Vowels That Condition	Word Example/Examples
g	/g/ /j/	When *a*, *o*, *u* follow g, g usually encodes /g/. When *i*, *e*, *y* follow g, g usually encodes /j/.	game, gem
s	/s/ /z/ /sh/	none	same, rose, sugar

3. *y* may be a consonant at the beginning of a word—*yellow*.
   y may be a vowel in the middle of words—/ĭ/ gym, /ī/ cycle.
   y may be a vowel at the end of words—/ē/ pretty, /ī/ apply.
   y may be part of a vowel digraph as ay /ā/ stay and ey /ē/ money.
   y may be part of the diphthong oy /oy/ toy.
4. A consonant blend occurs when two or three adjacent letters encode consonant sounds that cluster together and are pronounced very rapidly.
   a. *r cr*eam, *pr*ize b. *l bl*ame, *fl*ight c. *s sn*ail, *str*eam d. *tw tw*irl, *tw*ist
5. *ck* is used after a short vowel. *ke* is used after a long vowel.
6. Answers will vary: b*a*t, b*e*t, b*i*t, b*o*p, b*u*t are some examples.
7. *ä* /ä/ father
   o /o͞o/ to
   u /u/ bush
8. *ai* maid *ay* tray *oa* oats *ee* sleep
9. *ou* soup *u* rude *ui* fruit
   o prove *ue* clue *ew* flew
10. *chance*, *change*. Final *e* indicates the preceding *c* and *g* have the respective sounds of /s/ and /j/.
    pipe. Final *e* indicates the preceding vowel is long. This differentiates pipe from pip.
    have. Final *e* is used after *v* because English words do not end in *v*.
    able. Final *e* completes a needed second syllable; otherwise the word would be unpronounceable as *abl*.
    awe. Historical reasons.

11. *ee* sheep *ie* brief *ey* monkey
    ea treat *ei* conceive *y* candy
12. A *diphthong* is a gliding sound from one vowel to another.
    oo /o͞o/ /o͝o/ spool, shook
    ou /ow/ /ŭ/ crouch, touch
    ow /ow/ /ō/ crowd, snow
    oi /oy/ moist
    oy /o/ employ
13. *y* cry *ie* pic *igh* right
14. They all encode /er/; *or* encodes /er/ when *w* precedes it.
15. The schwa is the vowel sound in unstressed syllables with a sound similar to short *uh* written as ə.
16. The final consonant is doubled to show the preceding vowel is short. This differentiates between words such as *stripper* and *striper*.
17. blath blathing blathed
    gute guting guted
    pem pemming pemmed
    shane shaning shaned
    colnep colnepping colnepped
    theg thegging thegged
    cay caying cayed
18. First see if the sentence context can help.
    Check for structural parts such as roots and affixes.
    Check for syllable and phonics clues.

Part II

character	afraid	relative	coarse
shook	flight	back	chaise
receive	known	surprise	athlete
treasure	✓ toil	illustration	whether

Part III

1. (a) They are "heavy duty" words such as *at*, *the*, *be*, *of* that appear frequently.
   (b) They must be recognized immediately, as it is difficult to read any extended passage without meeting a large number of them.
2. A regular prefix changes the word's meaning as in *preview* (to see before). In an absorbed prefix the *pre* or other like-seeming prefix is part of the word (*presume*).
3. Inflectional suffixes number only eight and are taught early in the reading program. They do not change the part of speech. Derivational suffixes are numerous and are of four kinds: noun, verb, adjective, and adverb. These do change the part of speech, their main function.
4. A semantic clue is a meaning clue; a syntactic clue is a grammar clue.
5. See if a word is compound or has affixes.
   See if the word has double consonant letters or two unlike consonants.
   Do not divide blends or digraphs.
   If the word ends in *le*, place the preceding consonant before it.
   Always check to see if the word makes sense!

Appendix E

Basic Sight Words for Older Readers

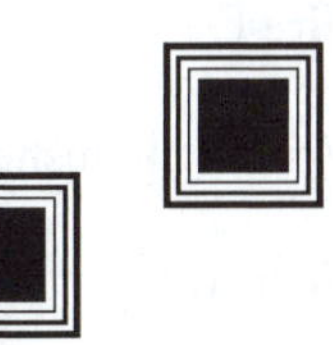

Adult Survival Words

Adults Only
Antidote
Beware
Bus Station
Caution
Combustible
Condemned
Contaminated
Detour
Do Not Enter
Don't Walk
Do Not Inhale Fumes
Do Not Refreeze

Do Not Incinerate
Dry Clean Only
Do Not Puncture
Do Not Induce Vomiting
Dosage
Do Not Use Near Heat
Doctor
Dynamite
Do Not Use Near Open Flame
Elevator
Emergency Exit
Employees Only
Enter At Your Own Risk

Entrance

Exit

Explosives

External Use Only

Emergency Vehicles Only

Floods When Raining

Fire Escape

Fire Extinguisher

First Aid

Flammable

Fragile

Gasoline

Gentlemen

Handle With Care

High Voltage

High Water

Inflammable

Information

Instructions

Keep Closed At All Times

Keep Out

Keep Out of Reach of Children

Ladies and Gentlemen

Last Chance for Gas

Left Turn Only

Loading Zone

Listen

Log Trucks 300 Feet

Merging Traffic

No Admittance

No Fires

No Left Turn

No Minors

No Parking

No Passing

No Right Turn

No Smoking

No Smoking Area

No Swimming

Not a Through Street

Noxious

Office

Out of Order

Put on Chains

Pedestrians Only

Pedestrians Prohibited

Poisonous

Police (Station)

Private Property

Pull-Push

Railroad Crossing

Restrooms

Right Turn Only

Road Ends

Slide Area

Slippery When Wet (Frosty)

Stop

Smoking Prohibited

Turn Off

Use in Open Air

Use Other Door

Violators Will Be Prosecuted

Watch for Flagman

Winding Road

Wind Gusts

Watch Out for Log Trucks

Women

X-ing

Yield: Right of Way

Adult Survival Transportation Words

Alternate Route

Bike Route

Bridge Freezes Before Road

Bridge May Be Slippery

Bridge Out

Camping

Cattle Xing (Crossing)

Caution

Children Crossing

Congested Area Ahead

Construction Ahead

Curve

Danger

Dangerous Curve

Dangerous Intersection

Dead End

Deer Xing (Crossing)

Detour Ahead

Dip

Divided Highway

Do Not Block Entrance

Do Not Enter

Do Not Pass

Emergency Parking Only

End Construction

Entrance

Exit

Exit Only

Express Lane

Expressway

Falling Rock

Farm Machinery

Fine for Littering

Food

Four-way Stop

Freeway

Gasoline

Go Slow

Hidden Driveway

Highway Ends

Hill—Trucks Use Lowest Gear

Hospital Zone

Information Center

Intersection

Interstate

Junction

Keep Right

Left Lane Ends

Left Lane Must Turn Left

Left Turn on Signal Only

Local Traffic Only

Low Clearance

Low Shoulder

Maximum Speed

Mechanic on Duty

Men Working

Merge

Merge Left

Merge Right

Merging Traffic

Minimum Speed

Narrow Bridge

Next Gas Miles

Next Left

Next Right

No Dumping

No Left Turn

No Parking This Side

No Passing Zone

No Right Turn on Red

No Thoroughfare

No Trucks

No Turns

No Turn on Red

North

Not a Through Street

No U Turn

One Way

One Way—Do Not Enter

Parking Ahead

Parkway

Pavement Ends

Pedestrian Crossing

Pedestrians Prohibited

Ped Xing (Pedestrian Crossing)

Plant Entrance

Private Road—Keep Out

Railroad Crossing

Ramp Speed

Reduce Speed Ahead

Restricted Lane Ahead

Resume Speed

Right Lane Must Turn Right

Right Turn Only

Right Turn on Red After Stopping

Road Closed

Road Construction Next Miles

Roadside Table

Route

Runaway Truck Ramp

School Bus Crossing

School Zone When Flashing

Signal Ahead

Slippery When Wet

Slow

Slower Traffic Keep Right

Soft Shoulder

South

Speed Checked by Radar

Speed Limit

Speed Zone Ahead

Steep Grade

Stop

Stop Ahead

Towaway Zone

Trail

Truck Route

Turnpike

Two-way Traffic

Use Low Gear

Walk

Watch for Fallen Rocks

Wayside Park

Weigh Station

Weight Limit Tons

West

Wrong Way

Yield

Yield Right of Way

Reprinted with permission. State of Oregon. (n.d.). Training effective literacy tutors. Retrieved February 25, 2005, from http://www. nwlincs.org/NWLINCSWEB/Teltv2/ABE.doc

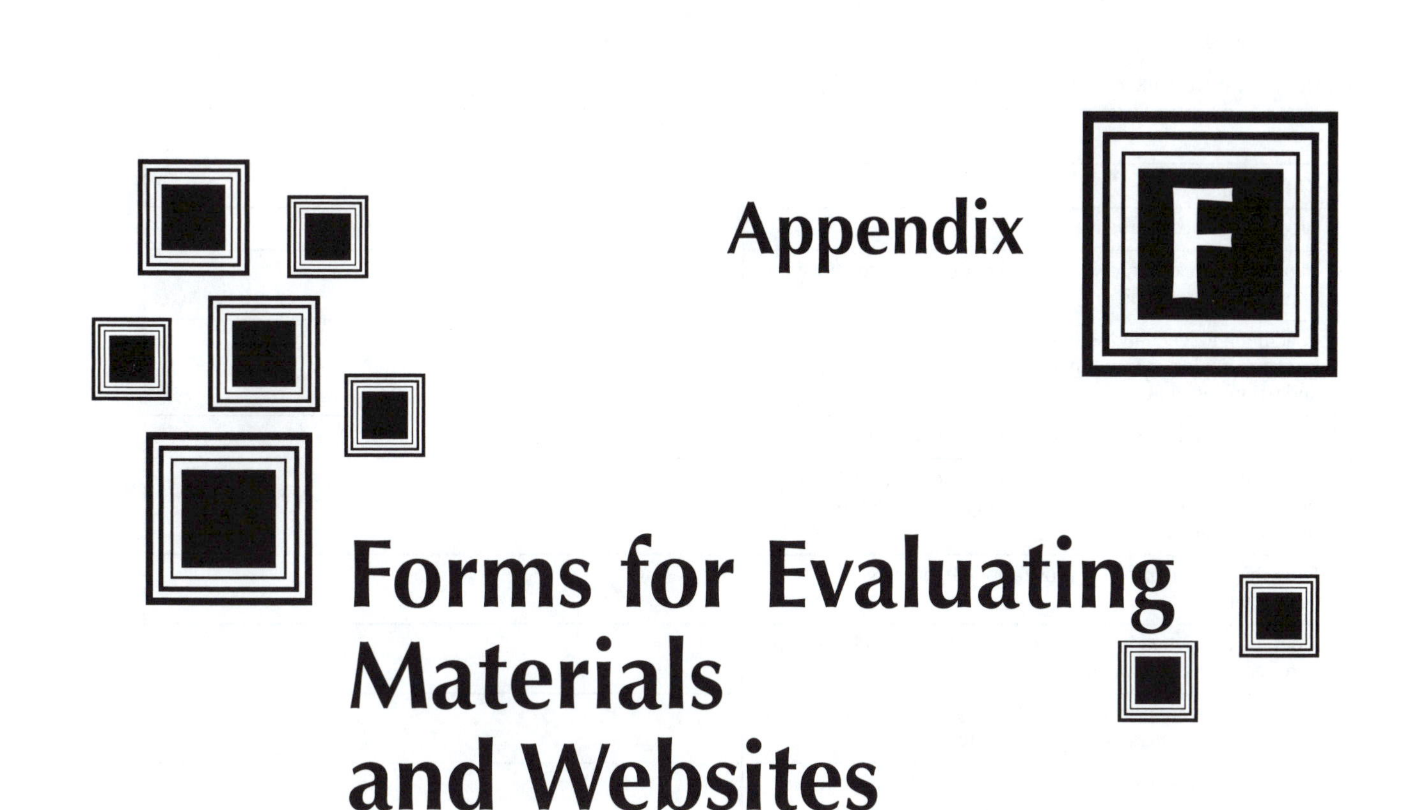

Appendix F

Forms for Evaluating Materials and Websites

PHONICS MATERIALS EVALUATION FORM

Software	
What are the developer's goals and claims?	
How long has the software/program been on the market?	
What are the qualifications of the people who developed the software/program?	
Is there credible evidence that the software/program has been effective over time and with large numbers of students?	
For what age children is the software/program intended?	
What is the cost?	
Does the software/program have reasonable time demands?	
Is there any reason to suspect that the software/program may be confusing or frustrating to use?	
Are the instructions clear?	
Do the explanations include a lot of special terminology?	

(Continued)

Software	
Are the activities instructive?	
Can the phonics instruction fit into a comprehensive program of reading instruction?	
In addition to letter and sound instruction, does the software/ program provide or recommend including other types of reading and writing activities?	
Does the software/program include rhyming activities?	
Does the software/program include other activities that will provide children with practice in distinguishing sounds in spoken words?	
Does the software/program provide for the teaching of letter names?	
Does the instruction help children understand the relationship between letters and sounds?	
Does the software/program provide interesting and high-quality stories and other materials for children to read?	
Do the materials provided include many words that children can figure out by using the letter and sound relationships they are being taught?	
Does the software/program provide opportunities for children to apply what they are learning by writing? If not, Is the software/program flexible enough to allow you to include spelling and writing opportunities along with the instruction?	
Overall assessment of the program?	

Adapted from Osborn, J., Stahl, S., & Stein, M. (1997). *Teachers' guidelines for evaluating commercial phonics packages*. Newark, DE: International Reading Association.

Questions to Ask About Computer-Based Reading Programs*

1. *Cost.*
   - ❒ Is the program copy protected?
   - ❒ Is there a charge for back-up copies or multiple copies?
   - ❒ Are there expenses for supplemental or resource materials?
   - ❒ Can the program be returned?
   - ❒ Are there opportunities for program upgrading as new versions appear?
2. *Equipment.* Does the program require:
   - ❒ special monitors?
   - ❒ extensive memory?
   - ❒ storage data?
   - ❒ a printer?
   - ❒ a speech synthesizer, or other additional equipment?
   - ❒ other requirements?
3. *Curriculum?*
   - ❒ What grade level?
   - ❒ What types of students?
   - ❒ What types of teaching styles?
   - ❒ What types of materials are compatible?
   - ❒ How long do the activities take?
4. *What is read on/off screen?* Do students:
   - ❒ read passages?
   - ❒ read sentences?
   - ❒ read individual words or phrases?
   - ❒ recognize letters?
   - ❒ read program or activity direction?
   - ❒ read or recognize anything else?

*Adapted from Blanchard, (1985). "Questions to Ask about Computer-Based Reading Programs," *The Reading Teacher*, pp. 250–252.

5. *Program content.* Does the program include:
   - ❒ instructional activities?
   - ❒ practice activities?
   - ❒ vocabulary activities?
   - ❒ comprehension activities?
   - ❒ study skills activities?
   - ❒ syllable or alphabet activities?
   - ❒ gamelike format?
   - ❒ testing items?
   - ❒ other?
   - ❒ multiple activities on one topic?

6. *Video presentations.* Does the program:
   - ❒ present information with appropriate speed and legibility?
   - ❒ present print appropriately spaced and sized?
   - ❒ use graphics (with color)—what types, when, and why?
   - ❒ use animation—when and why?
   - ❒ have color that interferes with legibility of print?

7. *Audio (and speech) presentation.* Does the program:
   - ❒ use speech (synthesized space-age voice or digitalized human voice)—when and why?
   - ❒ use nonspeech sound—when and why?
   - ❒ allow control of volume or eliminate the audio?

8. *Reading and language arts goals.* Does the program identify objectives and goals:
   - ❒ for teachers (achievement, motivational, behavioral, management)?
   - ❒ for students?
   - ❒ for parents, administrators, supervisors?
   - ❒ that meet state, provincial, or local educational requirements?
   - ❒ that meet objectives and goals of required tests?

9. *Prerequisite skills.* Of the following skills, what kinds are needed?
   - ❒ computer literacy?
   - ❒ keyboard?
   - ❒ spelling?
   - ❒ entry-level reading?
   - ❒ background knowledge?
   - ❒ other?

10. *Reinforcement in the program.*
    - ❒ What behaviors are reinforced—why, when, how?
    - ❒ What control does the teacher have over the reinforcement?

11. *Program operation.*
    - ❒ Can the students use the program with little or no assistance from the teacher?
    - ❒ Can the teacher or the students:
      - ❒ change the contents of the activity?
      - ❒ change the format of the activity?
      - ❒ control on-screen prompts or help?
      - ❒ make mistakes or press keys accidentally without deleting the activity?
      - ❒ correct entries?
      - ❒ work on unfinished sections of an activity without repeating completed sections?
      - ❒ reread previous screens easily without restarting?
      - ❒ access multiple activities simultaneously?
      - ❒ move freely from one part of the program to another?
    - ❒ Can the program give pretests or posttests?
    - ❒ Can the activity be used with both groups or individuals?

12. *Program reviews and field-testing.* What's available?
    - ❒ Critical reviews?
    - ❒ Descriptive reviews?
    - ❒ Field testing reports?

13. *Supplemental or resource material.* Are supplemental materials available for examining:
    - ❒ the contents of the activities before using them with the computer?
    - ❒ background information about the contents of the activity?
    - ❒ information about instructional strategies used?
    - ❒ other educational resources?

14. *Scoring and recordkeeping.* Does the program:
    - ❒ score and record student performance or other information—how?
    - ❒ permit students and teachers to see records?
    - ❒ provide summary data?

Keep the question, "What does this program offer my students that I cannot give them?"

A Model Sheet for Evaluating Reading Materials

TITLE:

PUBLISHER:

COST:

	Yes	*So-So*	*No*
1. Gives instructions for use that are clear and understandable.	_____	_____	_____
2. Is interesting and acceptable to students at designated age groups.	_____	_____	_____
3. Presents concepts or skills thoroughly and accurately.	_____	_____	_____
4. Uses language suitable for students who will be using the material.	_____	_____	_____
5. Provides for students to apply what they learned to other related areas.	_____	_____	_____
6. Presents follow-up activities for reinforcement.	_____	_____	_____
7. Provides for self-correction.	_____	_____	_____
8. Challenges students.	_____	_____	_____
9. Is easily presented to students.	_____	_____	_____
10. Provides the activity individually, or in a group.	_____	_____	_____

Strengths: ____

____

Weaknesses: ____

____

Website Evaluation

Name of Website: ______________________________ Date Visited: __________

URL: ____

Intended Audience:	Primary	Intermediate	Both
Item	**3**	**2**	**1**
Content	Offers a wealth of information about specific phonics skills	Offers limited information about specific phonics skills	Lacks information about specific phonics skills
Content Accuracy	All information is accurate	Some information is accurate	Site not accurate
Spelling/Grammar	No errors in spelling and grammar	1–5 errors in spelling and grammar	More than 5 errors in spelling and grammar
Layout	Attractive and usable layout—easy to find information	Useable layout, but somewhat difficult to find information	Cluttered or confusing layout, unable to locate information
Links	Three or more additional, working links included	1–2 additional working links included	Additional links included, with at least one working
Contact Information	Contact person or information included	Contact person included but lacks information	No contact person or information included
Graphics and Color	Very interesting, does not distract reader	Somewhat interesting, does not distract reader	Not interesting or available, distracts reader
Last Updated	1 day to 6 months since last update	7 months to 1 year since last update	Over a year since last update or no date on site
Standards	Standards posted on site	Standards linked to site	Standards not available
Extension to Other Environments	Many activities and ideas provided to extend learning at home/school	Few activities and ideas provided to extend learning at home/school	No activities and ideas provided to extend learning at home/school
	Total: /30	Total: /20	Total: /10

Total Score:
Comments:

Glossary

accented syllable: The syllable that receives more emphasis or stress than the other syllables in a word.

affix: A combination of letters that can be added to a root word/base word to change the meaning or grammatical function of the word. Affix is an umbrella term that includes both prefixes and suffixes.

alphabetic method: A teaching approach that emphasizes knowing the letter names and attaching sounds to the letter names.

alphabetic principle: The English writing system is based on a relationship between spoken sounds (approximately 44) and written symbols (26 letters) that allow each sound to be represented by a grapheme.

analytic phonics: A teaching approach that emphasizes beginning with whole words and then identifying the sounds of the parts; a whole-to-part approach. Also known as implicit phonics, inductive phonics instruction, or embedded phonics instruction.

automaticity: "Fluent processing of information that requires little effort or attention, as sight-word recognition" (Harris & Hodges, 1995, p. 16).

balanced literacy instruction: Literacy instruction that is characterized by using a combination of authentic reading experiences, methods, and materials in combination with direct instruction.

basal reading program: Instructional materials (generally designed for grades K–6 or K–8) consisting of sequential lessons that incorporate the use of student books, teacher guides, assessment materials, and other ancillary materials.

base word: A word to which affixes (prefixes and suffixes) are added; also known as a root word.

blending: The ability to join individual phonemes (sounds) into words.

blends: Two or more consonant sounds together, with each retaining its own identity.

breve: A symbol (˘) used to indicate a short vowel sound.

circumflex: A symbol (ˆ) used to indicate pronunciation of vowel graphemes.

closed syllable: A syllable that ends with a consonant sound.

cluster: The graphemes (letters) that make up the blends (sounds).

compound word: A word that includes two or more base words.

configuration cues: The shape of a word provides features that aid in word identification, such as the "*oo*" in look, the "tail" on monkey, the "*ll*" in yellow.

consonants: Letters and sounds that represent all the letters of the alphabet except the vowels, *a*, *e*, *i*, *o*, *u*, and sometimes *y* and *w*. The airflow is interrupted partially or completely to form consonants.

consonant blend: Two or more consonants grouped together with the sound of each of the consonants retained (street).

consonant cluster: The graphemes (letters) that make up the consonant blends (sounds).

context cues: Information in surrounding text that may assist the reader in pronouncing the unknown word or in gaining meaning of an unknown word.

contractions: Shortening a word by omitting letters and using an apostrophe to indicate missing letters.

decode: To translate graphemes (written letter or letters) into phonemes (sounds). Sometimes called sounding out, this is the process of attaching appropriate sounds to letters.

deductive instruction: The teaching methods whereby students are given phonics rules and then practice applying the rules to new words.

diacritical marks: A mark or sign affixed to a letter to specify the sound it represents in a given situation.

digraph: Two or more letters (either consonants or vowels) that stand for a single sound (*th*ink, b*oy*, l*oo*k, *sh*op, ca*sh*, si*ng*, b*ee*t, c*oa*t).

diphthong: Two vowels together that produce a gliding sound when pronounced. The most common diphthongs are *oi*, *oy*, *ou*, and *ow*. When *ou* and *ow* "say" *ow* as in *about* and *how*, they are diphthongs; when *ou* and *ow* "say" *o* as in *soul* and *tow*, they act as single vowels.

embed: To deliberately place selected words into a sentence for instructional purposes.

embedded phonics: A teaching approach that includes phonics instruction as part of authentic reading.

encoding: Writing the appropriate letters for sounds heard in words (spelling).

explicit phonics: A clearly identified sequential set of phonics elements that are directly taught in a particular sequence. An example would be when the teacher tells children that the sound of *d* is the first sound of the word *duck* and that it is written with the letter *d*. The teacher continues to directly teach the sound/symbol relationships.

fluency: To read with expression, meaning, and appropriate phrasing at an appropriate rate.

fricative consonants: Consonants that, when pronounced, cause friction in the mouth (*f*, *v*, *z*, *s*).

glide: Sound made when the tongue moves from one position to another.

grapheme: The written representation of a phoneme. Graphemes are written or printed symbols used to represent a speech sound (phoneme). Graphemes can be one letter or more than one letter.

grapheme-phoneme correspondence: Letter-sound relationship.

graphophonic clues: A within-word clue that helps indicate which of the 44 sounds (phonemes) each letter (26 graphemes) represents.

homographs: Words that share the same sound and same spelling such as read/read, lead/lead.

homonym: Words that look and sound alike such as bear/bear, base/base, will/will, right/right.

homophones: Words that share the same sound, such as two, too, to.

inductive instruction: Instruction that begins with specific examples from which generalizations are generated, similar to analytic.

invented spelling: A writer's rendition of a word based on his/her knowledge of sound-letter relationships.

italics: Used to represent the letter *p*, not the sound of *p*.

juncture: The pauses made between and within sentences.

L-controlled vowel: Vowel sound produced when the letter *a* is followed by an *l*.

language experience: Language experience refers to the type of instruction whereby children either dictate to the teacher or write sentences themselves. Subsequently the teacher, based on these sentences, teaches the children alphabetic principles such as sound/symbol relationships, capitals, and periods.

linguistic phonics: A patterned approach to teaching phonics that shows minimal differences between pairs of words such as *Dan ran to the tan van*.

long vowels: Are generally identified by the vowel "saying its name.

macron: A (-) over a vowel indicates a long vowel sound.

meaning vocabulary: Words that a child knows for which he/she attaches meaning.

miscue: A deviation from the text during oral reading; the errors made by a student while reading orally.

morpheme: The smallest unit of meaning in oral and written language. Box is a morpheme. If *es* were added to box, then *es* would be a morpheme because it changes meaning. Free morphemes are individual words (box) but bound morphemes, such as prefixes, suffixes, compounds, and contractions, must be attached to a free morpheme (box-es).

nasal consonants: Air is forced through the nose when these consonants are pronounced (n, m).

onset: The part of the syllable that includes all consonants before the vowel. May also be thought of as the initial consonant or consonant cluster at the beginning of a syllable.

open syllable: A syllable that ends with a vowel sound (phoneme).

orthography: Symbols or letters in a writing system; the spelling system.

phoneme: The smallest unit of sound that distinguishes one word from another. For example, *get* and *got*. The *e* and *o* are the smallest units that make the two words different. The English language is said to have 44 phonemes (25 consonant, 19 vowel).

phoneme addition: Adding new phonemes to a word.

phoneme deletion: Removing one or more phonemes from a word.

phoneme segmentation: The ability to separate spoken words into individual sounds.

phoneme substitution: Deleting a phoneme from a word and replacing it with a new phoneme.

phonemic awareness: The knowledge that spoken words are made of a series of discrete sounds that are related in some way to an alphabetic principle.

phonics: The study of sound-symbol relationships. Also perceived as a method of teaching that emphasizes the sound-symbol (grapheme) relationship.

phonics instruction: Teaching a child that printed letters in written words represent the speech sounds heard when the words are pronounced; teaching which sound is associated with a particular letter or combination of letters.

phonogram: Rimes or word families. A cluster of vowel and consonant blends such as *ent* and *ild* to which beginning sounds are added, forming words such as *sent* and *wild*.

phonological awareness: Knowing that speech is a sequence of phonemes that can be manipulated by adding, subtracting, and/or substituting one or more phonemes for others and that words are multiple phonemes blended together.

picture clues: Graphic devices such as photographs and pictures that assist the reader in attaching meaning to print.

pitch: The rise and fall in the voice during oral reading.

plosive consonants: These consonants produce a burst of air when pronounced (*b*, *p*, *d*, *t*, *k*, and hard *g*).

prefix: A combination of letters added at the beginning of a base word to change the meaning.

R-controlled vowel: The vowel sound heard when a vowel is followed by the letter *r*. The letter *r* following a vowel (in the *same* syllable) modifies the vowel sound, as in *her* and *stare*.

rhyme: The part of the syllable that contains the vowel and any consonants after the vowel; rhyme in which the parts that sound alike are not spelled alike (*toes*, *knows*).

rime: Similar to a word family, or phonogram. The part of the syllable that contains the vowel and any consonants after the vowel; rhyme in which the parts that sound alike are spelled alike (hose, nose).

root: A word to which affixes (prefixes and suffixes) are added; also known as a base word.

schwa sound: The sound made by unaccented syllables in a multisyllabic word (generally an "uh" sound) and represented by an upside down *e*.

semantics: The study of the meaning of language.

short vowels: The sound a vowel makes when it does not "say its name."

sight word: A word that is recognized immediately (automatically) as a whole word without decoding.

silent letter: A letter in a word with no corresponding sound.

stem: Another term for a base word or word part to which affixes may be added. For young children, this term is sometimes used instead of *root*.

stress: The emphasis placed on words or syllables when spoken orally.

structural analysis: Determining the pronunciation of a word by analyzing the structure (roots, prefixes, suffixes).

suffix: A combination of letters added to the end of a base word to change the meaning or grammatical function of the word. *Derivational*: There are many of these suffixes such as *ment (argument)* and *ism (capitalism)*. They often change the part of speech of the root word and sometimes the word's meaning. *Inflectional*: There are only eight simple inflectional suffixes, such as *ing* and *ed*. These do not change the part of speech.

suprasegmental phoneme system: Consists of stress, pitch, and juncture, which collectively make up the intonation used in spoken language and reading.

syllable: A group of letters that contain one and only one vowel sound. The number of syllables is dependent on the number of vowel sounds.

syntax: The word order in sentences and phrases.

synthetic phonics: An approach that involves learning letter-sound relationships and then blending the sounds to form words. This is also referred to as the deductive approach to teaching phonics. Or explicit phonics, in which teachers directly teach the sound/symbol relationships.

umlaut: The symbol (¨) placed above vowels to indicate pronunciation.

virgules: Slash marks: // used to represent sounds. /m/ represents the sound *m* makes, and italics represent the letter *m*.

vowels: Sounds represented by the letters *a*, *e*, *i*, *o*, *u*, and sometimes *y* (cry) and *w* (owl). Air flows through the mouth unobstructed.

vowel digraph: Two vowels grouped together with only one sound (usually the long vowel sound of one of the vowels) being heard.

vowel diphthong: Two vowel sounds grouped together and blended to make one sound.

whole word method: An approach to teaching that involves memorizing whole words.

word family: Phonograms or rimes.

word recognition: Determining the pronunciation and meaning of words in print. Synonymous with word identification, and/or word analysis.

References

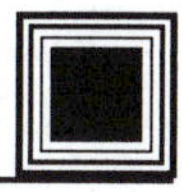

Adams, M. (1990). *Beginning to read: Thinking and learning about print.* Cambridge, MA: The MIT Press.

Adams, M. & Bruck, M. (1995). Resolving the 'Great Debate'. *American Educator, 8,* 7–20.

Ahmann, L. (1982). Some tips on teaching vowel-sound discrimination. *Academic Therapy, 17,* 570–71.

Allen, N., McClellan, C., & Stoeckel, J. (2005). *NAEP 1999 long-term trend technical analysis report: Three decades of student performance.* Washington, DC: National Center for Educational Statistics.

Allington, R. (1983). Fluency: The neglected reading goal. *The Reading Teacher, 36,* 556–561.

American Library Association. (2005). Children's dictionaries. Retrieved from http://www.ala.org/ala/booklist/speciallists/speciallistsandfeatures3/ChDictionaryRU. htm

Anderson, R., Hiebert, E., Scott, J., & Wilkinson, I. (1985). *Becoming a nation of readers: The report of the commission on reading.* Washington, DC: National Institute of Education.

Anderson, W., & Fordham, A. (1991). Beware the magic phonics program! *Childhood Education, 68* (1), 8–9.

Angeletti, S. (1993). Spelling dictionaries. *Learning, 21* (7), 36.

Antonaci, P., & O'Callaghan, C. (2004). *Portraits of literacy development: Instruction and assessment in a well-balanced literacy program, k-3.* Columbus, OH: Pearson, Merrill/Prentice Hall.

Austin, T. (n.d.). *The hornbook.* Retrieved from http://www.nd.edu/~rbarger/www7/hornbook.html

Barr, R., Blachowicz, C., Katz, C., & Kaufman, B. (2002). *Reading diagnosis for teachers: An instructional approach.* Boston: Allyn and Bacon.

Base, G. (1986). *Animalia.* New York: Harry Abrahams.

Baumann, J., Edwards, E., Font, G., Tereshinski, C., Kame'enui, E., & Olejnik, S. (2002). Teaching morphemic and contextual analysis to fifth-grade students. *Reading Research Quarterly, 37,* 150–173.

Bear, D. (2001). Learning to fasten the seat of my union suit without looking around: The synchrony of literacy development. *Theory Into Practice, XXX,* 149–157.

Bear, D., Invernizzi, M., Templeton, S., & Johnson, F. (2004). *Words their way: Word study for phonics, vocabulary, and spelling instruction* (3rd ed.). Upper Saddle River, NJ: Pearson.

Beck, I. & Juel, C. (1995). The role of decoding in learning to read. *American Educator, 19* (2), 8, 21–25, 39–42.

Beech, J. (2004). Using a dictionary: Its influence on children's reading, spelling, and phonology. *Reading Psychology, 25,* 19–36.

Blachman, B. (2000). Phonological awareness. In M. Kamil, P. Mosenthal, P. Pearson, & R. Barr (Eds.), *Handbook of reading research: Volume III* (pp. 483–502). Mahwah, NJ: Lawrence Erlbaum Associates.

Blachowicz, C. (1987). Vocabulary instruction: What goes on in the classroom? *The Reading Teacher, 41,* 132–137.

Blachowicz, C. (1993). C(2) QU: Modeling context use in the classroom. *The Reading Teacher, 47,* 268–269.

Blachowicz, C. & Lee, J. (1991). Vocabulary development in the whole literacy classroom. *The Reading Teacher, 45,* 188–194.

Blackwell Museum. (1999). Retrieved from http://www.cedu.niv.edu/blackwell/books.htm.

Blevins, W. (1998). *Phonics from A to Z.* New York: Scholastic.

Block, C. (2003). *Literacy difficulties: Diagnosis and instruction for reading specialists and classroom teachers.* Boston: Allyn & Bacon.

Bloomfield, L., & Barnhart, C. (1961). *Let's read: A linguistic approach.* Detroit, MI: Wayne State University Press.

Bond, G., & Dystra, R. (1967). The cooperative research program in first-grade reading instruction. *Reading Research Quarterly, 2,* 5–142.

Burns, M., & Snow, C. (Eds.). (1999). *Starting out right: A guide to promoting children's reading success.* Washington, DC: National Academy Press.

Chall, J. (1967). *Learning to read: The great debate.* New York: McGraw-Hill.

Chall, J. (1983). *Learning to read: The great debate* (2nd ed.). New York: McGraw-Hill.

Chall, J. (1996). *Learning to read: The great debate* (3rd ed.). San Diego: Harcourt Brace.

Chall, J. (1999). Some thoughts on reading research: Revisiting the first-grade studies. *Reading Research Quarterly, 34*, 8–10.

Chard, D., & Dickson, S. (1999). Phonological awareness: Instructional and assessment guidelines. *Intervention in School and Clinic, 34*, 261–270.

Chisholm, H. (1911). *Encyclopedia Britannica.* New York: Cambridge University Press.

Chomsky, C. (1976). After decoding: What? *Language Arts, 53*, 288–296.

Chomsky, C. (1978). When you still can't read in third grade: After decoding, what? In S. Samuels (Eds.), *What research has to say about reading instruction* (pp. 13–30). Newark, DE: International Reading Association.

Clark, C. (1995). Learning to read. *CQ Researcher, 5*, 443–461.

Clay, M. (1990). *Reading recovery in the United States: Its successes and challenges.* Boston, MA: American Educational Research Association.

Clymer, T. (1963). The utility of phonic generalizations in the primary grades. *The Reading Teacher, 16*, 252–258.

Collins, C. (1987). Content mastery strategies aid classroom discussion. *The Reading Teacher, 40*, 816–817.

Cooper, J., Boschken, I., McWilliams, J., & Pistochini, L. (1998). *Stopping reading failure: Reading intervention for intermediate grade students.* Boston: Houghton Mifflin.

Crawley, S., & Merritt, K. (2004). *Remediating reading difficulties.* Boston: McGraw Hill.

Cunningham, J. (1979). An automatic pilot for decoding. *The Reading Teacher, 32*, 420–424.

Cunningham, P. (1980). Teaching were, with, what and other 'four-letter' words. *The Reading Teacher, 34*, 160–163.

Cunningham, P. (1981). A teacher's guide to material shopping. *The Reading Teacher, 35*, 181–184.

Cunningham, P. (2005). *Phonics they use: Words for reading and writing* (4th ed.). Boston: Allyn and Bacon.

Cunningham, P., & Cunningham, J. (1992). Making words: Enhancing the invented spelling-decoding connection. *The Reading Teacher, 46*, 106–115.

Davis, D. (1989). First and fifth graders co-author books. *The Reading Teacher, 42*, 652.

DeVries, B. (2004). *Literacy assessment and intervention for the elementary classroom.* Scottsdale, AZ: Holcomb Hathaway, Publishers.

Dolch, E. (1936). A basic sight vocabulary. *The Elementary School Journal, 36*, 456–460.

Dowhower, S. (1987). Effects of repeated reading on second-grade transitional readers' fluency and comprehension. *Reading Research Quarterly, 22*, 389–406.

Dreyer, L., Futtersak, K., & Boehm, A. (1985). Sight words for the computer age: An essential word list. *The Reading Teacher, 38*, 12–15.

Durkin, D. (1990). Dolores Durkin speaks on instruction. *The Reading Teacher, 43*, 474–476.

Dykstra, R. (1968). Summary of the second-grade phase of the cooperative research program in primary reading instruction. *Reading Research Quarterly, 4*, 49–71.

Ehri, L. (1989). The development of spelling knowledge and its role in reading acquisition and reading disability. *Journal of Learning Disabilities, 22*, 356–364.

Ehri, L. (1994). Development of the ability to read words: Update. In R. Ruddell, M. Ruddell, & H. Singer (Eds.), *Theoretical models and processes of reading* (pp. 323–358). New York: Longman.

Ehri, L., & McCormick, S. (1998). Phases of word learning: Implications for instruction with delayed and disabled readers. *Reading and Writing Quarterly, 14*, 135–163.

Ehri, L., & Nunes, S. (2002). The role of phonemic awareness in learning to read. In A. Farstrup & S. Samuels (Eds.), *What research has to say about reading instruction* (3rd ed.) (pp. 110–139). Newark, DE: International Reading Association.

Eldredge, J. (2005). *Teach decoding: Why and how* (2nd ed.). Columbus, OH: Pearson, Merrill/Prentice Hall.

Eldredge, J., & Butterfield, D. (1986). Alternatives to traditional reading instruction. *The Reading Teacher, 39*, 32–37.

Elkonin, D. (1963). The psychology of mastery elements of reading. In B. Simon and J. Simon (Eds.), *Educational psychology in the USSR* (pp. 165–179). London: Routledge & Kegan Paul.

Eller, R., Pappas, C., & Brown, E. (1988). The lexical development of kindergartners: Learning from written context. *Journal of Reading Behavior, 20*, 5–24.

Fleming, D. (2003). *Alphabet under construction.* New York: Holt.

Flesch, R. (1955). *Why Johnny can't read.* Cutchogue, NY: Buccaneer Books.

Foss, K. (1995). Finger spelling. *Reading Today, 12*(3), 28.

Frith, U. (1985). Beneath the surface of developmental dyslexia. In K. Patterson, J. Marshall, & M. Coltheart (Eds.), *Surface dyslexia* (pp. 301–330). London: Erlbaum.

Fry, E. (1980). The new instant word list. *The Reading Teacher*, 34, 284–289.

Fry, E. (1998). The most common phonograms. *The Reading Teacher, 51*, 620–622.

Garan, E. (2001). Beyond the smoke and mirrors: A critique of the National Reading Report on phonics *Phi Delta Kappan, 82*, 500–566.

Goswami, U. (2000). Phonological and lexical processes. In M. Kamil, P. Mosenthal, P. Pearson, & R. Barr, (Ed.), *Handbook of Reading Research: Volume III* (pp. 251–269). Mahwah, NJ: Lawrence Erlbaum Associates.

Graves, M., Juel, C., & Graves, B. (2001). *Teaching reading in the 21st century* (2nd ed.). Boston: Allyn and Bacon.

Groff, P. (1991). Word recognition and critical reading. *Reading, Writing, and Learning Disabilities*, 7, 17–31.

Gunning, T. (2001). *Building words: A resource manual for teaching word analysis and spelling strategies.* Boston: Allyn and Bacon.

Hahn, M. (1994). *Time for Andrew.* New York: Clarion Books.

Harris, A., & Jacobson, M. (1972). *Basic elementary reading vocabularies.* New York: Macmillan.

Harris, T., & Hodges, R. (1995). *The literacy dictionary: The vocabulary of reading and writing.* Newark, DE: International Reading Association.

Heckelman, R. (1969). The neurological impress method of remedial reading instruction. *Academic Therapy, 4,* 277–282.

Heilman, A. (1998). *Phonics in proper perspective* (8th ed.). Columbus, OH: Merrill/Prentice Hall.

Heilman, A. (2005). *Phonics in proper perspective* (9th ed.). Columbus, OH: Merrill/Prentice Hall.

Hempenstall, K. (2004). How might a stage model of reading development be helpful in the classroom? *Educational Psychology, 24,* 727–751.

Hendricks, C., & Osborne, J. (2005). *The helping hand.* Unpublished manuscript.

Herman, P. (1985). The effects of repeated readings on reading rate, speech pauses, and word recognition accuracy. *Reading Research Quarterly, 20,* 553–565.

Higdon, P. (1987). Sticker books sight words. *The Reading Teacher, 41,* 369.

Holdaway, D. (1979). *The foundations of literacy.* Portsmouth, NH: Heinemann.

Honig, B. (1996). *How should we teach our children to read: The role of skills in a comprehensive reading program, a balanced approach.* San Francisco, CA: Far West Lab.

International Reading Association. (1998). *Phonemic awareness and the teaching of reading: A position statement from the board of directors of the International Reading Association.* Newark, DE: International Reading Association.

International Reading Association. (2002). *what is evidence-based reading instruction? A position statement of the International Reading Association.* Newark, DE: International Reading Association.

Jacobs, V., Baldwin, E., & Chall, J. (1990). *The reading crisis: why poor children fall behind.* Cambridge, MA: Harvard University Press.

Jenkins, J., Matlock, B., & Slocum, T. (1989). Two approaches to vocabulary instruction: The teaching of individual word meanings and practice in deriving word meaning from context. *Reading Research Quarterly, 24,* 215–35.

Johns, J. (1978). The revised Dolch list: Data and rationale. *Reading World, 18,* 24–26.

Johns, J., Lenski, S., & Elish-Piper, L. (1999). *Early literacy assessments & teaching strategies.* Dubuque, IA: Kendall/Hunt Publishing Company.

Johns, J., VanLeirsburg, P., & Davis, S. (1994). *Improving reading: A handbook of strategies.* Dubuque, IA: Kendall/Hunt Publishing Company.

Johnson, D., & Baumann, J. (1984). Word identification. In P. Pearson (Ed.), *Handbook of Reading Research* (pp. 583–608). New York: Longman.

Johnston, F. (2004, April). Phonics, phonological awareness, and the alphabet. EPS Update (www. epsbooks. com).

Juel, C. (1991a). Beginning reading. In R. Barr, M. Kamil, P. Mosenthal, & P. Pearson (Eds.), *Handbook of reading research: Volume II* (pp. 759–788). New York: Longman.

Juel, C. (1991b). Cross-age tutoring between student athletes and at-risk children. *The Reading Teacher, 45,* 178–83.

Kame' enui, E. (1995). Response to Deegan: Keep the curtain inside the tub. *The Reading Teacher, 48,* 700–702.

Kame' enui, E. (1996). Shakespeare and beginning reading: The readiness is all. *Teaching Exceptional Children, 27*(2), 77–81.

Kemp, J. (1990). Reading buddies. *The Reading Teacher, 44,* 356.

Koren, S. (1997). Quality versus convenience: Comparison of modern dictionaries from the researcher's, teacher's and learner's points of view. *TESL-EJ,* 2 (3), pp. 1–16.

Kraske, R. (1975). *The story of the dictionary.* New York: Harcourt Brace Jovanovich.

Krieger, V. (1981). Differences in poor readers' abilities to identify high-frequency words in isolation and context. *Reading Research Quarterly, 20,* 263–269.

Lane, H., & Pullen, P. (2004). *Phonological awareness assessment and instruction: A sound beginning.* Boston: Pearson Education, Inc.

Lauritzen, C. (1982). A modification of repeated readings for group instruction. *The Reading Teacher, 35,* 456–458.

Learning First Alliance. (1998). *Every child reading: An action plan.* Washington, DC: Learning First Alliance.

Learning First Alliance. (2000). *Every child reading: A professional development guide.* Washington, DC: Learning First Alliance.

Lenz, B. K., & Hughes, C. A. (1990). A word identification strategy for adolescents with learning disabilities. *Journal of Learning Disabilities, 23*(3), 149–158, 163.

Logan, J., Rupley, W., & Erickson, L. (1995). *Phonics research and instruction.* Dubuque, IA: Kendall/Hunt Publishing Company.

Martin, B., & Archambault, J. (1989). *Chicka chicka boom boom.* New York: Simon & Schuster.

McGuffey's Eclectic Primer. (1909). New York: Van Nostrand Reinhold.

McGuffey's readers. (n.d.). Retrieved from http://www.howtotutor.com/guffy.htm

McKee, P. (1948). *The teaching of reading.* Cambridge: Houghton Mifflin Company.

McKeown, M. (1985). The acquisition of word meaning from context by children of high and low ability. *Reading Research Quarterly, 10,* 482–496.

Moats, L. (1994). The missing foundation in teacher education: Knowledge of the structure of spoken and written language. *Annals of Dyslexia, 44*, 81–102.

Moats, L. (1995). The missing foundation in teacher preparation. *American Educator, 19*(9), p. 43–51.

Moats, L. (2000). *Speech to print: Language essentials for teachers.* Baltimore: Paul H. Brookes Publishing Co.

National Institute for Literacy. (1971). *Put reading first: The research building blocks for teaching children to read.* Washington, DC: The National Institute for Literacy.

National Institute of Child Health and Human Development. (2000). *Report of the national reading panel. Teaching children to read: An evidence-based assessment of the scientific research literature on reading and its implications for reading instruction: Report of the subgroups.* Washington, DC: U.S. Government Printing Office.

Nicholson, T. (2000). The flashcard strikes back. In T. Rasiniski & N. Padak (Eds.), *Teaching word recognition, spelling, and vocabulary: Strategies from The Reading Teacher* (pp. 37–44). Newark, DE: International Reading Association.

Novelli, J. (1993). Strategies for spelling success. *Instructor 102*(9), 41–42.

Palmer, B. (1985). Dolch list still useful. *The Reading Teacher,* 38, 708.

Pemberton, J. (2003). Integrated processing: A strategy for working out unknown words. *Intervention in School and Clinic, 38*, 247–250.

Peterson, S., & Phelps, P. (1991). Visual auditory links: A structural analysis approach to increase word power. *The Reading Teacher, 44*, 524–25.

Pikulski, J., & Templeton, S. (2004). *Teaching and developing vocabulary: Key to long-term reading success.* Boston: Houghton Mifflin.

Pressley, M. (2002). *Reading instruction that works* (2nd ed.). New York: Guilford Press.

Raphael, T. (1984). Teaching learners about sources of information for answering questions. *The Reading Teacher, 27*, 303–311.

Rashotte, C., & Torgesen, J. (1985). Repeated reading and reading fluency in learning disabled children. *Reading Research Quarterly, 20*, 180–188.

Rasinski, T., & Padak, N. (2001). *From phonics to fluency: Effective teaching of decoding and reading fluency in the elementary school.* New York: Longman.

Rasinski, T., & Padak, N. (2004). *Effective reading strategies: Teaching children who find reading difficult* (3rd ed.) Columbus, OH: Merrill/Prentice Hall.

Rasinski, T., Padak, N., Linek, W., & Sturtevant, B. (1994). Effects of fluency development on urban second-grade readers. *Journal of Educational Research, 87*, 158–165.

Reutzel, D., & Hollingsworth, P. (1993). Effects of fluency training on second graders' reading comprehension. *Journal of Educational Research, 86*, 325–331.

Rhoder, C., & Huerster, P. (2002). Use dictionaries for word learning with caution. *Journal of Adolescent and Adult Literacy 45*, 730–735.

Richek, M., & McTague, B. (1988). The "Curious George" strategy for students with reading problems. *The Reading Teacher, 42*, 220–226.

Rosenshine, B., & Stevens, R. (1984). Classroom instruction in reading. In P. Pearson (Ed.), *Handbook of reading research* (pp. 745–798). New York: Longman, 1984.

Rosso, B., & Emans, R. (1981). Children's use of phonics generalizations. *The Reading Teacher, 34*, 653–657.

Routman, R. (1993). The use and abuse of invented spellings. *Instructor, 102* (9), pp. 37–39.

Rubin, D. (2002). *Diagnosis and correction in reading instruction.* Boston: Allyn & Bacon.

Samuels, S. (1979). The method of repeated readings. *The Reading Teacher, 32*, 403–408.

Samuels, S. (2002). Reading fluency: Its development and assessment. In A. Farstrup & S. Samuels (Eds.), *What research has to say about reading instruction* (pp. 166–183). Newark, DE: International Reading Association.

Samuels, S., & Farstrup, A. (Eds.). (1992). *What research has to say about reading instruction.* Newark, DE: International Reading Association.

Savage, J. (2004). *Sound it out! Phonics in a comprehensive reading program* (2nd edition). Boston: McGraw Hill.

Shannon, T. (2001). History 341: Colonial America homepage. Retrieved from http://www3.gettysburgs.edu/~tshannon/his341/colonialamer.htm.

Snow, C., Burns, M., & Griffin, P. (1998). *Preventing reading difficulties in young children.* Washington, DC: National Academy Press.

Snowball, D. (1993). A sensible approach to teaching spelling. *Teaching K-8, 23*(8), 49–50.

Snyder, G. (1981) Learner's verification of reading games. *The Reading Teacher, 34*, 686–691.

Spiegel, D. (1990). Decoding and comprehension games and manipulatives. *The Reading Teacher, 44*, 258–259.

Spiegel, D. (1998). Silver bullets, babies, and bath water: Literature response groups in a balanced literacy program. *The Reading Teacher, 52*, 114–124.

Stahl, S. (1992). Saying the "p" word: Nine guidelines for exemplary phonics instruction. *The Reading Teacher, 45*, 618–625.

Stahl, S. (1998). Understanding shifts in reading and its instruction. *Peabody Journal of Education, 73* (3/4), 31–67.

Stahl, S., Duffy-Hester, A., & Stahl, K. (1998). Theory and research into practice: Everything you wanted to know about phonics (but were afraid to ask). *Reading Research Quarterly, 33*, 338–355.

Stanovich, K. (1993/1994). Romance and reality. *The Reading Teacher, 47*, 280–291.

Strickland, D. (1998). *Teaching phonics today: A primer for educators.* Newark, DE: International Reading Association.

Sutton, C. (1989). Helping the nonnative English speaker with reading. *The Reading Teacher, 42*, 684–688.

Swaby, B. (1982). Using repeated readings to develop fluency and accuracy. *The Reading Teacher, 36*, 317–318.

Temple, C., Ogle, D., Crawford, A., & Freppon, P. (2005). *All children read: Teaching for literacy in today's diverse classroom.* Boston: Pearson.

Tuer, A. (1897). *History of the hornbook.* London: The Leadenhall Press.

Une Education Pour Demain, Association. (2002). Caleb Gattegno's words in color. Retrieved from: http://assoc,orange.fr/une.education.poor.demain/lectureenc/wcprese.htm.

U. S. Department of Education. (2005). *No child left behind: Expanding the promise, guide to president Bush's FY 2006 education agenda.* Washington, DC: U.S. Department of Education.

Visser, C. (1991). Football and reading do mix! *The Reading Teacher, 44*, 710.

White, T., Sowell, J., & Yanagihara, A. (1989). Teaching elementary students to use word-part clues. *The Reading Teacher, 42*, 302–309.

Wiesendanger, K., & Bader, L. (1987). Teaching easily confused words: Timing makes the difference. *The Reading Teacher, 41*, 328–332.

Wilde, S. (1997). *What's a schwa sound anyway?* Portsmouth, NH: Heinemann.

Williams, J. (1985). The case for explicit decoding instruction. In J. Osborn, P. Wilson, & R. Anderson, *Reading education: Foundations for a literate America* (pp. 206–213). Lexington, MA: Lexington Books.

Wisconsin Department of Public Instruction. (1985). *A guide to curriculum planning in reading.* Madison, WI: Wisconsin Dept. of Public Instruction.

Yatvin, J. (2002). Babes in the woods: The wanderings of the National Reading Panel. *Phi Delta Kappan, 83*, 364–369.

Yopp, H. (1992). Developing phonemic awareness in young children. *The Reading Teacher, 45*, 696–703.

Yopp, H. (1995). Read-aloud books for developing phonemic awareness: An annotated bibliography. In T. Rasiniski & N. Padak (Eds.), *Teaching word recognition, spelling, and vocabulary: Strategies from The Reading Teacher* (pp. 3–12). Newark, DE: International Reading Association.

Yopp, H., & Yopp, R. (2000). Supporting phonemic awareness development in the classroom. *The Reading Teacher, 54*, 130–143.

Index